Riveting Read-Alouds
for Middle School

35 Selections to Spark Deep Thinking,
Meaningful Discussion, and Powerful Writing

Janet Allen & Patrick Daley

■ SCHOLASTIC

New York • Toronto • London • Auckland • Sydney
Mexico City • New Delhi • Hong Kong

FOR PATRICK DALEY

In Mary Oliver's "The Summer Day," the poet asks:

Tell me, what is it you plan to do

with your one wild and precious life?

Thousands of children's and educators' lives have been changed by your work, and my life has been richer for your presence in it—as a friend, a colleague, and an author. Your "one wild and precious life" lives on in those fortunate enough to have been part of your journey.

~Janet Allen

Note from the editor:

I worked with author Patrick Daley on and off for the past 20 years, first as part of his team in Scholastic's Classroom Magazines division, and most recently as his editor for this book. As my supervisor, he was supportive and generous, always offering words of encouragement. Our work relationship transitioned into a friendship when he moved to READ 180, the reading-intervention program started by Scholastic. Every time I ran into him, there was a sparkle of mischief in his eyes, and I knew he'd have a story to tell that would soon have me laughing out loud. But anyone who has worked with Patrick knows that behind his charming façade was a man with lots of big, brilliant ideas. He was passionate about reaching struggling readers and making reading fun for them. As a former middle school teacher, he had a keen sense of what kinds of stories would make kids want to read. That came through in the reading programs and products he developed for Scholastic, including this book. He meticulously chose the stories he wanted to feature in this book, continually searching for even more engaging texts. I asked him to please finalize his list by Thanksgiving 2015 so we could get started on the book. He did. A few weeks later, Patrick had a heart attack. He passed away on February 5, 2016. Working on this book without Patrick was very difficult; there were times when it felt like my heart would break. But with the help and support of Patrick's co-author, Janet Allen, and his former assistants, Julia Graeper and Tim Crino, we were able to finish it. I would like to think this book is exactly the way Patrick envisioned it. Here's to you, Patrick! Love and miss you.

~Maria L. Chang

· · · · ·

Editor: Maria L. Chang
Cover designer: Tannaz Fassihi
Interior designer: Sarah Morrow
Cover photo: Adam Chinitz

ISBN: 978-0-545-09600-3
Copyright © 2017 by Janet Allen and Patrick Daley
All rights reserved. Printed in the U. S. A.
First printing, January 2017.

1 2 3 4 5 6 7 8 9 10   40   25 24 23 22 21 20 19 18 17

Contents

Read Aloud: Prime-Time Instruction

by Janet Allen

> *"The fire of literacy is created by the emotional sparks between a child, a book, and the person reading. It isn't achieved by the book alone, nor by the children alone, nor by the adult who's reading aloud—it's the relationship winding between all three, bringing them together in easy harmony."*

—Mem Fox, *Reading Magic*

I had a rich reading life as a child, due in large part to those around me who read to me constantly. When my mother was looking for someone to take care of me while she worked, she said the only thing she was looking for was someone who would read to me as that was the only time I wasn't getting into trouble. Fortunately, she found that in Helen Taylor. Helen abandoned housework, cooking, and all other responsibilities so she could read to me the entire time I was there. One of my earliest memories is being curled up with her on the couch, listening to her read while I ate a peanut-butter-and-pink-marshmallow sandwich. Life was good.

Flash forward to the early 1970s, when I started teaching. Life was not so good. I was not prepared for one class after another where students refused to read, write, or take part in anything academic. The superintendent had told me when I signed my contract that I had to teach for 60 days before I could quit. Each day I marked another day off on the calendar as I struggled to find anything that would capture my students' attention. In my search for materials in our book room, I found two sets of young adult novels. I had never heard of young adult literature, but as I looked at the cover of *Mr. and Mrs. Bo Jo Jones* (Head, 1967), I remembered my mother's goal: find someone who would read to me. It was in those early days of teaching that I learned the significance of reading aloud to my students. Reading aloud was a practice I refined but never abandoned.

In these days of strict pacing guides, assessments that require us to try to determine everything each child is thinking, extensive data collection, and classrooms where teachers don't have time or permission to read aloud, I want to cry. I think often of Helen Taylor's cluttered house and realize she had it right. She took time away from other responsibilities to do what mattered most—read aloud. A few years ago, I wrote a children's picture book and did book signings in the city where I had taught. The majority of those who came to get their books signed were former students. Each had a story to tell. Not one talked about strategy lessons or grammar; all talked about the impact reading had made on their lives and the lives of their children. Many of the conversations started with, "I remember when you read to us every day." As they stood in line, they shared titles from those memories. Reading aloud develops a set for literacy that will last a lifetime and be passed along to another generation.

Making a Case for Reading Aloud: Engagement

It is easy to make a case for reading aloud, because reading aloud impacts learning in so many positive ways. The first, and most important, benefit of reading aloud is that we have the opportunity to get students engaged in reading. This engagement applies to many aspects of literacy and learning.

- Reading aloud shows learners that texts offer enjoyment and information. Students begin to see that books can amuse, delight, comfort, raise questions, and provide answers.

- Reading aloud helps students see that text has meaning—or that it should have meaning. Researcher Thomas Sticht discovered that children's reading comprehension doesn't catch up to their listening comprehension until around middle school. In other words, students who have problems decoding texts on their own can easily comprehend those texts when they are read aloud (1984). When the teacher is doing the decoding, students have a greater opportunity to generate meaning from the text.

- Reading aloud helps students develop fluency. "During read-aloud, the listener hears how the voice can be used to create and extend meaning" (Rasinski, 2003).

- Reading aloud can help students develop skills for listening, thinking, and responding.

- Reading aloud can help develop readers who make time to read and who see the value in rereading.

- Reading aloud increases vocabulary. If using a wide variety of texts, students will be exposed to new and specialized vocabulary they otherwise might never encounter.

- Reading aloud helps students focus on meaning first and expand their understanding with repeated or related readings.

- Reading aloud develops community. The text, and the feelings related to the text, becomes a touchstone for a group as they connect to new shared texts.

Maya Angelou said, "I've learned that people will forget what you said, people will forget what you did, but people will never forget how you made them feel." The positive feelings of being read to can last a lifetime, and you are the one who can make that possible.

Making a Case for Reading Aloud: Instruction

I titled this introduction "Read Aloud: Prime-Time Instruction" because reading aloud can set the stage for instruction. A text that is read for engagement can be reread to help students focus on content details, writer's craft, or strategies for comprehension. Television shows vie for the best time slots during prime time; reading aloud is prime time in the classroom because you have used the time to get students engaged.

If you have read the first *Read-Aloud Anthology* (Allen & Daley, 2004), you will notice this collection is different. In addition to engaging texts for reading aloud, we have included a teaching page for each selection to offer you opportunities for extending the read-aloud experience. Each teaching page comes with a summary of the text as well as its source. We also provide a recommended number of reading sessions. Some texts are longer than others, and you may want to read them over two or more sessions. You will find section breaks in the text (indicated by a dotted line) so you know when it's a good time to end each read-aloud session. You will also find ideas for teaching language and vocabulary—often accompanied by a graphic organizer—as well as prompts for thinking, talking, and writing about the text.

Let's look at some other instructional opportunities provided when you read aloud.

- **Background Knowledge:** Much of the content students encounter beyond the primary grades is new to them. The teaching page offers several sources of important background information to help students understand and connect with the content. A short **summary** for each text provides an overview. Additionally, a **Language and Vocabulary** previewing activity is provided to help students anticipate unfamiliar language. If there are words critical to understanding the read-aloud, those words are highlighted in **Background Language**.

- **Extending Strategy Instruction:** Reading aloud thought-provoking texts can help students continue developing strategies as thoughtful readers and writers. Each teaching page includes a section called **Think, Talk, and Write About Text**. These literacy activities support students as they do a close reading, think deeply about the content, and discuss the text structures.

- **Types of Text:** The texts we chose for this collection include short stories and excerpts from novels, literary nonfiction, informational texts, and poetry. You can find the **source** for each selection in the teaching pages. Some of the activities in Think, Talk, and Write About Text offer suggestions for extending students' reading with other texts.

- **Writing:** Richard Peck said, "None but a reader ever became a writer." Reading aloud provides mentor texts for student writers. The teaching pages offer several opportunities for students to write about the text. Some prompts serve to help students think carefully in order to discuss the texts, and others give students the opportunity to create their own texts inspired by the read-aloud.

In Marcia Freeman's *Listen to This: Developing an Ear for Expository*, she encourages reading aloud so that students hear a variety of genres.

> "Just as students develop an ear and a preference for different styles of music, so can they develop an ear and preference for different genres of writing. You can help your students become better expository writers by reading well-written expository samples to them" (1997).

Reading aloud can lead students to reading others' texts and guide them in writing and reading their own.

Our Role as the Reader

Being prepared for reading aloud is as critical as the preparation you would do for any other teaching times of your day. Effective oral reading takes practice. Some people are uncomfortable with reading aloud, while others turn the read-aloud into a theatrical performance. If you are one of the former (or even if you belong to the latter group), we've included a **read-aloud tip** for each selection to help you "bring life to the text." Each of us has to read aloud with a method that is comfortable for us; however, all of us have to practice the reading *prior* to reading aloud to the class. I'm always a bit amazed when teachers tell me they were reading a novel and they were shocked that there was profanity or something offensive in the book. Even with prereading, I have still been shocked with the content—not because I hadn't read it, but because I didn't notice it! Previewing the text and practicing by reading aloud help you plan for an effective reading experience.

There are many aspects of preparing for a read aloud. One of those is text selection. I love Steven Layne's advice: "Selecting a great read aloud is a lot like selecting a great movie—it's all a matter of opinion." This is certainly true. When I taught in northern Maine, Gary Paulsen's *Hatchet* was a huge favorite. When I moved to Orlando, Kyle Gonzalez asked for a recommendation and I suggested *Hatchet*. It was a terrible suggestion on my part because I hadn't met her students and had no idea that *Hatchet* was not the book for them. So, I think choosing the right text is a matter of opinion combined with knowing the audience. Learning who your students are as readers, writers, and teens is critical to your book choice. Taking time during the first week of school to get to know them will go a long way. Here are a few suggestions for accomplishing that.

- Interest surveys definitely help you know what your students' interests are. I did find that many of my students didn't know genres, so having a checklist of each different type of writing often fell short of my expectation.

- Ask students to create a mixtape where each song on the mix represents something about them. Introduce it with a tape you have made and ask students to make inferences about you based on the song selection.

- Read aloud Lisa Delpitt's opening in *Fires in the Bathroom*: "Wanted: One Teacher." Have students write a "Wanted" ad for the kind of teacher they would like. Some teachers model the process by writing a "Wanted" ad for the students they are hoping to teach this year.

Get Started!

So, you are prepared—you've practiced reading aloud and you know the instructional implications for consistently reading aloud. You know your students (as well as you can) and you know the texts you will read. What now?

- Jump in and give it a try. Start with something you think will be very engaging. Begin with a relatively short text and work up to longer texts.

- Don't interrupt the reading so often that students miss the read-aloud experience. There is no need to stop and explain every word or event. In *The Call of Stories: Teaching and the Moral Imagination*, Robert Coles said: "But the beauty of a good story is its openness—the way you or I or anyone reading it can take it in, and use if for ourselves" (1989).

- Read in a way that demonstrates fluent reading. Students are listening to your expression, your emotion, and your ability to bring the words to life. One of my students said she used my voice in her head until she read so much she found her own. In *Making the Match: The Right Book for the Right Reader at the Right Time, Grades 4–12*, Teri Lesesne reminds us of the importance of fluent reading: "It is important to remember that reading aloud is a performance of sorts. We should keep in mind what I call the three P's of reading aloud: *preview, practice,* and *personalize*" (2003).

- Help students make a connection with a brief introduction before you start reading the text. It might be a simple question that segues into the reading: "Do you know what a *phobia* is? Let's read 'The Escape' by J. B. Stamper and see if we can find out."

- Enjoy the experience. Kids are resilient and forgiving. They want you to succeed because almost everyone loves a great read-aloud.

I've been in education for many years now, and I know there is ample research that demonstrates the importance of reading aloud to your students. But you already know that. You know it in the students who come back from last year's class to tell this year's class how much they are going to enjoy a book you read to them. You know it when a student wants to borrow the book that holds the poem you read that morning. One of the most touching experiences in my career happened on the last day of school. I was reading Mazer's *War on Villa Street* and misjudged how long it would take to complete the book. When the bell rang signaling the end of school for the summer, the students just sat there waiting. Finally, one of them said, "Hold that thought. We'll go across the street and grab something to eat and you can finish the book when we get back." Life was good again.

References

Allen, J., & Daley, P. (2004). *Scholastic read-aloud anthology.* New York, NY: Scholastic Inc.

Coles, R. (1989). *The call of stories: Teaching and the moral imagination.* Boston, MA: Houghton Mifflin Company.

Delpit, L. (2005). Wanted: One teacher. In K. Cushman and What Kids Can Do, Inc., *Fires in the bathroom: Advice for teachers from high school students.* New York, NY: The New Press.

Fox, M. (2001). *Reading magic: Why reading aloud to our children will change their lives forever.* Orlando, FL: Harcourt, Inc.

Freeman, M. S. (1997). *Listen to this: Developing an ear for expository.* Gainesville, FL: Maupin House Publishing, Inc.

Head, A. (1967). *Mr. and Mrs. Bo Jo Jones.* New York, NY: New American Library.

Layne, S. (2015). *In defense of read-aloud: Sustaining best practice.* Portland, ME: Stenhouse Publishers.

Lesesne, T. S. (2003). *Making the match: The right book for the right reader at the right time, Grades 4–12.* Portland, ME: Stenhouse Publishers.

Mazer, H. (1978). *The war on villa street.* New York, NY: Dell.

Oliver, M. (1992). The summer day. In *New and selected poems.* Boston, MA: Beacon Press.

Rasinski, T. V. (2003). *The fluent reader: Oral reading strategies for building word recognition, fluency, and comprehension.* New York, NY: Scholastic Inc.

Sticht, T., & James, J. (1984). Listening and reading. In P. Pearson, ed., *Handbook of research on reading.* New York, NY: Longmans.

1 For Pete's Snake

by Ellen Conford

SUMMARY

One 4th of July, Will agrees to watch his sister Petra's ("Pete") boa constrictor, Coily. Only Will's pretty nervous about it, and all of his friends have other plans. And then Coily escapes. And there's a thunderstorm. And the electricity goes out. By the time Will's family returns home, he is huddled under the covers, scared to death. And then there is one more surprise that might just push Will over the edge.

SOURCE: *"For Pete's Snake"* was written by Ellen Conford. Ms. Conford has written more than 40 books for children and teens.

READING SESSIONS: 2

LANGUAGE AND VOCABULARY

The effective use of irony helps make a story or event more interesting. Use the organizer to help students identify irony in this story and create a vocabulary card for use in other reading.

Literary Terms: *Irony*

Information From the Context	*Information From Resources (teacher, other students)*
"Not the lights. A boa constrictor and a thunderstorm aren't enough for one night?" As if in *ironic* answer, a flash of lightning—very close … illuminated the room … And the giant brown reptile twined around the curtain rod flicking his forked tongue at me."	
In my own words, irony or ironic means …	*Mnemonic to help me remember (visual, jingle)*

THINK, TALK, AND WRITE ABOUT TEXT

In literary terms, setting includes time, place, mood, and tone. **Think about** and **discuss** how the setting of this story influences the plot or sequence of events in this story. Use a sequence chart to identify the events that make this story interesting.

The story is told from Will's point of view. Assign students to collaborative writing groups and give each group a character: Pete, Will's friends, mother, father, and Coily. Ask each group to **write** a retelling of the story from the point of view of the character they were assigned.

Riveting Read-Alouds for Middle School © Janet Allen and Patrick Daley, Scholastic Inc.

For Pete's Snake

by Ellen Conford

Have you ever agreed to help out a friend or a sibling when you really, actually, kind of didn't want to? One day, Will ends up having to watch his sister's pet boa constrictor. He has really mixed feelings about it—for good reason!

READ-ALOUD TIP

The narrator, who is very melodramatic, controls this humorous short story. The rising panic in his tone as the story unfolds helps students imagine how they would feel if they were stuck in a house with a boa constrictor. When reading this text aloud, being dramatic will help students relate to Will's dilemma and his fear.

BACKGROUND LANGUAGE

The narrator uses the word *ironic* as a way to describe the events in this story. An understanding of this term would be important for students to get some of the humor in the situation.

The last, tearful words my sister, Petra, said to me as they drove her off to the hospital were, "Please, Will, take care of my Coily!"

It was Saturday evening, on the Fourth of July weekend. My parents didn't know how long they'd have to wait in the emergency room. But they were used to it. This was not the first time Pete had fallen out of a tree. Or off the roof. Or off her skateboard.

Pete is a major klutz. She breaks things. Mostly her bones. Whenever anyone asks my father for a credit card, he says, "Visa, American Express, or County General?"

So there was really nothing new about Pete being carried off to the hospital again.

Except that this time I had promised to baby-sit a boa constrictor.

Well, I hadn't really promised. But I had nodded. I'm her brother, what else could I do? The kid was in pain, in tears, and in the car. If I'd said no, she might have jumped out of the car and tried to take Coily with her to the hospital. Then my mother and father would probably have argued over who would get to shoot me.

And besides, I thought, as I sat down on the front steps, it's a snake, not a baby. It's not as if I'd have to pick him up, or rock him, or burp him or anything.

As Pete told my mother when she begged to adopt the beast, "They're really no trouble at all. You don't have to walk them, and you only have to feed them every two weeks. And they eat mice."

"We don't have any mice," my mother had pointed out.

"So we'll get some," Pete said.

The sky was beginning to turn a coppery color, and I could see hard-edged dark clouds on the horizon. The air was heavy and still. I hoped we weren't going to have a thunderstorm.

It's not that I'm really afraid of storms. It's just that when I was five, I wandered away from our tent during a family camping trip. I got lost, and this monster thunderstorm came up—

Well, ever since then I've been a little tense about thunder and lightning.

Except for the occasional sound of a distant firecracker, the neighborhood was unnaturally quiet. A lot of people were away for the holiday weekend, and the others were at Waterside Park, waiting for the fireworks display.

Which is where we were planning to go before Petra fell out of the tree.

I can go anyway, I realized. After all, it wasn't as if I had to do anything for Coily. Mostly he lay on the flat rock in his tank, or wrapped himself around the tree branch in there, or hid inside the copper water pipe Pete had found for him.

"They like to hide," Pete explained. "Where they can't be seen."

"Great," I'd told her. "The less I see him, the better."

Not that I'm afraid of snakes—but, hey, even Indiana Jones thinks they're repulsive. So I'd just look in on Coily— very briefly—and then go off to see the fireworks. If I could find someone to drive me.

I went into the house, flipping on light switches as I made my way to the kitchen. It was getting pretty dark. The fireworks would probably begin in about an hour.

I phoned my friend Josh, hoping he was home.

"Hey, Will!" he shouted. "Boy, am I glad to hear somebody who doesn't sound like Popeye the Sailor Man."

"Excuse me?"

"There's a six-hour Popeye marathon on cable. We're into the fourth hour here."

"Then you'll be glad to know why I'm calling," I said. "Though it does involve water." I explained about Pete and the hospital, and how I wanted to go down to Waterside Park.

"That would be great," he said.

"Okay, come over and pick me up and—"

"Except that I have to sit with Steffie." Steffie is Josh's five-year-old sister.

"Bring her along," I said.

"She's got a strep throat," Josh said. "I can't take her anywhere."

"It's hot out," I said. "It wouldn't hurt her to just lie on a blanket and watch—"

"She's got a hundred-and-one fever," he said. "Hey, I have to go. I think I hear her croaking for something. Enjoy the fireworks."

"How can I—" But he'd already hung up. How can I enjoy the fireworks, I'd been about to ask, with no one to drive me there? The park is four miles away.

Shelly! I thought. My friend Shelly had a brand-new driver's license and was always looking for an excuse to drive somewhere.

I heard a lot of noise in the background when Mrs. Getz answered the phone. Kid noise. Like a bunch of preteenies squealing and giggling.

"Hi, Mrs. Getz. It's Will. May I speak to Shelly?"

"She's sort of tied up at the moment," said Mrs. Getz. "Can she call you back?"

"What's going on there?" I asked. "Is that Shelly screaming?"

"I think so," Mrs. Getz answered. "She's supposed to be running Carol's birthday party."

Carol is Shelly's eleven-year-old sister.

 Riveting Read-Alouds for Middle School © Janet Allen and Patrick Daley, Scholastic Inc.

"I forgot about the party," I said glumly. "I guess she'll be tied up for a while then."

"She will until I go untie her," said Mrs. Getz. "I believe they're playing Joan of Arc."

"Boy," I said, thinking of Pete and Steffie, "kids can sure be a pain sometimes."

Mrs. Getz snorted. "Tell me about it," she said, and hung up.

I dropped the phone back on the hook. I peered out the window over the kitchen sink. It was only seven thirty, but the darkness was closing in fast.

I called three other friends. Two weren't home. Chip, the third, had to shout over the sound of an electric guitar, and some horrible wailing.

"Family reunion!" he yelled. "That's my cousin Dennis."

"What's he doing?"

"Elvis Presley. Why don't you come over? We're barbecuing."

"Dennis, I hope," I muttered.

"What? I can't hear you."

"I said, great, I'll be right there." It was only half a mile to Chip's, and even if I'd have to listen to Dennis, it was better than sitting alone in the house with a boa constrictor.

And then I heard a distant rumble.

"Was that thunder?" I asked.

"I can't hear a thing," Chip shouted. "Dennis is doing 'Hound Dog.'"

Another rumble, closer.

"I think it's starting to rain," Chip said. "It doesn't matter. Come on over."

"Well, maybe not," I said. "I mean, if it's raining."

"That's okay. We'll go inside. Whoo, there goes the lightning."

"I'd better stay here," I said. "My folks might try to call."

"Oh, yeah," Chip said. "You have this thing about thunderstorms."

"I do *not* have a thing about thunderstorms," I said defensively. "I just don't feel like walking half a mile in a downpour, that's all." With lightning striking all around me.

"Suit yourself," Chip said. "I'd better help Dennis get his amp inside before he's electrocuted."

"Right." I slammed the phone down. Okay. Fine. I'll stay home. I'll read. I'll watch TV. I'll listen to music. I'll worry about my sister.

I'll be alone in the house with a boa constrictor.

Big deal. It doesn't scare me. All he ever does is lie on his rock. Or curl up inside his pipe. I won't bother him, he won't bother me. I'm not really afraid of snakes anyway. I just happen to find them repulsive, disgusting, and evil looking.

But I'm not afraid of them.

And I'm certainly not afraid of being alone in the house. And even though it's starting to thunder, I'm perfectly safe, as long as I don't talk on the telephone, stick my toe in a light socket, or stand under a tree.

So there's nothing to be afraid of. Even if it is getting so dark that the light over the kitchen table is barely making a dent in the gloom.

So don't stay in the kitchen, dummy, I told myself. There's a whole, brightly lit house to wander around in. I'll just go check the stupid snake, I thought, then settle down in front of the TV. There's nothing like a Popeye festival to calm your nerves.

* * * * *

I turned on the light in the hallway and headed toward Pete's room.

One quick look into the glass tank and I could say that I'd kept my promise. Coily will be curled up on his rock, and I'll go curl up with Popeye and Olive. The rumbles of thunder that had seemed so far away a moment ago were louder now. The storm was coming closer.

That's okay, I told myself. The closest thing to a tree in this house was Coily's branch, and I would hardly climb into the tank and wedge myself under it, so there was nothing to worry about.

The door to Pete's room was wide open. This was a major violation of rules. Ever since she'd gotten the boa, Pete had strict orders to keep her door closed. That way, in case Coily ever managed to escape from his tank, he'd be confined to Petra's room and be reasonably easy to recapture.

Not that any of us, except Pete, would ever try to recapture him. My father said, "If that thing gets loose, I'm moving to a motel and putting the house up for sale."

So far the only time the snake had been out of Pete's room was when she would occasionally drape Coily around her shoulders and parade around the house so we could admire his exotic markings and alleged tameness.

When Pete "walked" her scaly pet, the rest of us found urgent business to attend to in rooms with doors that locked.

Anyway, it disturbed me that Pete's door was wide open, but I figured that in her hurry to get to the yard and climb a tree so she could fall out of it, she'd forgotten the rule.

I reached inside the room and flicked the light on. From the entrance I peered at the snake tank. It was a large, glass rectangle with gravel on the bottom and plastic mesh screening over the top. Pete had taped a little sign on the side that said COILY'S CORNER.

I couldn't see the beast at first, but that didn't throw me. As Pete had said, snakes like to hide, so I figured Coily was scrunched inside his copper pipe.

I moved into the room. A clap of thunder made me jump, but it wasn't too bad, and I didn't see any lightning flash.

"Miles away," I reassured myself. "Just get the stupid snake check over with and go watch something dumb on the tube."

Okay. I cleared my throat so Coily would know I was coming and not feel he had to rear up and do anything dramatic to protect his territory. I know snakes can't hear. But why take chances?

I edged closer to the tank. I could see it all, the whole thing. But I couldn't see Coily. Inside the pipe, I reminded myself. Just squat down, look inside the pipe, barf, run out of the room, and shut the door.

The lights flickered with another burst of thunder. Lights flicker in a storm, I reminded myself. No need to panic. I squatted down and looked into the copper pipe. I could see through it to the other side. There was nothing inside it but air.

"Yikes!" I straightened up, and as I did, I noticed that the plastic mesh screening on top of the tank had a jagged rip in one corner.

As if something—something with fangs—had gnawed right through it.

"Yikes!" I was repeating myself, but this was no time to worry about being clever. I raced out of Pete's room and slammed the door. I leaned against the wall, panting, even though I'd only sprinted ten feet.

What a narrow escape. I could have been standing—or squatting—right there in front of the tank, with the boa lurking under a chair just waiting to slink up and constrict me.

And then it hit me.

Pete's door had been open when I went into her room. It had been open for almost an hour. The snake might not be in there at all. In fact, it could be anywhere in the house by this time.

I hugged the wall, wanting to climb up it. If I could hang from the light fixture on the ceiling, chances were the creature couldn't reach me.

Don't lose it, Will, I told myself. This is stupid. I could see all the way up and down the hall. And the boa was nowhere in sight.

There are seven rooms in this house, I reminded myself. Plus the hall. The odds are eight to one that I won't be in the same place as the snake. As long as I keep my eyes open—

Two deafening bursts of thunder, one right on top of the other. Instinctively I shut my eyes and clapped my hands over my ears. Then I thought of the twelve-foot-long snake slithering along the hall toward me. I snapped my eyes open and did a 360 to make sure I was still alone.

Another clap of thunder. The lights went out.

"No!" I yelled. "*No! Don't let the* electricity go off!"

The lights came back on.

"Thank you."

A drenching rain began to pound the house. It sounded as if I were standing in the middle of Niagara Falls.

Flashlight! I thought. Candles. Quick, while I could still find them.

I ran for the kitchen. I opened the utility cabinet, next to the refrigerator.

Something smacked against the window. It was probably a branch of the mimosa tree, driven by a sudden, howling wind that had seemed to come from nowhere.

"Just the tree," I told myself. "It happens all the time when it's windy."

As I turned around to make sure it was nothing more sinister than the tree branch, the room went black.

Another flicker. I tried to keep calm. The electricity would come back on in a moment.

But it didn't.

"Aw, no!" I begged. "Not the lights. A boa constrictor and a thunderstorm aren't enough for one night?"

As if in ironic answer, a flash of lightning—very close, extremely close—illuminated the room with a harsh, chalky light. For three seconds I could see as clearly as if it were daytime. The mimosa tree, the sink, the white curtains at the window . . .

And the giant brown reptile twined around the curtain rod flicking his forked tongue at me.

I screamed and jumped backward, crashing against the open door of the utility cabinet. Shrieking, I stumbled out of the kitchen, flailing my arms in front of me to keep from banging into anything else.

Which didn't work. I tripped over the stepladder, bounced off a wall, and staggered into the dining room, where I met the china cabinet head-on. Every dish on the shelves clattered as I careened into it and landed on the floor. I moaned and wondered which part of my body hurt the most.

I sat huddled there for a moment, dazed and whimpering. Now, accompanying the torrential rain, there was a loud, rattling sound, as if someone were hurling handfuls of gravel against the windows. Hail, I thought. You sometimes get hail with severe thunderstorms. And tornadoes.

Great. A tornado. Just what I need. Thunder and lightning and hail and total darkness and a wandering boa constrictor and a tornado.

Mommy!

The hail and rain were making so much noise that I could hardly hear myself think. If you could call what I was doing thinking. If I can't hear myself think, I realized, I can't hear the brown monstrosity unwind himself from the curtain rod.

I can't hear him slip down off the sink, and across the floor, and out of the kitchen, and into the dining room, where I'm curled up here on the floor like a sitting—

"Ayiee!"

I leaped to my feet—or at least I crawled to my knees and stood up as quickly as I could with an entirely black-and-blue body. *Think, Will,* I ordered myself. *Just shut the kitchen door, and—*

Good idea. Except we don't have a kitchen door, only an archway that separates the kitchen from the dining room. At this very moment Coily could be slithering past the refrigerator, heading for the dining room.

I'll go to my room. I'll go to my room and shut the door. No problem. Just grope around the table, through the living room, down the hall, and into my room. I can certainly move faster than a snake can slither—at least I can when the lights are on.

Of course there is another archway that leads from the kitchen and into the hall. The snake could be creeping out that way and into the hall just as I—

Don't even think about it.

Move.

I moved. As fast as I could, in the dark, with only an occasional flash of lightning to help me around the maze of furniture that clutters the living room.

"Why is this room so crammed?" I wondered, as I banged my shin against a footstool. "Does anyone really need this much furniture?"

I flung my arm against a plant stand. A flowerpot crashed to my feet.

"Please don't let it be my mother's African violet that didn't bloom for three years up until last week," I prayed.

I made it to my room without further damage to myself or to our overfurnished house. I slammed the door behind me. I was sure the snake couldn't haven gotten to my room before I did.

Well, I was pretty sure.

Call Josh, I thought. *Maybe his parents are home by now. Maybe he can come over with a flashlight, find the boa, and put him back in his tank.*

The phone next to my bed has a lighted keypad, which is convenient if you have to call the police in the middle of the night, or if a boa constrictor gets loose in the dark.

When Josh picked up his phone, I didn't even say hello. I just shrieked.

"You have to come over and help me! I don't know where Coily is!"

"Did you check with Larry and Moe?" he asked.

"*What?*"

"A Three Stooges joke," he explained. "You know Larry, Moe and—"

"This is no time for jokes!" I yelled. "I'm alone in the house with a rampaging boa constrictor, and the lights are off, and—"

"I can't take my sister out in this storm," he cut in.

"When will your parents be home?" I asked desperately.

"Monday," he answered.

"ARRGGHH!" I slammed down the phone.

There was only one thing to do. Only one intelligent, mature way of coping with the situation.

I dived into bed and pulled the covers over my head.

The snake couldn't be in my room. He just couldn't be. I'd be perfectly safe here under the covers. If I didn't pass out from the heat or smother myself.

I cowered there, sweating and shaking, waiting for my parents to come home. Once in a while I'd think I'd heard a car door slam. Then I'd poke my head out and listen. And gasp for air. But the only sounds were the rain—softer now—and distant rumbles of thunder.

I don't know how long I stayed there, trying to breathe, feeling my clothes getting wetter and wetter with sweat, telling myself that there was no snake in my room and even if there was, he preferred curtain rods to beds.

And I felt something soft graze my leg.

For a moment I froze. I couldn't breathe, couldn't even scream, which is what I really wanted to do.

It can't be a twelve-foot boa constrictor, I told myself. *It's just a beetle or a mosquito or something. But it didn't feel like a beetle or a mosquito.*

I threw the covers off, howling. Just as I did, the electricity came back on. My room blazed with light. I blinked, and like a kid waking up from a nightmare, clutched my pillow to my chest. I forced myself to look down,

down toward the end of the bed, where I had flung off the covers.

And saw a procession of brown, foot-long snakes writhing up my sheet, heads darting, tongues flicking, coming straight at me. Screaming uncontrollably, I threw myself out of bed. I could still feel something on my leg. When I looked down, I saw that one of the creatures was hanging from my ankle like a loose boot strap.

"NO! *NO!*" I shook my leg violently, and the snake fell to the floor. I felt as if there were snakes crawling all over my body. I twisted around frantically, smacking my pillow against my legs, my arms, my chest.

What if they're in my shorts?

I screamed even louder, dropped my pillow, and scrambled out of my cutoffs. Through my screaming I heard feet pounding down the hall.

"Will! *Will!*" My father threw my door open and grabbed me by the shoulders.

"Snakes! Snakes!" I screamed. "In my pants! In my bed!"

My mother was right behind him. Dimly, through a haze of terror, I saw Pete peer into my room. She had a splint on one arm and a boa constrictor wrapped around the other.

"Coily!" she cried delightedly. "You're a girl!"

Maybe the biggest surprise was that my hair did *not* turn completely white. Although I was afraid to look in a mirror for two days.

Coily has been adopted by one of my sister's weird friends. My mother put her foot down. She told Pete, "Look, your brother cannot live in the same house with that snake."

"So let him move," Pete said.

They think they found all the babies.

But since no one knows how many snakes Coily actually gave birth to, no one is positive they're really all gone. Pete says if there are any left, they ought to come out pretty soon, because they'll be hungry.

In the meantime, they could be anywhere. In the pipes under the toilet, in the back of a closet, behind the refrigerator.

So I did move. I'm staying at Josh's house for a while. My parents have been very understanding about my traumatic experience. Especially my father.

He's checked into a motel for two weeks.

2 The Child Laborer

by J. Patrick Lewis

SUMMARY

This poem is about Iqbal Masih, a Pakistani boy who at age 5 was sold into slavery and forced to spend long days weaving carpets. He escaped and became an outspoken activist against child labor, but was shot and killed in Pakistan at age 12. Many people believe that it was because of Iqbal's crusade against the exploitation of children that he was murdered.

SOURCE: Heroes and She-roes: Poems of Amazing and Everyday Heroes *is a collection of poems about extraordinary people who have devoted their lives to making the world a better place.*

READING SESSION: 1

LANGUAGE AND VOCABULARY

Before reading "The Child Laborer," allow students time to define *crusade* and discuss who usually leads crusades using the "5 W's and H of Knowing a Word" chart below.

W	**What** is a crusade?	
W	**Who** usually leads crusades?	
W	**When** did Iqbal Masih lead a crusade?	
W	**Where** did he lead the crusade?	
W	**Why** did Iqbal think a crusade was necessary?	
H	**How** successful was his crusade?	

  After reading, give students an opportunity to extend their understanding by completing the remaining cells in the organizer.

THINK, TALK, AND WRITE ABOUT TEXT

Think about what your life was like when you were 5. Now, discuss Iqbal's life as a 5-year-old. How was his life different from the lives of most 5-year-olds? Capture the details of your conversation by listing the positives and negatives in Iqbal's life.

Positive Experiences	Negative Experiences

Use, or adapt, the "Once upon a time" template below to write a poem from Iqbal's point of view.

Once upon a time in a land not so far away

I spent my days _____ .

My only concern was _____ .

I went to sleep at night thinking about _____ .

Each day was filled with _____ .

But then my worst nightmare happened.

Now, I'm caught in _____ .

I'm worried that _____ .

I keep thinking I _____ .

My worst fear is _____ .

Now, I know that happily ever after is _____ .

The Child Laborer

by J. Patrick Lewis

Iqbal Masih was a young Pakistani boy who used to work long hours for almost no pay. But Iqbal was very brave; he escaped the factory where he worked, later becoming an activist who spoke out against child labor all across the world. One day, Iqbal was killed not far from his home in Pakistan. This poem about Iqbal considers his impact on the world and whether his bold ideas cost him his life.

READ-ALOUD TIP

This powerful poem may have to be read more than once for students to internalize its content. Using the line punctuation to guide your read-aloud will allow you to change the tempo as your read. In the first stanza, each of the first four lines is a sentence; then there is a two-line sentence followed by a four-line sentence. The second stanza is a six-line sentence. The dashes and commas set off content that expands upon the basic facts.

BACKGROUND LANGUAGE

Two words that will help students understand Iqbal's life are **crusade** and **fortitude**. After a first reading, reread the poem, highlighting these two words to help students make inferences about Iqbal's life.

Iqbal Masih

Pakistan, 1982–1995

Iqbal Masih—Pakistan.
Father sold him to a man.
Sixteen dollars, the going price.
Five-year-olds were merchandise.
The factory owner—dealer in doom—
Chained him to a carpet loom.
Slaving long hours without food,
Iqbal found the fortitude
To escape an inhumane
Never-ending house of pain.

Men occasionally destroy
Youth and spirit, but the boy,
Ten years old, led a crusade—
Life, the highest price he paid—
Against some of the greatest crimes
Perpetrated in modern times.

3 Malala's Address to the United Nations

by Malala Yousafzai

SUMMARY

Malala Yousafzai is a Pakistani activist who fights for the right of girls and women to pursue education. In 2012, when Malala was 16, she was shot by the Taliban, who tried to assassinate her in retaliation for her education advocacy. She survived and went on to be recognized on a global scale for her work. In 2013, she addressed the United Nations and declared her ongoing commitment to fighting illiteracy, poverty, and terrorism.

SOURCE: *Speech to United Nations (2013) At the age of 15, Malala Yousafzai began speaking up so that young women in her country could attend school in Pakistan. Though the Taliban tried to silence her, Malala made her voice heard throughout the world.*

READING SESSION: 1

We suggest reading this twice: the first reading for the impact of the message and the second reading to connect her words to those who inspired her.

LANGUAGE AND VOCABULARY

After reading, invite students to generate language that describes Malala. Have them use the words to write a description of Malala for someone who has never heard of this brave young woman.

Descriptive Language

Discuss the words in the word box below with members of your group. Circle the words you think you would use to describe Malala Yousafzai to help someone understand this remarkable young woman and her actions.

activist	fearful	nonviolent
outspoken	educated	powerful
shy	silenced	rich
angry	weak	tolerant
peaceful	extremist	prejudiced
respectful	frightened	strong

Based on your group discussion, what other words would you now add to the ones you chose from the list above in order to write your description?

THINK, TALK, AND WRITE ABOUT TEXT

Think about how you might have responded to your attackers had you been in Malala's circumstances. Where do you think she gets the strength to stay with her mission after the attack?

In her speech to the United Nations, she says: "Malala Day is not my day. Today is the day of every woman, every boy and every girl who have raised their voices for their rights." **Discuss** what these lines tell us about Malala's character and sense of purpose.

Malala calls on world leaders to change their policies. What does she ask these leaders to increase and what does she ask them to decrease? **Discuss** the way you think these new world policies might change the world.

Visit https://secure.aworldatschool.org/page/content/the-text-of-malala-yousafzais-speech-at-the-united-nations/ to read Malala's entire speech at the Youth Takeover of the United Nations. If the participants who attended wrote a bill of rights for the world's children, what would the rights be? How could you get involved?

"One child, one teacher, one book, and one pen can change the world. Education is the only solution." In what way does this quote remind us of what we take for granted?

Malala's Address to the United Nations

by Malala Yousafzai

On October 9, 2012, a group of armed men boarded a bus in Mingora, Pakistan, looking for a girl named Malala Yousafzai. Malala had spoken out for the right of girls and women to get an education. The men, part of a terrorist group called the Taliban, disagreed with Malala and wanted her dead. They shot her three times, but Malala survived and went on to become recognized across the world for her work on behalf of girls and children. In 2013, the United Nations declared July 12th to be "Malala Day." Following is an excerpt from Malala's speech on that day.

READ-ALOUD TIP

This thought-provoking speech will challenge students to think about what they might be taking for granted. Read aloud this speech in a voice filled with courage and determination, placing particular emphasis on sentences such as: "So here I stand," or "Their right to . . ." or "We call upon . . ."

BACKGROUND LANGUAGE

Many political, cultural, and geographic terms are used in this speech. Some words and names that might need attention include: *activists*, *extremists*, Martin Luther King, Nelson Mandela, Gandhi, and Mother Teresa.

Honorable UN Secretary General Mr. Ban Ki-moon,

Today it is an honor for me to be speaking again after a long time.

Dear brothers and sisters, do remember one thing: Malala Day is not my day. Today is the day of every woman, every boy, and every girl who have raised their voice for their rights.

There are hundreds of human rights activists and social workers who are not only speaking for their rights, but who are struggling to achieve their goal of peace, education and equality. Thousands of people have been killed by the terrorists and millions have been injured. I am just one of them.

So here I stand. So here I stand, one girl, among many. I speak—not for myself, but for all girls and boys. I raise up my voice—not so that I can shout, but so that those without a voice can be heard. Those who have fought for their rights:

- Their right to live in peace
- Their right to be treated with dignity
- Their right to equality of opportunity
- Their right to be educated

Dear friends, on 9 October 2012, the Taliban shot me on the left side of my forehead. They shot my friends, too. They thought that the bullets would silence us, but they failed. And out of that silence came thousands of voices. The terrorists thought they would change our aims and stop our ambitions. But nothing changed in my life except this: weakness, fear and hopelessness died. Strength, power and courage were born.

I am the same Malala. My ambitions are the same. My hopes are the same. And my dreams are the same.

Dear sisters and brothers, I am not against anyone. Neither am I here to speak in terms of personal revenge against the Taliban or any other terrorist group. I am here to speak up for the right of education of every child. I want education for the sons and the daughters of all the extremists, especially the Taliban. I do not even hate the Talib who shot me. Even if there was a gun in my hand and he was standing in front of me, I would not shoot him. This is the compassion I have learned from Mohammed, the prophet of mercy, Jesus Christ and Lord Buddha. This is the legacy of change I have inherited from Martin Luther King, Nelson Mandela and Mohammed Ali Jinnah.

This is the philosophy of nonviolence that I have learned from Gandhi, Bacha Khan and Mother Teresa. And this is the forgiveness that I have learned from my father and from my mother. This is what my soul is telling me: be peaceful and love everyone.

Dear sisters and brothers, we realize the importance of light when we see darkness. We realize the importance of our voice when we are silenced. In the same way, when we were in Swat, the north of Pakistan, we realized the importance of pens and books when we saw the guns. The wise saying, "The pen is mightier than the sword," is true. The extremists are afraid of books and pens. The power of education frightens them.

Peace is a necessity for education. In many parts of the world, especially Pakistan and Afghanistan, terrorism, war and conflicts stop children from going to schools. We are really tired of these wars. Women and children are suffering in many parts of the world, in many ways.

In India, innocent and poor children are victims of child labor. Many schools have been destroyed in Nigeria. People in Afghanistan have been affected by the hurdles of extremism for decades. Young girls have to do domestic child labor and are forced to get married at an early age. Poverty, ignorance, injustice, racism and the deprivation of basic rights are the main problems, faced by both men and women.

Dear fellows, today I am focusing on women's rights and girls' education because they are suffering the most. There was a time when women social activists asked men to stand up for their rights. But this time we will do it by ourselves. I am not telling men to step away from speaking for women's rights, but I am focusing on women to be independent and fight for themselves.

Dear sisters and brothers, now it's time to speak up.

So, today, we call upon the world leaders to change their strategic policies in favor of peace and prosperity.

We call upon the world leaders that all the peace deals must protect women's and children's rights. A deal that goes against the dignity of women and their rights is unacceptable.

We call upon all governments to ensure free compulsory education for every child all over the world.

We call upon all governments to fight against terrorism and violence, to protect children from brutality and harm.

We call upon the developed nations to support the expansion of educational opportunities for girls in the developing world. We call upon all communities to be tolerant, to reject prejudice based on cast, creed, sect, color, religion or gender. To ensure freedom and equality for women so they can flourish. We cannot all succeed when half of us are held back.

We call upon our sisters around the world to be brave, to embrace the strength within themselves and realize their full potential.

So let us wage, so let us wage a glorious struggle against illiteracy, poverty and terrorism, and let us pick up our books and our pens. They are the most powerful weapons.

One child, one teacher, one book and one pen can change the world. Education is the only solution. Education first. Thank you.

4 A Child Slave in California

by Kristin Lewis

SUMMARY

Shyima was born into a poor family in Alexandria, Egypt. When she turned 8, her parents sent her to work for a wealthy family in Cairo. When the family moved to California, Shyima was forced to go with them. She lived and worked in servitude until 2002, when she was rescued by the police. Later, she was adopted by a loving family, attended school, and even earned U.S. citizenship.

SOURCE: *Scholastic* SCOPE *is an ELA magazine for secondary school that features engaging, multigenre content, and rich skill-building support material.*

READING SESSIONS: 2

LANGUAGE AND VOCABULARY

Prior to reading the text, read students the title and ask them to brainstorm words or phrases they think will appear in the text. Then, read each of these words, which appear in the text: *enslaved, free will, shaghala* (servant), *captors, domestic servitude, human trafficking, protective custody, involuntary servitude.* Ask students to write each word in the box that best describes their understanding of the word or phrase.

I don't know this word.	I've seen or heard the word but don't know what it means.
I think I know this word.	I know this word.

After reading, ask students to look at the words or phrases again and list one in the box that now describes their understanding of the word.

THINK, TALK, AND WRITE ABOUT TEXT

The author writes: "Today, slavery is illegal everywhere. Yet more people are enslaved today than at any other time in history." **Think about** this quote. Does this shock you? What does this make you wonder or question?

Talk about Shyima's journey. How do you think Shyima's life would have been different had she remained living with her family in Egypt?

Talk about the role of a bystander in this type of situation. An "anonymous caller" reported that something suspicious was happening at the Ibrahims' house. Why do you think others who were suspicious didn't get involved earlier? What was the impact of the call to authorities on Shyima's life? In what ways might this person's actions impact the lives of other children and adults who are enslaved?

Think about Shyima's life as a road she is traveling. Create a road map that includes markers (signs) that show major events or turning points in her life. After you complete your map, use the map to help you write about what you think Shyima's life will be like now that she is no longer enslaved.

A Child Slave in California

by Kristin Lewis

Slavery is outlawed everywhere today. Yet millions of people, many of whom are children and teens, are enslaved around the world, including in the United States. This is the story of one young girl who was sold into slavery by her own family.

READ-ALOUD TIP

Pacing will be critical when reading this informational text. The narrative segments can be read with the same pace you would use for a story. Read the informational sections more slowly, emphasizing significant details.

BACKGROUND LANGUAGE

Knowledge of *human trafficking* and *servitude* will be critical for students to understand Shyima's life in America. Students may already know about trafficking from television, so adding this language to the images they already own will provide effective support for them to make connections.

Shyima stood at the sink in the elegant kitchen of a fancy Southern California home. She was barely tall enough to reach the counter. Elbow-deep in soapy dishwater, she methodically washed the plates, scrubbing off bits of food and carefully rinsing them under the faucet. When she finished washing and drying, she stood on a chair to put the dishes away.

Seems like an ordinary chore for a 12-year-old girl, right?

But washing dishes was not just an ordinary chore for Shyima, something she did before watching TV or doing her homework. It was one of an endless series of chores she did all day long, every day of the year.

Shyima was a modern-day slave.

Nearly every culture on nearly every continent on Earth has had slaves. Slavery has existed since the beginning of recorded history. Indeed, the citizens of Mesopotamia, where the first cities were built, enslaved those they defeated in battle.

In the United States, more than 12 million Africans were forced into slavery from 1619 to 1865. Slaves helped build many of our early government buildings, including the White House and the U.S. Capitol. It took a bloody Civil War and a constitutional amendment, passed in 1865, to outlaw slavery in the U.S. for good.

Today, slavery is illegal everywhere. Yet more people are enslaved today than at any other time in history. Many are children and young teens—hauling bricks in India, harvesting cocoa beans in West Africa, or weaving carpets in Pakistan. They are in restaurants, factories, mines, homes, and on farms. Although their plights are different, what they have in

 Riveting Read-Alouds for Middle School © Janet Allen and Patrick Daley, Scholastic Inc.

common is this: They are held captive and forced to work.

"Slavery is about the loss of free will; it's about coming under the violent control of another who is going to exploit you," says Kevin Bales, who runs an organization called Free the Slaves. According to Bales, there are as many as 27 million slaves in the world—about 50,000 of them in the U.S. "Slavery is like someone is mugging you and stealing your life," he says.

For four years Shyima, 12, had been living a nightmare. She was not allowed to go to school. She was not allowed to have friends or go to the movies or play sports or go to the doctor when she was sick. Instead, she was forced to work as a maid in the home of Abdel Nasser Ibrahim, his wife, Amal Ahmed Motelib, and their five children in Irvine, California.

Shyima often worked 18 hours a day. Many nights, while the family slept, she stayed up ironing their outfits for the next day. Each morning, she woke the kids, got them ready for school, and cooked breakfast. In return, they called her *shaghala* (servant) and "stupid."

During the day, Shyima cleaned the enormous house. She vacuumed, made the beds, dusted, and did laundry. Once, she tossed her own clothes in the washing machine. When Motelib found out, she slapped Shyima. "She told me my clothes were dirtier than theirs, that I wasn't allowed to clean mine there," Shyima remembers. After that, she washed her clothes in a bucket and dried them outside, by the trash cans.

Victims of slavery are controlled by the physical and emotional power of their captors. The Ibrahims threatened Shyima that if she told anyone about her situation, she would be beaten by the police. They forbade her from going anywhere alone. Sometimes they even locked her in her room.

How had this happened to her?

Shyima was born in Alexandria, Egypt. She lived with her parents and 10 brothers and sisters, sharing a small one-bathroom home with three other families. They slept on blankets on the floor. They had no money for dentists or doctors or school. But though life was often hard, Shyima felt loved.

All that changed when Shyima turned 8. That's when her mother decided it was time for Shyima to help out. Shyima was sold to the Ibrahims, who at the time lived in Cairo, Egypt's capital. (In Egypt, selling children is illegal but widespread.)

The arrangement was simple: Shyima would live with and work for the Ibrahims. In exchange, they would pay her family $45 a month.

The price that Shyima paid, however, was immeasurable. Being a slave meant that she would live in loneliness, cut off from everyone who cared for her. It meant that every day, she would be treated as if her life had no value.

Yet for poor families like Shyima's, domestic servitude often seems like the best option for their children. As servants, children are at least guaranteed food to eat. Some "employers," like the Ibrahims, even see themselves as benefactors who are doing a kind thing by taking on a less-fortunate child. Shyima's family firmly believed that she would have a better life with the Ibrahims.

They were wrong.

* * * * *

From the start, Shyima desperately missed her family and didn't understand why she couldn't go home. Then came the news that the Ibrahims were moving to America and that she was going with them.

Complicating the situation was the fact that Shyima's parents had borrowed money from the Ibrahims for medical expenses. The only way to repay the debt, said the Ibrahims, was to let Shyima go to America.

It was against the law to bring Shyima into the United States as a maid, but that did not stop the Ibrahims. Each year, thousands of children are smuggled into the U.S. to work. They come mainly from China, Mexico, and West Africa.

Human trafficking, as it is called, is the fastest-growing criminal industry in the world. More than 800,000 people are trafficked worldwide every year—as many as 17,500 in the U.S. No one knows the exact number because once here, they disappear like Shyima did, hidden behind locked doors, invisible to the outside world.

Shyima arrived in California on August 3, 2000. The Ibrahims' opulent house had a beautiful fountain with two angels spouting water. The bathrooms were marble, the furnishings expensive.

Shyima would not, however, sleep in one of the grandly appointed bedrooms. Her room was the garage—a tiny windowless room with no heating or air-conditioning. Soon after she arrived, the only light bulb burned out. The Ibrahims never bothered to replace it. And so Shyima lived in darkness.

The Ibrahims tried to keep Shyima a secret, but eventually their neighbors became suspicious. Finally, in 2002, an anonymous caller reported that something sinister was going on in the Ibrahim house—a young girl seemed to be living in the garage.

That call changed Shyima's life.

One April morning, a police detective knocked on the Ibrahims' door. He wanted to know if any children other than the Ibrahims' were living in the house.

Nasser Ibrahim said no. Then he contradicted himself. "Yes," he said, "a distant relative."

The detective wanted to know why that distant relative wasn't going to school. Ibrahim explained that he hadn't enrolled her "yet." A few moments later, he went to get Shyima. He threatened that if she said anything to the police, she would never see her parents again.

The detective wasn't fooled. He questioned one of the Ibrahims' children, 12-year-old Heba, about Shyima. "She's, uh, my uh . . . " Heba stammered. "She's like my cousin, but—she's my dad's daughter's friend. Oops! The other way. Okay, I'm confused."

The detective immediately took Shyima into protective custody.

As Shyima was driven away from the Ibrahims forever, she was petrified. She spoke no English. She had no idea what would happen to her in this mysterious land that she knew little about. Frightened, she lied to the police interpreter, saying exactly what the Ibrahims had told her to say.

As the investigation continued, the shocking details of Shyima's life tumbled out. The Ibrahims claimed Shyima was part of their family, describing the time they all went to Disneyland. In fact, Shyima hadn't been allowed on any of the rides. They had brought her along to carry their bags.

Slowly, Shyima came to understand that what had been done to her was wrong. At one point, officials arranged for her to call her family back in Egypt. She told her parents what had happened and that she wanted to come home. "They kept telling me that [the Ibrahims] are good people," Shyima remembers. "That it's my fault. That because of what I did, my mom was going to have a heart attack."

After that conversation, Shyima made a decision: She wanted to stay in the U.S. and start a new life.

And that is exactly what she did.

Shyima learned English and started going to school. For the first time, she had friends, opportunities, a life. She was soon adopted by Chuck and Jenny Hall. (They have since taken her to Disneyland many times.) Remarkably, Shyima not only graduated from high school at age 18—despite having never been to school before she was rescued—but also went on to college. Today, she dreams of becoming a police officer or an immigration agent, working to help victims of human trafficking.

As for the Ibrahims? They pleaded guilty to involuntary servitude and forced labor. The judge ordered them to pay Shyima $76,000, the amount she would have earned at minimum wage. They went to prison and were later deported.

On December 15, 2011, Shyima stood in a packed room in Montebello, California. She was dressed in a stylish black top and pants. In her hand was a tiny American flag. Her nails were perfectly manicured, her hair and makeup flawless. There was little trace of the frightened young girl who was rescued from the dark nine years earlier.

"I solemnly swear," she began in perfect English, her hand raised to take the oath. "To support and defend," she continued, her eyes glistening, "the Constitution and the laws of the United States."

Shyima Hall, 22, had just become an American citizen.

"I can be who I want to be now," Shyima told reporters after the ceremony, smiling broadly. "And that is the most important part for me . . . that I can be who I want to be."

5 IU

by Tavis Smiley

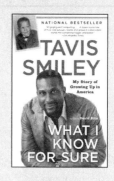

SUMMARY

Tavis Smiley is proud to be the first in his family to go to college, with or without his parents' approval. But although he is admitted to Indiana University, he neglects to officially register. When he arrives, no one knows who he is. Luckily, he meets two people who are sympathetic to his story. Smiley officially enrolls at IU, having learned that perseverance and some help from others can make things happen.

SOURCE: *Tavis Smiley's memoir speaks of his childhood in rural Indiana, and how poverty, race, religion, and his family's love shaped him into the person he is today.*

READING SESSIONS: 2

LANGUAGE AND VOCABULARY

As you fill in the flow chart below, discuss with students each step of the process. Encourage them to discuss what might go into each step. Encourage them to ask questions about each step.

How Do I Get to College?

Apply to a College

Wait for Acceptance Letter

Fill Out Proper Paperwork

Apply for Financial Aid

Obtain Welcome/New Student Information

Sign Up for Courses

Arrive at College

THINK, TALK, AND WRITE ABOUT TEXT

How is it possible that Tavis Smiley ended up at school not having filled in any of the right paperwork? What might have happened?

What do you think his brother, father, and mother were feeling as he left for school that day?

Why do you think the two men who Tavis met that first day helped him as they did?

The word *perseverance* means "the act of sticking to something or going through something even when there are a lot of obstacles." **How** did Tavis show perseverance?

Today Tavis Smiley is a successful writer. He is also a successful radio and TV host. What can we **infer** about him since that first week at Indiana University?

IU

by Tavis Smiley

So you got into college—great! But you never registered or paid tuition—oops! The following essay is a memoir, or an autobiographical account, of what happened to one man who forgot a few details before the first day of school.

READ-ALOUD TIP

IU is an autobiographical account of Tavis Smiley's college experience. As you read aloud this text, try to take on Smiley's persona. Use your reading voice to help listeners experience the range of his emotions: sadness at leaving home, insecurity, confusion, determination, and accomplishment.

BACKGROUND LANGUAGE

Students may not know the responsibilities of the various university officials who met with and ultimately supported Tavis Smiley's journey. Give a brief overview of these individuals: *secretary, director of admissions, bursar, associate bursar,* and *director of financial aid.*

I went off to Indiana University with nothing more than $50 in my pocket and a small suitcase.

A friend, Councilman Hogan's son Danny, drove me to Bloomington. I gave him half my money for gas for the two-and-a-half-hour drive. As we headed down the state, I was both excited and nervous. It was a day of firsts. I was leaving home for the first time. I was the first in my family to step into the world of higher education. And for the first time I would be living on my own, without restrictions, without rules, without the nightly church meetings and our cleaning work for Smiley and Sons.

I had excelled in high school, but would I measure up in college? I had no idea what to expect. Going without my parents' approval or help didn't make matters any easier. I had no dorm assignment, no money for tuition, no financial aid. I had nothing but my letter of acceptance.

"What are you going to do when you get there?" my brother Garnie had asked when the family had gathered outside the house. Our family had moved from the trailer to a house in Kokomo that my parents had bought from the estate of deceased members of New Bethel Tabernacle Church.

"I'm not sure," I said. "But I'll figure it out."

"You scared to be going so far from home?" asked my brother Maury.

"I'll miss you guys, sure," I said. "But you'll come to visit me. You'll come down to Bloomington."

As my siblings all gathered around to hug me, I saw Mama and Dad looking on. Then Dad stepped forward and shook my hand.

"You'll do fine, Tabo," he said. "God gave you a good mind."

When Mama slowly approached me, I saw tears in her eyes. We didn't know what to say to each other. Finally she hugged me with all her might and simply said, "Oh, Tavis. I love you so much."

Tears came to my eyes. I didn't want to break down with my siblings all around, so I broke away, saying, "I love you too."

The campus was enormous, a lot bigger in size than the town of Bunker Hill. The university population, perhaps thirty-two thousand strong, was on par with the city of Kokomo. The sprawling landscape of buildings—science labs, athletic fields, auditoriums, chapels, dormitories—was overwhelming.

Standing there in front of a dormitory on the campus of Indiana University, holding my little suitcase and my letter, I felt like a country hick.

Where was my place in all this?

All I knew was that I was standing in front of a dorm that housed students, and I needed a place to put down my suitcase. I walked into a front lobby filled with boxes and suitcases. Young men and women accompanied by their parents streamed in and out carrying portable stereos and boxes of books and bedspreads. I looked at a large piece of paper pinned to the bulletin board listing room assignments. I looked for my name. Of course, it wasn't there. As far as Indiana University knew, I didn't exist. I had never returned the form accepting admission because my parents had never signed it.

With a combination of naïveté and determination, I had simply shown up.

I could have lost it and gone running back to Kokomo. I could have let the feeling of intimidation turn me right around. I could have shrunk within myself and given in to feelings of isolation and fear.

Turn the fear to energy.

And that's what I did. I turned my apprehension into action. The action involved taking one step at a time. To begin with, I needed to find a place to put down my suitcase and sleep for the night. It was after 6 P.M. and the administration offices were closed. No one was going to give me a room tonight. At the end of the hallway, though, I saw a small sitting area with an easy chair and a couch. No one was using the space. Nor were there any signs declaring the area off limits. So I put down my suitcase on the couch and silently claimed the space as my own. I sat there for a long while, thinking how amazing it was to be in college, with no idea how any of this was going to work out.

One step at a time.

Next, I went down to the dorm cafeteria. Fortunately, no one was taking names or asking for food passes. First-day chaos allowed me to move through the line and get a free meal.

Families were gathered together. Old friends, reunited after the summer, excitedly discussed what they had done and where they had been. I sat alone, not really feeling sorry for myself, but feeling anonymous. And in fact, I was anonymous. And that feeling was new. After all, for the past four years I'd been a big shot at Maconaquah High School. I knew everyone and everyone knew me. People respected my accomplishments, and I reveled in that recognition. My place in that universe was secure. Here I had no place—not now, maybe not ever.

After dinner I went back to the public area of the dorm, sat on the couch, and read the *Indiana Daily Student*, a college newspaper more sophisticated than the *Kokomo Tribune*. I was surprised at the diversity of articles, movie reviews, music reviews, and editorials. I was amazed at the variety of activities on campus. Once I was through with the paper, though, I had nothing to do. It was only nine o'clock, too early to go to sleep. With the assistance of their parents, students were still moving in, carrying lamps and trunks, tennis rackets and cartons of clothes. I noticed how helpful the other parents were. I couldn't help but feel the advantages of family bonds at such a critical time in the students' lives. Right around now, my brothers would be getting home from church.

By eleven, the noise had died down. I could have used the bathroom down the hall and changed into my pajamas, but that would have made me even more conspicuous. I decided just to stretch out on the couch and sleep in my clothes. Chances were, no one would notice. And no one did. I drifted off, my overstimulated mind scrambled with thoughts. My dreams were a wild surreal movie, with tornadoes roaring through cornfields and demolishing trailer parks in their wake. I was in a version of the *The Wizard of Oz* set in Indiana. Senator Bayh was in the dream and so was Elder Rufus Mills, who was the Wizard. Dr. King worked as professor at Indiana University, where he welcomed me to his class. The fictitious Boxcar Children figured into the dream—I don't remember exactly how—and all the Smiley children were under my protection as we huddled together in the dark woods.

When morning broke, I didn't know where I was. Then I remembered—on a couch in a dorm in Bloomington, Indiana. I yawned and stretched.

"Don't you have a room?" asked a student who noticed me.

"Not yet," I said.

He just nodded and moved on.

I needed to eat, and once again, was able to join the cafeteria line and treat myself to a free breakfast. I picked up the local paper, the *Bloomington Herald-Times*, and scanned the news: Reagan at an economic summit, Princess Grace of Monaco had been killed in a horrific car wreck on the Riviera. It all seemed so far away. The *Indiana Daily Student* was filled with articles on how and where to register for classes; the information went over my head.

I knew one thing: I had to find the admissions office.

A pretty coed told me where it was, and I was off.

"May I help you?" asked the first secretary I encountered.

I told her my story.

"I'm not sure what to tell you," she said quizzically. So she sent me to a second secretary. Again, I told my story. Again, the secretary was confused.

"I've never heard of a case like yours," she said. "I'm not sure you belong here."

"Oh, I belong here," I replied. "I have this letter that says so."

"But that letter's not enough. You need proof of tuition payment, a room assignment, and any number of other documents. You can't just waltz in here and go to college."

"I *have* to go to college," I said. "I *am* going to college."

· · · · · ·

The process went on and on. I moved from one secretary to another. Finally, nearly three hours after I had arrived, I found myself sitting across the desk from the director of admissions, a white man in his fifties. He, too, had a puzzled look on his face.

"We've called the bursar's office, Mr. Smiley," he said, "but they have no information on you. You're nowhere to be found in their records. You never applied for aid, and you never sent in payment for tuition."

"I know," I said.

"In fact, there's no real reason you should be here."

"I understand, sir, except I do have my letter of admission."

"I've looked up your high school record, Mr. Smiley, and it's outstanding. That's why you were admitted. But you never wrote us back to say you were coming."

I explained that was because of my parents' refusal to sign any of the forms.

The director scratched his head. "Mr. Smiley," he said, "I'm going to send you to see David Hummons, our associate bursar. I'm hoping David can help you."

Much to my amazement, David Hummons was a tall, barrel-chested black man with a full-flown Afro and a laid-back attitude.

"What's happening, brother?" he asked me as we crowded into his cubicle.

I didn't know whether to call him "brother" or "sir." In high school, I didn't have a single black teacher or administrator. This was new territory. To me, David Hummons looked like someone out of the movie *Superfly*.

"Man," he said, "how you gonna go to this school—you got no room assignment and you got no money. I bet you don't even have the funds to pay for your books."

"No, sir, I don't."

Hummons laughed so loudly a secretary came in to see what was so funny. The laugh, though, wasn't mean; it was a warm and engaging laugh, almost a laugh of appreciation.

"Tell you what, young Tavis Smiley, I have no notion how all this will work out, but I do have a friend who might have an idea or two."

Hummons picked up the phone, dialed a number, and said, "Jimmy, I have a young man here with the strange name of Tavis. You won't believe his story. I'll let him tell it to you, but bottom line is that he just showed up as a freshman with nothing but a toothbrush and a smile. The smile ain't all that pretty, but something tells me this kid's all right. Can I send him up?"

Five minutes later I was waiting outside the office of Jimmy Ross, director of financial aid. I waited for nearly an hour.

"Mr. Ross will see you now," the secretary finally announced.

Sitting behind a big desk in a big office was, much to my unspoken delight, another black man. Jimmy Ross was also a brother!

Jimmy Ross totally understood my story. He understood the Pentecostal church and its resistance to the outside world. I didn't have to explain.

"What you will have to do," said Ross, "is fill out a million forms. We're going to straighten you out, Brother Smiley, but it's going to take a mountain of paperwork to do it."

And so I began to climb that mountain. I filled out forms till my fingers practically fell off. I filled out admissions forms, financial forms, forms for student employment and forms for Pell Grants. At the end of the day, when the forms were completed and I took them into Ross's office, he and David Hummons were standing together in the middle of a conversation. They both turned to me with broad beautiful smiles on their faces.

"Welcome to IU," said Ross.

"Make us proud, young brother," added Hummons, slapping me on the back.

"I will, sir," I promised solemnly. "You know I will."

It's a lesson I'll never forget. No one in this life gets ahead without the help of a lot of other people. Even the most talented need others to point out the way or lend a hand. Without Councilman Hogan and so many others, I never would have made my way to IU. Without the help of David Hummons and Jimmy Ross, my career at IU would have been over before it started. Anyone who thinks he's gotten ahead in life without the help of others is living in a fool's paradise.

6 Day of Disaster: The Eruption of Mt. Vesuvius 79 A.D.

by Lauren Tarshis

SOURCE: *Scholastic SCOPE is an ELA magazine for secondary school that features engaging, multigenre content, and rich skill-building support material.*

READING SESSIONS: 2

SUMMARY

Mt. Vesuvius looms over the bustling streets of Pompeii, which are packed with vendors, merchants, shoppers, even Roman gladiators. The volcano has been dormant for more than a thousand years. But one catastrophic day, it erupts, burying the city and its people under ash and rock. In 1748, Pompeii was rediscovered by scientists, who found a city destroyed but preserved, providing a glimpse into this ancient civilization.

LANGUAGE AND VOCABULARY

Prior to reading, share the title "Day of Disaster" and ask students to predict words they think will be included in this article.

During reading, ask students to collect words from the article to build a specialized vocabulary to use when writing about this event.

Words Related to Pompeii	Words Related to Volcanoes	Words Related to Emotions
amphitheater	erupted	surprised
		.

After reading, allow students to combine word lists so they are available when students discuss and write about this disaster.

THINK, TALK, AND WRITE ABOUT TEXT

Think about the way we depend on emergency preparedness information and instructions when we experience, or anticipate, a disaster. Discuss how that disaster information compares to what the citizens of Pompeii had before Mt. Vesuvius erupted.

Talk about why archaeologists have been so fascinated with the ruins since they were rediscovered in 1748.

Think and talk about how those citizens who survived might have felt when they saw the devastation. What do you think they might want to say to those who live in the eruption zones?

Write a letter from the point of view of one of the survivors, directed to someone who is living in the eruption zones today. What would a survivor want people to know?

Write an informational piece explaining the science behind the preservation of Pompeii. Use your specialized vocabulary and text features (e.g., maps, diagrams, pictures) to help the reader understand why Pompeii is described as a *time capsule.*

Day of Disaster: The Eruption of Mt. Vesuvius 79 A.D.

by Lauren Tarshis

Nearly 2,000 years ago, a volcanic eruption destroyed the city of Pompeii. Thousands died. It was one of the worst disasters of the ancient world. Now, imagine that you were there.

READ-ALOUD TIP

This informational text is told using a narrative format, inviting readers to imagine what it would have been like to walk through Pompeii before the eruption. As the volcano starts to erupt, intensity will be an important factor in your read-aloud. To help students relive this disastrous event, read short sentences with increasing urgency.

BACKGROUND LANGUAGE

Geographical information will be important for students. If possible, show a map of Pompeii and visuals of volcanic eruptions to add to students' understanding.

It's a typical summer day in the beautiful city of Pompeii in the year 79 A.D. The main street is packed with people—women swishing by in long robes, men in tunics, children with leather sandals that slap against the hot stone streets.

Vendors shout for your attention, offering you slices of juicy melons or sizzling hunks of roasted meats. From the shoulder of a shopkeeper, a parrot squawks, *"Salve!"—hello* in Latin, the language of the Roman Empire.

You're surprised by how modern this city seems. It has a library, theaters, and grand temples. There are shops and restaurants and a market where you can taste dozens of delicacies, from sweet dates and figs to fattened roasted mice stuffed with nuts and rose petals. Beautiful marble and bronze statues stand all over the city, monuments to the famous citizens, mighty emperors, and fierce generals who built Rome into the most powerful empire in the world.

The heat makes you thirsty, so you stop at a public fountain made of carved stone. You scoop up some of the cool, clean water. No wonder Romans are proud of their water. Nowhere else in the world has such a sophisticated system of aqueducts, underground tunnels that deliver fresh water to fountains, bathhouses, and private homes.

As you rest by the fountain, an enormous man lumbers past, his arms scarred, his muscled legs thick as tree trunks. This man is a famous gladiator—a fighter set to do battle that afternoon in Pompeii's amphitheater, a stadium that holds 20,000 people. Romans love to watch gladiators fight each other with fists, swords, clubs, or knives. Sometimes men are pitted against ferocious lions or bears. If it sounds gruesome, that's because it is. Gladiators often die in the arena.

Maybe by now you've noticed it: the massive mountain that looms behind the city.

That's Mount Vesuvius. You haven't given it much thought—and neither do the people of Pompeii. Why should they? It's just a big mountain, silent and still, its gentle slopes covered with trees and grape vineyards.

Except Mount Vesuvius is not just a mountain. It is a volcano. Vesuvius sits atop a crack in the earth's crust—the hard, rocky layer that covers the surface of our planet like the shell of an egg. From miles below, molten rock called magma seeps up through this crack.

The people of Pompeii have no idea that a huge lake of magma is boiling under Vesuvius, steaming with poisonous, explosive gases. How could they? There is not even a word for *volcano* in Latin.

Vesuvius has been dormant for 1,500 years, but now it is waking up. For months, magma has been rising through the center of the volcano, filling it like fiery blood. Pressure is building.

Over the past few weeks, there have been warning signs. Talk to the farmers who tend the vineyards around Vesuvius. They'll tell you about a stinging smell—like rotten eggs—wafting from the mountaintop. Is it a warning from the gods? Like the ancient Greeks before them, the Romans believe that gods and goddesses control everything in the world. Some say that mighty Jupiter, god of the sky, is angry at the people of Pompeii. Of course, nobody understands that the terrible smell is sulfurous gas, part of the explosive brew simmering inside Vesuvius.

There have been other signs of a coming disaster. The extreme heat underground has dried up streams. Goats and sheep are dropping dead on the mountain, their lungs seared by the poisonous gases. Most alarming of all: Small earthquakes have jolted the city, a sign of growing strain on the land.

All this is evidence that a huge eruption will come at any moment. The people of Pompeii should have evacuated days or even weeks before. But no one understands the signs. So what are you doing standing around? You should run. *Now.*

At this point, it's too late for the people of Pompeii . . . and it may be too late for you.

Boom! Boom!

Two powerful explosions, seconds apart, shatter the sky. The ground shakes so violently that people fall. Horses and donkeys scream. Birds scatter by the thousands. You see a terrifying sight: a gigantic column of what looks like gray smoke spewing from the top of Mount Vesuvius.

It's not smoke though. The intense heat produced by the eruption has turned millions of tons of solid rock into superheated foam. The boiling plume shoots 12 miles into the sky at rocket speeds. When it hits the freezing air in the lower atmosphere, the melted rock cools into tiny pebbles called pumice. Carried by wind, they spread through the air and pour down on Pompeii.

The pumice falls with painful force. It is mixed with hot ash, which clogs your nose and throat. Many people are fleeing. Go with them! Push past the donkey carts and through the gates of the city. Grab the hand of a little boy who has become separated from his family. Keep moving.

Riveting Read-Alouds for Middle School © Janet Allen and Patrick Daley, Scholastic Inc.

The farther you get, the more likely you are to live.

Other people decide to stay behind, to guard their homes and businesses. Crime is bad in Pompeii. An empty home or shop will almost certainly be ransacked by thieves. People hide in their homes. They think this strange storm of ash and rock will end soon.

They are wrong.

• • • • •

The sky turns black. As hours pass, the weight of the pumice causes roofs to collapse, trapping people in their homes.

Then more terror.

As the volcano loses energy, the molten rock and ash mix together to create a superheated wave that rushes down the mountain at 80 miles an hour. This burning avalanche is known as a pyroclastic flow. When it hits Pompeii, death for those who stayed behind is almost instant.

Over the next few hours, millions of tons of ash and rock fall on the city. In the weeks that follow, people return to Pompeii to search for survivors.

There are none.

In fact, the entire city seems to have vanished. Pompeii is buried under 12 feet of rock. Within a few decades, Pompeii is all but forgotten, wiped off the face of the Earth.

You survived your day in Pompeii. You are one of the lucky few who made it far enough away from the city to escape being crushed. But before you go home, let's take one more trip, to Pompeii today. The ruins lie near the city of Naples, in southern Italy. For nearly 1,700 years, Pompeii was forgotten. It was rediscovered in 1748 and has been studied ever since.

The layers of pumice and ash that fell on Pompeii formed a shell over the city, preserving it as a time capsule of Roman life. Archaeologists have unearthed dazzling treasures, like jewels, mosaic artwork, and statues. They even found a basket of petrified eggs and the remains of a bowl of chicken soup.

As you walk through the ruins of Pompeii, you can admire the remnants of houses, shops, and temples. You can almost hear the voices of the citizens. And you can see Mount Vesuvius. It is silent and still.

But don't be fooled.

Vesuvius has erupted more than 80 times since Pompeii was destroyed, the last time in 1944. These eruptions were small, but scientists have no doubt that the volcano will erupt again, possibly with the same devastating force as it did in 79 A.D. They worry about the millions who live in the eruption zones. Will they have enough warning before the next eruption? Or will people suffer the same fate as ancient Pompeiians—swallowed by fire, buried in ash, and lost to time?

And would you want to be there to find out?

7 Priscilla and the Wimps

by Richard Peck

SOURCE: *Richard Peck is the author of several children's stories and novels. He currently lives in Manhattan, NY.*

READING SESSION: 1

SUMMARY

Told from a spectator's point of view, this short narrative relates the story of a gang of school bullies called Klutter's Kobras. Led by Monk Klutter, the Kobras have picked on practically every guy in school. But when they target little Melvin Detweiler one day, they finally met their match in Melvin's friend, Priscilla Roseberry, the largest student in school. She quickly teaches Monk and his thugs not to mess with her or her friend.

LANGUAGE AND VOCABULARY

There are many different types of figurative language. Figurative language goes beyond the actual meaning (literal language) to give the reader new insights. Some common types of figurative language include comparisons (simile, metaphor); exaggerations (hyperbole); representations of something else (symbolism); and, giving human characteristics to inanimate objects, animals, or ideas (personification). After reading, analyze some of the figurative language Peck used and see if you can find other examples not shown here.

Quote	Literally means . . .	Figuratively means . . .	Type of figurative language . . .
"Monk ran a tight ship."			
"This school was old Monk's Garden of Eden."			
" . . . neck popping like gunfire."			
" . . . frog-marches Monk . . ."			

THINK, TALK, AND WRITE ABOUT TEXT

Think about the school you attend. Are there groups that have more power than the rest of the students? What gives them that power? Is that power typically used in positive or negative ways?

There is clearly bullying with violence and extortion at this middle school. **Discuss** whether anti-bullying messages have changed this, or do these behaviors still exist? How are the Kobras getting away with this?

Visit this website to see what recommendations these authors make for dealing with bullies: http://kidshealth.org/en/teens/bullies.html. Do you think these recommendations would have helped students at this school? What is one strategy you learned from reading about bullying?

Use this point-of-view guide as a prewriting exercise to help you **write an article** for the newspaper that expresses Monk's point of view.

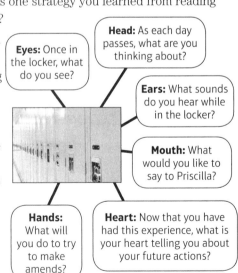

Eyes: Once in the locker, what do you see?

Head: As each day passes, what are you thinking about?

Ears: What sounds do you hear while in the locker?

Mouth: What would you like to say to Priscilla?

Hands: What will you do to try to make amends?

Heart: Now that you have had this experience, what is your heart telling you about your future actions?

Priscilla and the Wimps

by Richard Peck

Monk Klutter and his gang of Kobras have all the students cowering in fear . . . except for Priscilla Roseberry, who's not even aware they exist. What happens when they come face to face?

READ-ALOUD TIP

Use the action of the story to establish pacing. When reading this short story, pause slightly to anticipate the encounter between Monk and Priscilla, which is about to occur when Monk says: "Who is it around here doesn't know Monk Klutter?" Pause again just before the last paragraph.

BACKGROUND LANGUAGE

In order to grasp the subtleties of language used, students may need to know what a pun is as well as understand the reference to the Garden of Eden.

L isten, there was a time when you couldn't even go to the *rest room* around this school without a pass. And I'm not talking about those little pink tickets made out by some teacher. I'm talking about a pass that could cost anywhere up to a buck, sold by Monk Klutter.

Not that Mighty Monk ever touched money, not in public. The gang he ran, which ran the school for him, was his collection agency. They were Klutter's Kobras, a name spelled out in nailheads on six well-known black plastic windbreakers.

Monk's threads were more . . . subtle. A pile-lined suede battle jacket with lizard-skin flaps over tailored Levis and a pair of ostrich-skin boots, brass-toed and suitable for kicking people around. One of his Kobras did nothing all day but walk a half step behind Monk, carrying a fitted bag with Monk's gym shoes, a roll of rest-room passes, a cash box, and a switchblade that Monk gave himself manicures with at lunch over at the Kobras' table.

Speaking of lunch, there were a few cases of advanced malnutrition among the newer kids. The ones who were a little slow in handing over a cut of their lunch money and were therefore barred from the cafeteria. Monk ran a tight ship.

I admit it. I'm five foot five, and when the Kobras slithered by, with or without Monk, I shrank. And I admit this, too: I paid up on a regular basis. And I might add: so would you.

This school was old Monk's Garden of Eden. Unfortunately for him, there was a serpent in it. The reason Monk didn't recognize trouble when it was staring him in the face is that the serpent in the Kobras' Eden was a girl.

Practically every guy in school could show you his scar. Fang marks from Kobras, you might say. And they were all highly visible in the shower room: lumps, lacerations, blue bruises, you name it. But girls usually got off with a warning.

Except there was this one girl named Priscilla Roseberry. Picture a girl named Priscilla Roseberry, and you'll be light years off. Priscilla was, hands down, the largest student in our particular institution of learning. I'm not talking fat, I'm talking big. Even beautiful, in a bionic way. Priscilla wasn't inclined toward organized crime. Otherwise, she could have put together a gang that would turn Klutter's Kobras into garter snakes.

Priscilla was basically a loner except she had one friend. A little guy named Melvin Detweiler. You talk about The Odd Couple. Melvin's one of the smallest guys above midget status ever seen. A really nice guy, but, you know—little. They even had lockers next to each other, in the same bank as mine. I don't know what they had going. I'm not saying this was a romance. After all, people deserve their privacy.

Priscilla was sort of above everything, if you'll pardon a pun. And very calm, as only the very big can be. If there was anybody who didn't notice Klutter's Kobras, it was Priscilla.

Until one winter day after school when we were all grabbing our coats out of our lockers. And hurrying, since Klutter's Kobras made sweeps of the halls for after-school shakedowns.

Anyway, up to Melvin's locker swaggers one of the Kobras. Never mind his name. Gang members don't need names. They've got group identity. He reaches down and grabs little Melvin by the neck and slams his head against his locker door. The sound of skull against steel rippled all the way down the locker row, speeding the crowds on their way.

"Okay, let's see your pass," snarled the Kobra.

"A pass for what this time?" Melvin asks, probably still dazed.

"Let's call it a pass for very short people," says the Kobra, "a dwarf tax." He wheezes a little Kobra chuckle at his own wittiness. And already he's reaching for Melvin's wallet with the hand that isn't circling Melvin's windpipe. All this time, of course, Melvin and the Kobra are standing in Priscilla's big shadow.

She's taking her time shoving her books into her locker and pulling on a very large-size coat. Then, quicker than the eye, she brings the side of her enormous hand down in a chop that breaks the Kobra's hold on Melvin's throat. You could hear a pin drop in that hallway. Nobody'd ever laid a finger on a Kobra, let alone a hand the size of Priscilla's.

Then Priscilla, who hardly ever says anything to anybody except to Melvin, says to the Kobra, "Who's your leader, wimp?"

This practically blows the Kobra away. First he's chopped by a girl, and now she's acting like she doesn't know Monk Klutter, the Head Honcho of the World. He's so amazed, he tells her. "Monk Klutter."

"Never heard of him," Priscilla mentions. "Send him to see me." The Kobra just backs away from her like the whole situation is too big for him, which it is.

Pretty soon Monk himself slides up. He jerks his head once, and his Kobras slither off down the hall. He's going to handle this interesting case personally.

"Who is it around here doesn't know Monk Klutter?"

He's standing inches from Priscilla, but since he'd have to look up at her, he doesn't. "Never heard of him," says Priscilla.

Monk's not happy with this answer, but by now he's spotted Melvin, who's grown smaller in spite of himself. Monk breaks his own rule by reaching for Melvin with his own hands. "Kid," he says, "you're going to have to educate your girlfriend."

His hands never quite make it to Melvin. In a move of pure poetry Priscilla has Monk in a hammerlock. His neck's popping like gunfire, and his head's bowed under the immense weight of her forearm. His suede jacket's peeling back, showing pile.

Priscilla's behind him in another easy motion. And with a single mighty thrust forward, frog-marches Monk into her own locker. It's incredible. His ostrich-skin boots click once in the air. And suddenly he's gone, neatly wedged into the locker, a perfect fit. Priscilla bangs the door shut, twirls the lock, and strolls out of school. Melvin goes with her, of course, trotting along below her shoulder. The last stragglers leave quietly.

Well, this is where fate, an even bigger force than Priscilla, steps in. It snows all night, a blizzard. The whole town ices up. And school closes for a week.

8 Dead Men Floating

by Danielle Denega

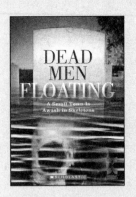

SUMMARY

In 1993, a natural disaster turned into a nightmare for the residents of Hardin, Missouri. The rain-swollen Missouri River overflowed, unearthing nearly 600 coffins and scattering the remains of the dead across Hardin. A team of forensic anthropologists came to the town to identify remains and rebury the dead.

SOURCE: *Dead Men Floating is from XBOOKS, an informational text program by Scholastic.* www.scholastic.com/xbooks

READING SESSIONS: 2

LANGUAGE AND VOCABULARY

Create a concept web like the one below. Put "Death and Burial Rites" in the center circle. Discuss the three words already connected to the circle. Ask students to contribute other words, ideas, and concepts that relate to death and burial rites. Reinforce that any word can go on the web if they can justify the connection.

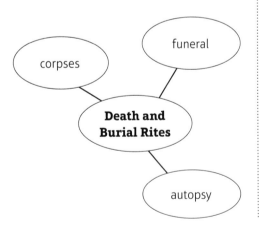

THINK, TALK, AND WRITE ABOUT TEXT

The author says that the rain turned from a "nuisance" to a "nightmare." What did he mean by that?

Why was the flooding in Harding like a "scene from a horror movie"?

What was the advantage of having a DMORT mission come into Hardin? Why couldn't the citizens handle this problem on their own?

Explain how the author helps us understand why this event was so devastating to the community (e.g., "You bury someone and you expect them to be buried for eternity.").

Why do you think it was so important for the citizens of Hardin to get all the bones identified and put back into the proper graves? Would it have mattered to you if you lived in Hardin?

What would you have liked or not liked about being on this DMORT mission?

Dead Men Floating

by Danielle Denega

When a huge storm caused the Missouri River to overflow in 1993, its waters swept through Hardin, destroying homes and buildings, and unearthing nearly 600 coffins from the local cemetery. What would it take to get the corpses back in their proper graves? And what did it matter anyway?

READ-ALOUD TIP

This information-heavy text is divided into two sections. Pause at the end of each section to allow for students' responses and reactions. The final sentence in each section will be an excellent place for you to review and emphasize critical events.

BACKGROUND LANGUAGE

You may need to explore the definition of *forensic* and the work of forensic scientists. Dictionary.com defines *forensic* as "pertaining to, connected with, or used in a court of law or public discussion and debate" and notes that *forensic science* uses "hands-on" lab work. The origin of *forensic* is Latin "belonging to the forum, public." Think aloud with your students about the work of forensic anthropologists and forensic pathologists in relation to the definition and origin of the word *forensic*.

When the rain started falling in the spring of 1993, no one could have imagined the devastation it would bring. As storm after storm pummeled the midwestern United States, rivers began to overflow their banks. Throughout the summer, floodwaters destroyed homes and businesses, and roads and bridges were washed away. The flooding didn't end until the fall, and by then, more than 500 counties in nine midwestern states had been hit hard. Floodwaters covered more than 20 million acres of land.

The wreckage from the flood was so terrible that much of the Midwest was declared a disaster area. Fifty people had died, and 55,000 homes were damaged or destroyed. All told, the Great Flood of 1993 was one of the worst natural disasters in American history and caused more than $15 billion in damage. Worse yet, the horrors it unleashed would haunt one small Missouri town forever.

Hardin is only six miles north of the Missouri River, so the people there knew it was only a matter of time before the flood reached their town. That horrible day arrived in July 1993. The rushing waters swept through Hardin, destroying homes and other buildings. Then something so terrible happened that the town would never be the same: the dead rose up from the cemetery.

Hardin's cemetery had been built in 1828 in a low-lying area of town. For over a century and a half, it was where most of the town's approximately 600 residents had buried their dead.

When the flood hit, water poured into Hardin Cemetery. It rushed into the graves and unearthed the coffins. Hundreds of headstones, burial vaults, and coffins were swept away, and about half of the 1,576 graves in the cemetery were destroyed. And then things got even worse when hundreds of coffins began to break open. It was like a scene from a horror movie. Human remains spilled out and floated through the streets and fields. Some of the corpses in Hardin were fresh and whole, while others had been underground for more than a century. The remains had broken apart and scattered across town, some ending up as far as 18 miles away.

The people of Hardin were powerless to stop the raging flood and the destruction of the cemetery, and they watched in horror as water tore apart the bodies of their loved ones. "People are just heartsick," one resident said to a reporter.

The town desperately needed help, so they turned to Dean Snow, the county coroner, hoping that he could identify the remains so their loved ones could be laid to rest once more. Snow organized a special team made up of members of DMORT, or the Disaster Mortuary Operational Response Team. DMORT are experts put together by the U.S. government, whose job it is to help identify bodies after major accidents. Some members of DMORT are forensic pathologists, medical experts who are in charge of figuring out how a person died. Once DMORT arrived in Hardin, the team members' mission was clear: to find and identify the human remains that were now spread across town.

First, they had to locate the remains. With the help of local volunteers, DMORT rounded up nearly 600 coffins. They also recovered 3,400 bones, including 129 human skulls, which they stored in barns and refrigerated trucks at the county fairgrounds.

Next, the team created antemortem profiles of the missing dead. (*Antemortem* means "before death.") These profiles included information about the people before they died—such as dental and medical records—that help the team identify remains. For example, if an antemortem profile showed that a person had once broken his leg, the experts would look for a skeleton with that injury. And yet, there was a problem. Paul Sledzik, a forensic anthropologist from the DMORT team said, "In the Hardin disaster, many of the missing had been dead for a very long time." This meant that for many of the missing dead, dental and medical records were simply not available.

Investigators tried to fill in the gaps by interviewing townspeople about their missing relatives. Did the dead have any broken bones? What clothes had they been buried in? The answers they collected helped investigators create antemortem profiles for most of the people who had been buried in the cemetery.

The corpses and bones were next.

• • • • •

When the DMORT team had finished the antemortem profiles, they moved on to postmortem profiles, or records and information that the team had collected about the corpses and bones. Postmortem profiles also noted personal items such as watches or blankets, which were often found inside the coffins.

They could then compare that information to what they knew about the missing dead, and try to make matches. Using that strategy, the DMORT team hoped to be able to identify the corpses.

However, the remains were in various states of decay. Some were new and well preserved, but some were dried up like mummies and others were skeletons or just pieces of bones. It was the forensic pathologist's job to handle the bodies that had a lot of soft tissue left, and the anthropology team handled remains that were mostly bones.

Some bodies had been torn from their coffins. Sledzik and the others did what they could to create profiles of these skeletons. Before long, thirty-five of the coffins held complete skeletons, and so the anthropologists measured the skulls and the long bones. ("Long bones" are longer than they are wide and are rounded at both ends.) They measured bones to discover a person's age, race, gender, and height. The anthropologists also looked for evidence of broken bones or diseases. But these were the easy cases; others would turn out to be more difficult—and gruesome.

As Paul Sledzik and his team continued their work on the postmortem profiles, they turned to the hundreds of loose bones they had found. The forensic anthropologists had to sort the bones by type. They put skulls in one place, and tibias—bones found in the shins— were put in another area. Femurs— thighbones—were grouped together, and so on. After sorting the bones, the anthropologists tried to "side" them, or figure out whether a bone came from the left or right side of a body. Next, the experts grouped the bones according to age, and then finally by gender.

The team found it extremely difficult to put together whole skeletons, but they were able to estimate the number of people whose remains they found. The flood had washed away the remains of 793 people, and the team estimated that they had found about 600 of these bodies.

As DMORT finished examining the remains, they moved on to their final task, which was to compare the postmortem profiles to the antemortem profiles. Some cases were easy to solve. A well-preserved body might be identified by a tattoo. A coffin could be linked to a name by a piece of jewelry found inside.

In the end, Sledzik and the rest of the DMORT team identified the remains of 119 people, and in October 1993, the DMORT team left Hardin. The townspeople prepared to rebury all the remains that DMORT had not been able to identify. Bones and pieces of bones were placed in 476 separate vaults, each of which was carefully tagged to link it with its postmortem profile.

Vernie Fountain, who led a team of funeral directors that helped respond to the disaster, told the *New York Times* how terrible the flood had been for families of the missing dead. "You bury someone and you expect them to be buried for eternity," he said.

9 Amigo Brothers

by Piri Thomas

SOURCE: *Piri Thomas has written several stories about growing up in Spanish Harlem. "Amigo Brothers" comes from his book,* Stories From El Barrio.

READING SESSIONS: 2

SUMMARY

Antonio Cruz and Felix Vargas are best friends, and both love boxing. Each dreams of becoming a champion. But when they are scheduled to fight each other for the division final, their friendship becomes strained. On the day of the fight, they must decide what is more important: their friendship or the title.

LANGUAGE AND VOCABULARY

Explain to students that the story they are about to hear is filled with boxing and fighting terms. The writer uses these words to make the listening and reading experience feel authentic. Use the chart below to preview some fighting words. Go through the list of boxing/fighting words on the left. Work as a class to come up with definitions on the right.

Fighting Terms	Definitions
draws	boxing contests left undecided or in a tie
elimination	the process of removing someone from a boxing competition
rights/lefts	right and left punches to an opponent
knockout	a blow that leaves an opponent unconscious
the ring	a raised, square platform in which a boxing match occurs
sparring	practice fighting, training
bout	a contest or fight
tournament	a series of contests between many competitors, who all compete to win

THINK, TALK, AND WRITE ABOUT TEXT

What was the upcoming fight doing to the friendship of Felix and Antonio? Why did they need time apart?

What was the big deal about this fight for the people of the neighborhood?

What does the term *ghetto grapevine* mean?

Listen again to the last five paragraphs of the selection (*They looked around . . .*). The writer doesn't really tell us what happens to the two guys just before they walk away. What do you think happened?

If Felix and Antonio were to **write** their definition of the term *amigo brothers*, what might they write? What would you write?

Amigo Brothers

by Piri Thomas

Antonio and Felix live in New York City and are best friends. They are also boxers, competitive and dedicated to their sport. But life is about to change when Antonio and Felix must face each other in the ring. Will their friendship survive the fight of their lives?

READ-ALOUD TIP

When reading a story with exciting events, most students will not want you to stop and discuss aspects of the story. Emphasize the relationship between Antonio and Felix by distinctly alternating between their voices. Change your tone according to the story's action: brotherly, determined, sensitive, or caring.

BACKGROUND LANGUAGE

Some students may not be aware of the fighting terms that are used: *bouts, draws, eliminations, sparring, barrage,* and *bobbed and weaved.* In addition, there are several words in Spanish that might need definition for some: *panin* (Puerto Rican Spanish slang for "pal" or "buddy"), *cheverote* (the greatest); *hermano* (brother), *suavecito* (take it easy), and *mucho corazon* (a lot of heart). For either set of words, you may have students who can explain and demonstrate some of the words.

Antonio Cruz and Felix Vargas were both seventeen years old. They were so together in friendship that they felt themselves to be brothers. They had known each other since childhood, growing up on the Lower East Side of Manhattan in the same tenement building on Fifth Street between Avenue A and Avenue B.

Antonio was fair, lean, and lanky, while Felix was dark, short, and husky. Antonio's hair was always falling over his eyes, while Felix wore his black hair in a natural Afro.

Each youngster had a dream of someday becoming lightweight champion of the world. Every chance they had the boys worked out, sometimes at the Boys' Club on 10th Street and Avenue A and sometimes at the pro's gym on 14th Street. Early morning sunrises would find them running along the East River Drive, wrapped in sweatshirts, short towels around their necks, and handkerchiefs around their foreheads.

While some youngsters were into street negatives, Antonio and Felix slept, ate, rapped, and dreamt positive. Between them, they had a collection of *Fight* magazines second to none, plus a scrapbook filled with torn tickets to every boxing match they had ever attended, and some clippings of their own. If asked a question about any given fighter, they would immediately zip out from their memory banks divisions, weights, records of fights, knockouts, technical knockouts, and draws or losses.

Each had fought many bouts representing their community and had won two gold-plated medals plus a silver and bronze medallion. The difference was in their style. Antonio's lean form and long reach made him the better boxer, while Felix's short and muscular frame made him the better slugger.

They rested their elbows on the railing separating them from the river. Antonio wiped his face with his short towel. The sunrise was now creating day.

Felix leaned heavily on the river's railing and stared across to the shores of Brooklyn. Finally, he broke the silence.

"Man, I don't know how to come out with it."

Antonio helped. "It's about our fight, right?"

"Yeah, right." Felix's eyes squinted at the rising orange sun.

"I've been thinking about it too, *panin*. In fact, since we found out it was going to be me and you, I've been awake at night, pulling punches on you, trying not to hurt you."

"Same here. It ain't natural not to think about the fight. I mean, we both are *cheverote* fighters and we both want to win. But only one of us can win. There ain't no draws in the eliminations."

Felix tapped Antonio gently on the shoulder. "I don't mean to sound like I'm bragging, bro. But I wanna win, fair and square."

Antonio nodded quietly. "Yeah. We both know that in the ring the better man wins. Friend or no friend, brother or no . . . "

Felix finished it for him. "Brother, Tony, let's promise something right here. Okay?"

"If it's fair, *hermano,* I'm for it." Antonio admired the courage of a tugboat pulling a barge five times its welterweight size.

"It's fair, Tony. When we get into the ring, it's gotta be like we never met. We gotta be like two heavy strangers that

want the same thing and only one can have it. You understand, don'tcha?"

Whenever they had met in the ring for sparring sessions, it had always been hot and heavy.

Now, after a series of elimination bouts, they had been informed that they were to meet each other in the division final that's scheduled for the seventh of August, two weeks away. The winner would represent the Boys' Club in the Golden Gloves Championship Tournament.

The two boys continued to run together along East River Drive. But even when joking with each other, they both sensed a wall rising between them.

One morning less than a week before their bout, they met as usual for their daily workout. They fooled around with a few jabs at the air, slapped skin, and then took off, running lightly along the dirty East River's edge.

Antonio glanced at Felix, who kept his eyes purposely straight ahead. He kept pausing from time to time to do some fancy leg work and throw some punches to an imaginary jaw. Antonio then beat the air with a barrage of body blows and short devastating lefts with an overhand jaw-breaking right.

After a mile or so, Felix puffed and said, "Let's stop a while, bro. I think we both have something to say to each other."

Antonio nodded. It was not natural to be acting as though nothing unusual was happening when two good buddies were going to be blasting each other within a few short days.

"*Sí,* I know." Tony smiled. "No pulling punches. We go all the way."

"Yeah, that's right. Listen, Tony. Don't you think it's a good idea if we don't see each other until the day of the fight? I'm going to stay with my Aunt Lucy in the Bronx. I can use Gleason's Gym for working out. My manager says he got some sparring partners with more or less your style."

Tony scratched his nose pensively. "Yeah, it would be better for our heads." He held out his hand, palm upward. "Deal?"

"Deal." Felix lightly slapped open skin.

"Ready for some more running?" Tony asked lamely.

"Naw, bro. Let's cut it here. You go on. I kinda like to get things together in my head."

"You ain't worried, are you?" Tony asked.

"No way, man." Felix laughed out loud. "I got too much smarts for that. I just think it's cooler if we split right here. After the fight, we can get it together again like nothing ever happened."

The *amigo* brothers were not ashamed to hug each other tightly.

"Guess you're right. Watch yourself, Felix. I hear there's some pretty heavy dudes up in the Bronx. *Suavecito,* okay?"

"Okay. You watch yourself too, *sabe?*"

Tony jogged away. Felix watched his friend disappear from view, throwing rights and lefts. Both fighters had a lot of psyching up to do before the big fight.

The days in training passed much too slowly. Although they kept out of each other's way, they were aware of each other's progress via the ghetto grapevine.

The evening before the big fight, Tony made his way to the roof of his tenement. In the quiet, early dark, he peered over the ledge. Six stories below, the light of the city blinked and the sounds of cars mingled with the curses and the laughter of children in the street. He tried not to

think of Felix, feeling he had succeeded in psyching his mind. But only in the ring would he really know. To spare Felix hurt, he would have to knock him out, early and quick.

Up in the South Bronx, Felix decided to take in a movie in an effort to keep Antonio's face away from his fists. The flick was *The Champion* with Kirk Douglas, the third time Felix was seeing it.

The champion was getting hit hard. He was saved only by the sound of the bell.

Felix became the champ and Tony the challenger.

The movie audience was going out of its head. The challenger, confident that he now had the championship in the bag, threw a left. The champ countered with a dynamite right.

Felix's right arm felt the shock. Antonio's face, superimposed on the screen, was hit by the awesome blow. Felix saw himself in the ring, blasting Antonio against the ropes. The challenger fell to the canvas.

When Felix finally left the theater, he had figured out how to psyche himself for tomorrow's fight. It was Felix the Champion vs. Antonio the Challenger.

He walked up some dark streets, deserted except for small pockets of wary-looking kids wearing gang colors. Despite the fact that he was Puerto Rican like them, they eyed him as stranger to their turf. Felix did a fast shuffle, bobbing and weaving, while letting loose a torrent of blows that would demolish whatever got in its way. It seemed to impress the brothers, who went about their own business.

Finding no takers, Felix decided to split to his aunt's. Walking the streets had not relaxed him, neither had the fight flick. All it had done was to stir him up. He let himself quietly into his Aunt Lucy's apartment and went straight to bed, falling into a fitful sleep with sounds of the gong for Round One.

Antonio was passing some heavy time on his rooftop. How would the fight tomorrow affect his relationship with Felix? After all, fighting was like any other profession. Friendship had nothing to do with it. A gnawing doubt crept in. He cut negative thinking real quick by doing some speedy, fancy dance steps, bobbing and weaving like mercury. The night air was blurred with perpetual motions of left hooks and right crosses. Felix, his *amigo* brother, was not going to be Felix at all in the ring. Just an opponent with another face. Antonio went to sleep, hearing the opening bell for the first round. Like his friend in the South Bronx, he prayed for victory, via a quick clean knockout in the first round.

· · · · ·

Large posters plastered all over the walls of local shops announced the fight between Antonio Cruz and Felix Vargas as the main bout.

The fight had created great interest in the neighborhood. Antonio and Felix were well liked and respected. Each had his own loyal following. Antonio's fans counted on his boxing skills. On the other side, Felix's admirers trusted in his dynamite-packed fists.

Felix had returned to his apartment early in the morning of August 7th and stayed there, hoping to avoid seeing Antonio. He turned the radio on to *salsa* music sounds and then tried to read while waiting for word from his manager.

The fight was scheduled to take place in Tompkins Square Park. It had been decided that the gymnasium of the Boys' Club was not large enough to hold all the people who were sure to attend. In Tompkins Square Park, everyone who wanted could view the fight, whether from ringside or window fire escapes or tenement rooftops.

The morning of the fight, Tompkins Square was a beehive of activity, with numerous workers setting up the ring, the seats, and the guest speakers' stand. The scheduled bout began shortly after noon, and the park had begun filling up even earlier.

The local junior high school across from Tompkins Square Park served as the dressing room for all the fighters. Each was given a separate classroom with desktops covered with mats, serving as resting tables. Antonio thought he caught a glimpse of Felix waving to him from a room at the far end of the corridor. He waved back just in case it had been him.

The fighters changed from their street clothes into fighting gear. Antonio wore white trunks, black socks, and black shoes. Felix wore sky blue trunks, red socks, and white boxing shoes. Each had dressing gowns to match their fighting trunks, with their names neatly stitched on the back.

The loudspeakers blared into the open windows of the school. There were speeches by dignitaries, community leaders, and great boxers of yesteryear. Some were very well-prepared, some improvised on the spot. They all carried the same message of great pleasure and honor at being part of such a historic event. This great day was in the tradition of champions emerging from the streets of the Lower East Side.

Interwoven with the speeches were the sounds of the other boxing events. After the sixth bout, Felix was relieved when his trainer Charlie said, "Time change. Quick knockout. This is it. We're on."

Waiting time was over. Felix was escorted from the classroom by a dozen fans in white T-shirts with the word FELIX across their fronts.

Antonio was escorted down a different stairwell and guided through a roped-off path.

As the two climbed into the ring, the crowd exploded with a roar. Antonio and Felix both bowed gracefully and then raised their arms in acknowledgment.

Antonio tried to be cool, but as the roar was starting to build, he turned slowly to meet Felix's eyes looking directly into his. Felix nodded his head and Antonio responded. And both as one, just as quickly, turned away to face their own corner.

BONG–BONG–BONG. The roar turned to stillness.

"Ladies and Gentlemen. *Señores y Señoras.*"

The announcer spoke slowly, pleased at his bilingual efforts.

"Now the moment we have all been waiting for—the main event between two fine young Puerto Rican fighters, products of our Lower East Side. In this corner, weighing 134 pounds, Felix Vargas. And in this corner, weighing 133 pounds, Antonio Cruz. The winner will represent the Boys' Club in the tournament of champions, the Golden Gloves. There will be no draw. May the best man win."

The cheering of the crowd shook the windowpanes of the old buildings surrounding Tompkins Square Park.

At the center of the ring, the referee was giving instructions to the youngsters.

"Keep your punches up. No low blows. No punching on the back of the head. Keep your heads up. Understand? Let's have a clean fight. Now shake hands and come out fighting."

Both youngsters touched gloves and nodded. They turned and danced quickly to their corners. Their head towels and dressing gowns were lifted neatly from their shoulders by their trainers' nimble fingers. Antonio crossed himself. Felix did the same.

BONG! BONG! ROUND ONE. Felix and Antonio turned and faced each other squarely in a fighting pose. Felix wasted no time. He came in fast, head low, half hunched toward his right shoulder, and lashed out with a straight left. He missed a right cross as Antonio slipped the punch and countered with one-two-three lefts that snapped Felix's head back, sending a mild shock coursing through him. If Felix had any small doubt about their friendship affecting their fight, it was being neatly dispelled.

Antonio danced, a joy to behold. His left hand was like a piston pumping jabs one right after another with seeming ease. Felix bobbed and weaved and never stopped boring in. He knew that at long range he was at a disadvantage. Antonio had too much reach on him. Only by coming in close could Felix hope to achieve the dreamed-of knockout.

Antonio knew the dynamite that was stored in his *amigo* brother's fist. He ducked a short right and missed a left hook. Felix trapped him against the ropes just long enough to pour some punishing rights and lefts to Antonio's hard midsection. Antonio slipped away from Felix, crashing two lefts to his head, which set Felix's right ear to ringing.

BONG! Both *amigos* froze a punch well on its way, sending up a roar of approval for good sportsmanship.

Felix walked briskly back to his corner. His right ear had not stopped ringing. Antonio gracefully danced his way toward his stool none the worse, except for glowing glove burns, showing angry red against the whiteness of his midribs.

"Watch that right, Tony." His trainer talked into his ear. "Remember Felix always goes to the body. He'll want you to drop your hands for his overhand left or right. Got it?"

Antonio nodded, spraying water out between his teeth. He felt better as his sore midsection was being firmly rubbed.

Felix's corner was also busy.

"You gotta get in there, fella." Felix's trainer poured water over his curly Afro locks. "Get in there or he's gonna chop you up from way back."

BONG! BONG! Round Two. Felix was off his stool and rushed Antonio like a bull, sending a hard right to his head. Beads of water exploded from Antonio's long hair.

Antonio, hurt, sent back a blurring barrage of lefts and rights that only meant pain to Felix, who returned with a short left to the head, followed by a looping right to the body. Antonio countered with his own flurry, forcing Felix to give ground. But not for long.

Felix bobbed and weaved, bobbed and weaved, occasionally punching his two gloves together.

Antonio waited for the rush that was sure to come. Felix closed in and feinted with his left shoulder and threw his right instead. Lights suddenly exploded inside Felix's head as Antonio slipped the blow and hit him with a piston-like left, catching him flush on the point of his chin.

Bedlam broke loose as Felix's legs momentarily buckled. He fought off a series of rights and lefts and came back with a strong right that taught Antonio respect.

Antonio danced in carefully. He knew Felix had the habit of playing possum when hurt, to sucker an opponent within reach of the powerful bombs he carried in each fist.

A right to the head slowed Antonio's pretty dancing. He answered with his own left at Felix's right eye, which began puffing up within three seconds.

Antonio, a bit too eager, moved in too close and Felix had him entangled into a rip-roaring, punching toe-to-toe slugfest. It brought the whole Tompkins Square Park screaming to its feet.

Rights to the body. Lefts to the head. Neither fighter was giving an inch. Suddenly, a short right caught Antonio squarely on the chin. His long legs turned to jelly and his arms flailed out desperately. Felix, grunting like a bull, threw wild punches from every direction. Antonio, groggy, bobbed and weaved, evading most of the blows. Suddenly his head cleared. His left flashed out hard and straight, catching Felix on the bridge of his nose.

Felix lashed back with a harsh punch, right off the ghetto streets. At the same instant, his eye caught another left hook from Antonio. Felix swung out, trying to clear the pain. Only the frenzied screaming of those along ringside let him know that he had dropped Antonio.

Fighting off the growing haze, Antonio struggled to his feet, got up, and ducked. Then he threw a smashing right that dropped Felix flat on his back.

Felix got up as fast as he could in his own corner, groggy but still game. He didn't even hear the count. In a fog, he heard the roaring of the crowd, who seemed to have gone insane. His head cleared to hear the bell sound at the end of the round. He was very glad. His trainer sat him down on the stool.

In his corner, Antonio was doing what all fighters do when they are hurt. They sit and smile at everyone.

The referee signaled the ring doctor to check the fighters out. He did so and then gave his okay. The cold water sponges brought clarity to both *amigo* brothers. They were rubbed until their circulation ran free.

BONG! Round Three—the final round. Up to now it had been tic-tac-toe, pretty much even. But everyone knew there could be no draw and that this round would decide the winner.

This time, to Felix's surprise, it was Antonio who came out fast, charging across the ring. Felix braced himself but couldn't ward off the barrage of punches. Antonio drove Felix hard against the ropes.

The crowd ate it up. Thus far, the two had fought with *mucho corazon*. Felix tapped his gloves and commenced his attack anew. Antonio, throwing boxer's caution to the wind, jumped in to meet him.

Both pounded away. Neither gave an inch and neither fell to the canvas. Felix's left eye was tightly closed. Bright red blood poured from Antonio's nose. They fought toe-to-toe.

The sounds of their blows were loud in contrast to the silence of a crowd gone completely mute. The referee was stunned by their savagery.

BONG! BONG! BONG! The bell sounds over and over again. Felix and Antonio were past hearing. Their blows continued to pound on each other like hailstones.

Finally the referee and the two trainers pried Felix and Antonio apart. Cold water was poured over them to bring them back to their senses.

They looked around and then rushed toward each other. A cry of alarm surged through Tompkins Square Park. Was this a fight to the death instead of a boxing match?

The fear soon gave way to wave upon wave of cheering as the two *amigos* embraced.

No matter what the decision, they knew they would always be champions to each other.

BONG! BONG! BONG! "Ladies and Gentlemen, *Señores y Señoras*. The winner and representative to the Golden Gloves Tournament of Champions is . . . "

The announcer turned to point to the winner and found himself alone. Arm in arm, the champions had already left the ring.

10 The Golden Arm

by J. B. Stamper

SUMMARY

A woman with a costly golden arm makes unending demands on her poor husband. She makes him promise that the arm will stay with her—even in death. He agrees to the promise but is overcome with thoughts of revenge. The golden arm ultimately causes the chilling death of the man—or does it?

SOURCE: *J. B. Stamper is known as the scariest woman in her neighborhood. Her stories can be found in many collections, including Tales for the Midnight Hour.*

READING SESSION: 1

(If you need to divide the story into two sessions because of time, stop after the wife's funeral on page 60.)

LANGUAGE AND VOCABULARY

Point out that the writer, J. B. Stamper, uses language to build suspense and fear in her readers. The sentence starters below come from the text. Encourage students to take them and turn them into sentences that might end up in a suspenseful story. Challenge students to expand on the sentences created by other students (i.e., keep the story going!).

Afraid of her terrible temper . . .
The man's meekness turned into . . .
Breathing heavily with anticipation . . .
When sleep refused to come . . .
With a sickening creak . . .

THINK, TALK, AND WRITE ABOUT TEXT

What happened to the man at the end of the story? What caused his death?

What were your feelings for this woman—who lost her arm in a tragic accident AND died suddenly of a mysterious disease? Why did you feel the way you do?

Read the opening three lines again. Why did the man resent the golden arm so much?

The story says that ". . . after the funeral, the man's mind settled into a heavy gloom that would not lift." What does that mean? What does that tell you about the man's state of mind?

What plan did he come up with? How might that plan have backfired?

The Golden Arm

by J. B. Stamper

In this chilling tale of greed and resentment, a man decides to take back what he feels rightly belongs to him—and pays the ultimate price for it.

READ-ALOUD TIP

As with most ghost stories, this passage is best read aloud with pacing that becomes increasingly suspense-filled. Read the beginning with an even tone so there's room to build up to the "surprise" ending. As the story starts to describe the wife with phrases such as "terrible temper" and "biting tongue," your tone of voice should become more shrill and insistent. After her death, speak slowly as the husband decides and then goes to the grave, then increasing the intensity and fearfulness as he proceeds with the horrible act. The story should be the most intense with the repetition of "WHOOO . . . WHOOO'S GOT MY GOLDEN ARM?"

BACKGROUND LANGUAGE

Most students will have heard ghost stories from camp, sleepovers, and television shows. Because of the suspense factor, this reading will be most effective if read aloud first, then discussed after the reading.

Once there was a woman who had a golden arm. She had lost her real arm in a terrible accident. But after she got the golden arm, she didn't even seem to miss her real one.

The golden arm was beautifully made. It was slender and elegant and shone with a warm glow from its shoulder down to its fingertips. The woman vainly decorated its gold fingers with jeweled rings. People who saw her thought she must be very rich to have such a lovely golden arm. But, in fact, the opposite was true.

The woman's husband made only enough money for them to get by modestly in life. For many years, he had carefully saved part of his paycheck. This money had added up to a considerable sum. But after her accident, his wife had demanded that he spend all the money on the golden arm and its decorations. Being a meek person, he did as she asked. But deep inside, he hated the arm.

Every morning, at the breakfast table, the man would stare at the golden arm lying on the table across from him. He would think of all the scrimping and saving he had done over the years. He would think of all the comforts the money could have brought him. Now it all rested in his wife's golden arm. He grew to hate its shapely curves and shiny golden fingers.

As the years passed, the woman seemed to grow more and more fond of her golden arm and less and less fond of her husband. She insisted on a new ring every birthday. Her husband, afraid of her terrible temper and biting tongue, scrimped and saved again to meet her demands. But, with each passing year, his resentment against the arm grew and grew.

One cold winter evening, as the couple was reading the newspaper, the wife read a notice about the death of a woman she had gone to school with. She dropped the paper suddenly and stared blankly at the wall, her face drained of color. The idea of death had crept into her mind, and it would not go away. The more the woman thought about dying, the more she found herself stroking the golden arm with her other hand. Slowly, an idea began to take form in her mind, an idea she had not considered before. She turned to her husband and met his eyes with a steely gaze.

"If I happen to die before you," she said to him, "promise to bury me with my golden arm."

Her husband clutched his newspaper so tightly that it ripped, and he stared at his wife in shocked amazement.

"But that arm is the only thing of value that we have," he said, his voice shaking. "All the money I've worked for and saved has gone into it."

"I want to be buried with it," his wife said in an insistent voice. "And I want all my rings on the fingers." She paused, picturing in her mind how she would look in her casket. "Just think how people will stare when they view my body."

At that very moment, the husband's heart turned as hard and cold as the golden arm. Any feelings of love that remained for his wife were turned to bitter disgust. But, still, he was afraid to cross her. Calmly, he looked her in the eye and promised to do as she asked. After all, he told himself, there was little chance that she would die before he did, anyway.

The future, however, proved him wrong. Just one year later, his wife died suddenly of a mysterious disease. In shock, the man went about the preparations for her funeral. He planned to tell the undertaker to remove the golden arm before laying his wife out in the casket. But then his wife's relatives arrived to help make the funeral arrangements. To his dismay, she had told them about her desire to be buried with the golden arm. She had even given them a signed, legal document stating her wishes. And, so, even in death, his wife got her way.

At the funeral, the man stared at the body laid out in the coffin, with the golden arm gleaming at its side. On the golden fingers sparkled all the jeweled rings. And as the coffin lid was closed for the final time, the man said goodbye—not only to his wife, but also to his life's savings.

After the funeral, the man's mind settled into a heavy gloom that would not lift. Day after day, he thought of his wife's coffin and the golden arm gleaming inside it. Why, he asked himself, should she still have the arm when he could sell the gold and live out the rest of his life without worry? Slowly, the man's meekness and timidity turned to anger and revenge.

Then, on one cold and windy night near the end of October, while the man lay in bed, an idea began to prey on his mind. What if the arm was no longer in the coffin? What if someone had already stolen it? After all, who would be so foolish as to let that much gold stay buried? The idea took root in the man's mind and grew like a poisonous weed.

Finally, not able to stand it any longer, the man jumped from his bed and pulled on his warmest clothes. He went out to the garage and found a pick and shovel. Then he hurried toward the graveyard in which his wife was buried under the hard, cold ground.

Breathing heavily with anticipation and fear, the man came up to the high iron gates of the graveyard. He hesitated and then pushed against them. The gates swung open like the jaws of a gigantic black mouth. Only the thought of the golden arm made the man force his legs forward, step by step, toward his wife's grave. His mind was still obsessed by the picture of the grave, dug up and disturbed. But when he reached the burial site, the grave lay tranquilly under the full moon, covered by bouquets of wilting flowers.

In a mad frenzy, the man began to work. He dug the pickax into the hard earth and then shoveled it away, digging deeper and deeper. At last, the pick struck the top of his wife's expensive coffin. An image of the golden arm began to burn in the man's mind. It gave him enough courage to pull open the coffin lid and look down at his wife's decaying body. In triumph, he pulled the golden arm from the grave and cradled it against his chest.

Quickly, the man shut the coffin back up and covered it again with the cold earth. He gathered the withered flowers back over the grave and then hurried toward home, clutching the golden arm under his coat.

The night had turned bitterly cold. Rain began to lash down on the man's head as he ran back to his house. He hugged the golden arm tighter and tighter under his coat, but its icy embrace sent a shudder through his whole body.

At last, the man reached his home, feeling sick with fear. He searched and searched for a place to hide the arm, but nowhere seemed safe. Finally, in desperation, he slipped it under the blankets of his bed and crawled in beside it.

Outside, the wind howled around the house, and the rain tapped like angry fingers against the windowpanes. The man huddled in his bed and tried to calm his shaking body. He pulled the covers up higher around his face, but, beside him, the golden arm was still icy cold. It seemed to draw all the heat out of his body, making him feel like a corpse in a coffin.

When sleep refused to come, the man tried to busy his mind thinking of all the things he would buy after selling the golden arm. But his mind was pulled away from these thoughts by a soft, strange wail that seemed to come and go with the howling of the wind. The man sat up in bed and strained his ears. Then he heard the sound again, just outside his bedroom window.

WHOOO . . . WHOOO'S GOT MY GOLDEN ARM?

The wailing voice made the man's blood run cold. It sounded like his wife's voice, mixed with the howling of the wind. He looked over to where the golden arm lay beside him in bed, and he shrank away from it.

Again, the man thought he heard the strange voice calling from outside the window. He strained his ears to hear. But the sound faded away into the night with the wind. Slowly, the man relaxed and smiled at his own stupidity. He told himself that he had let his imagination go wild. But, then, the wailing started up again, like a ghostly call from the grave.

WHOOO . . . WHOOO'S GOT MY GOLDEN ARM?

In panic, the man searched the darkness. The voice sounded closer now. It seemed to be coming from inside the house. All the man could think about was hiding the golden arm. He couldn't be discovered with it beside him in bed! Reaching under the covers, the man tried to pick up the arm. But it was so cold that it almost froze his fingers. He dropped it and stared at it in terror. In the pale moonlight, he saw one gold finger pointing at him in accusation. Then, again, the wailing voice echoed into the room.

WHOOO . . . WHOOO'S GOT MY GOLDEN ARM?

Now the voice was coming from the staircase. Then the man heard the sound of footsteps climbing the stairs, one by one, as the wailing voice came closer and closer to his bedroom door.

WHOOO . . . WHOOO'S GOT MY GOLDEN ARM?

With a sickening creak, the door to the bedroom opened. The man lay trembling under the covers, trying to hide from the thing that was coming nearer and nearer to his bed. His teeth began to chatter with fear, and he suddenly felt the icy-cold finger of the golden arm stab at him.

Now the footsteps had reached the bed. The arm's cold grip was reaching up around the man's neck. Then, softly, the voice beside his bed whispered into his ear.

WHO'S GOT MY GOLDEN ARM?

With a scream, the man tried to jump from the bed. But he couldn't, because the fingers of the golden arm had tightened around his neck.

The next day, neighbors found the man, dead from fright. He was buried a few days later in the cemetery beside his wife—and her golden arm.

11 Train of Death

by John DiConsiglio

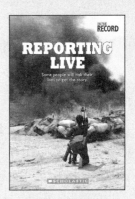

SUMMARY

In 2000, reporter Sonia Nazario began to investigate the "Train of Death," which many Central American children ride in order to enter the United States. She met Enrique, a teenage boy from Honduras who had ridden the train many times, trying to reach his mother in North Carolina. After learning Enrique's story, Nazario rode the Train of Death herself, and learned firsthand exactly how harrowing this journey is for so many children.

SOURCE: *"Train of Death" is featured in* Reporting Live, *part of* On the Record, *a supplemental ELA program featuring paired profiles of fascinating contemporary figures.* www.scholastic.com/ontherecord

READING SESSIONS: 3

LANGUAGE AND VOCABULARY

Create a concept web for the title "Train of Death." As you read this selection, have students add words, feelings, and ideas to the web. Encourage students to explain how their words or ideas connect to the web. To start the discussion, you may wish to add the words *dangerous* and *reporting* to the web. Model your thinking as to how these words connect to the web.

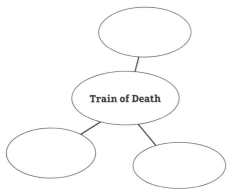

Train of Death

THINK, TALK, AND WRITE ABOUT TEXT

Why do so many kids take on this hard and dangerous journey?

Nazario says that she wanted to perfect the "fly on the wall" style of reporting. **What** is that? This kind of reporting prevented her often from helping kids who could have used help. Why do you think she did that?

The word *determination* means "the will to do something." The word *resilient* means "able to withstand and recover from obstacles." **How** are these kids determined? How are they resilient? What about Sonia Nazario—would you describe her as determined and resilient?

All of these young kids crossing the border illegally cause many problems for the U.S. **What** should the U.S. do about this? How do you feel about these kids' crossing the border?

What are some thoughts you have about *Enrique's Journey*, the book Nazario wrote about her research?

What are some thoughts you have about becoming a reporter like Sonia Nazario?

Train of Death

by John DiConsiglio

The Train of Death is one of the most dangerous rides on Earth. Every year, many kids ride this train from their homes in Central America over the border into the United States. Sometimes they are looking for family. Often, they are escaping political turmoil or violence back home. In this profile, you will meet a news reporter named Sonia Nazario who wanted to learn more about the Train of Death, so she took a ride on it—the most terrifying of her life.

READ-ALOUD TIP

This nonfiction text is filled with information, so you may need to pause occasionally when reading it aloud to allow students to process what they have just heard. There are many Spanish words in the text; each phrase is also in English. Practice the pronunciation of the words beforehand.

BACKGROUND LANGUAGE

Most students will have heard of illegal immigration, and some may have experienced similar journeys to the United States. It would be helpful to have a world map available so students can see the incredible distances these immigrants cover in order to get to the U.S.

Sonia Nazario clings to the top of an old freight train. Its wheels rattle along the tracks below. Rain slashes across her face. Lightning cuts through the Mexican night.

In the flashes of light, Nazario glimpses her fellow travelers. They are boys in their early teens, with wide eyes and hungry faces. A few are missing arms or legs. Some bear scars from machete blades. All of them hold tight to the guardrails, balancing as the train rumbles through the darkness.

The boys are desperately poor travelers on a long and dangerous journey. They have left their homes in Central American countries such as Honduras and Guatemala. Their destination is the United States. Most of them are trying to join parents who left to find a better life in the place they call *el norte*, or "the North." Each year, 50,000 of them reach their goal. Many more will never complete the journey.

The train they are riding is so dangerous it is nicknamed *el tren de la muerte*—the Train of Death. Gangsters, thieves, and corrupt policemen prowl the tracks, looking for easy prey. Many kids are robbed and beaten during their journey. Some are snatched from the trains by train or local authorities or worse—never to be seen again. Others fall off and are sucked under the grinding wheels.

Given the dangers, Nazario could be forgiven for wondering, *What am I doing here?*

In 2000, when Nazario boarded the Train of Death, she was a 39-year-old reporter for the *Los Angeles Times*. She wanted to tell the story of the migrant kids—and she wanted to get it right. "I wanted to put the reader on top of the train with these kids," she says. "I wanted to make people feel like they were riding with them. The only way to do that was to be there myself."

One boy in particular captured Nazario's imagination. She met Enrique in the middle of his journey from Honduras to the United States. He had already tried seven times to join his mother in North Carolina. He was risking everything to make the eighth attempt succeed.

On that hot summer night in 2000, Nazario was risking her own life to retrace Enrique's steps. She squinted into the trees that lined the tracks. Was that a gun muzzle between the bushes? Were gangsters about to attack the train? Nazario heard a shout from a distant car. "*Rama! Rama!*" Her mind raced to translate the word. *Rama?* Branch?

Suddenly, a tree branch struck her face. It knocked her over the edge of the train. As she fell toward the track, she grabbed a side rail just in time. She felt the sucking wind from the wheels below her pulling at her legs. She was just a few feet from falling to her death.

In the dark, she saw shadows of children running across the top of the freight car.

She heard voices yelling in Spanish. Hands reached over the side to her.

With the help of several boys, Nazario lifted herself to the top of the train. She lay on her stomach, panting and holding back tears. As the kids tried to calm her, she sobbed. Maybe, she thought, this trip had been a terrible mistake.

* * * * *

The Train of Death wasn't Nazario's first brush with danger. Since her teenage years, she has been drawn to stories of people living in poverty and violence.

Nazario grew up in Kansas, but her parents came from Argentina. When Sonia was 14, her father died of a heart attack. Her mother took Sonia, her sister, and twin brothers back to Argentina to live with family.

At the time, Argentina was in the middle of a crisis known as the "Dirty War." The army seized control of the country and set up a dictatorship. Then it cracked down on its critics, killing as many as 30,000 people.

Nazario recalls walking with her mother along a bloodstained sidewalk. "I asked what happened and my mom said that two people were killed there." Nazario says. "She said they were murdered because they were journalists and they were trying to tell the truth."

"At that moment, my teenage mind knew I wanted to be a reporter," Nazario recalls. "I wanted to write about what was happening in places like Argentina. These were stories the world needed to know."

To escape the violence, Nazario's mother moved the family back to Kansas. In high school, Nazario worked as a waitress. Her mother struggled to earn a living as a seamstress and a cook. Nazario's good grades led her to Williams College in Massachusetts. There, she says, "I was one of maybe ten Hispanics on the whole campus."

After college, Nazario went to work as a reporter. She wrote about "forgotten people"—drug addicts, the homeless, people with AIDS. And she perfected the "fly on the wall" style that became her hallmark. For a series on drugs, she spent months following a heroin-addicted mother and her three-year-old daughter. She came home each night covered in fleas and smelling like urine. Her husband made her change clothes in the garage.

Nazario learned about the migrants' journey in the late 1990s. She sat down one day to talk with her housekeeper, Maria del Carmen Ferrez. Carmen told Nazario that she had four children in Guatemala. She hadn't seen them in 12 years. One of them was an infant when she left.

Nazario was stunned. How could a mother leave her children behind to come to a strange country?

Choking back tears, Carmen told Nazario the full story. In Guatemala, her husband had deserted her for another, leaving the family in poverty. Some days she had nothing to feed her kids. She gave them glasses of water with a teaspoon of sugar. At night, she made them sleep face down to quiet their growling stomachs.

Carmen decided that she needed to leave to provide a future for her family. She made it to California. She earned enough to send money and clothes back to her family. But bringing her kids to the U.S. proved to be nearly impossible.

The U.S. takes in more than 1,000,000 legal immigrants annually. No other country in the world accepts anywhere near as many immigrants. But the law favors three categories of people: skilled workers with a job waiting for them, people with family living legally in the U.S., and political refugees who are persecuted in their home countries.

Millions of other people know they'll never get permission to come to the U.S. Every year, about half a million of them make the trip illegally. Carmen's teenaged son became one of the illegal immigrants. He hitchhiked through Guatemala and Mexico. He begged for food and ran from bandits. Eventually he found his way to his mother's door.

"As she spoke, I felt the hairs on my arm rise," Nazario says. "It was chilling. I felt I had to tell the story of these boys. It was the kind of story I became a journalist to tell."

Nazario planned to research her story by living like a migrant child. But she knew her limitations. She couldn't trail one boy for the entire 2,000-mile route. There was no way she could keep up with a teenager on such a dangerous journey.

Instead, Nazario searched for someone who had already made the trip. She called churches and shelters that harbored lost boys. She went to immigration detention centers. Kids at the detention centers had been arrested on the way to the United States. They were waiting to be sent back to their home countries.

As she interviewed children, Nazario was stunned by their stories. One 11-year-old boy had seen a band of gangsters hop a train, high on crack. The thugs snatched a young girl and threw her off the train, killing her.

Despite the horrors of the journey, many of the kids refused to give up. In a Mexican detention center, Nazario met a boy who had tried to reach the U.S. 27 times. He had been robbed and beaten. His girlfriend had been raped. "Tomorrow," he said, "they will send me back to Guatemala. And the next day, I will start on attempt number 28."

Finally, Nazario received a call from a nun in Nuevo Laredo, a Mexican town near the Texas border. "I have a boy here," she said. "I'll put him on the line."

Enrique got on the phone and began to tell his story.

He grew up in Tegucigalpa, the capital of Honduras. His mother, Lourdes, had almost no income. She couldn't even afford pencils for her children to take to school.

Lourdes left home when Enrique was five. She promised to send for him once she had settled in the U.S. But Enrique was devastated. He wondered what he had done wrong to drive his mother off. Every day he asked his grandmother when Lourdes would come home.

"*¿Dónde está mi mami?*" he cried over and over. "Where is my mom?"

In Lourdes's absence, Enrique grew into a troubled teen. He skipped school and got into fights. He hung out with gang members. He sniffed glue to get high.

At night, he'd sit on his grandmother's porch with his girlfriend, Maria Isabel. He'd look up at the stars and tell her about his dream. He wanted to go to America and find his mother.

At 16, Enrique resolved to make the journey. The only information he had was Lourdes's phone number, which he wrote on the waistband of a pair of blue jeans.

Over the next year, he set out seven times. Once, he stayed on the road for 31 days and covered about 1,000 miles. On his sixth trip he made it all the way to the U.S. border in just five days.

Each of Enrique's attempts ended in failure. On one trip he was stopped by *la migra*—the immigration police. The officers stole everything he had—a few crackers, some coins, and some dried-out tortillas. Another time a gang of thugs trapped him on the top of a freight car. They beat him nearly to death before he escaped.

The police caught Enrique several times and deported him to Guatemala. But he refused to give up. On his eighth try he made it all the way to the U.S. border. He was broke but determined to complete his journey.

• • • • •

In May 2000, Nazario went to meet Enrique in Nuevo Laredo. She hung out with him while he begged for money on the streets. She spent two weeks watching him search for a way across the border. Finally she left him to complete his journey by himself. She returned to California to plan her own trip.

Nazario knew what she was getting herself into. The director of a detention center in Texas told her, "For you to do this, you are either stupid or you have a death wish."

Nazario prepared as well as she could. She filled a small backpack with a cell phone, a credit card, toilet paper, cash, and a tape recorder. She also packed a letter from the office of the Mexican president. The letter explained what she was doing. She called it her *carta del oro,* or "golden letter." Its purpose was to keep her out of jail.

When she set out for Tegucigalpa, her husband asked her to make one promise: "Don't jump off moving trains." Nazario arrived in Tegucigalpa hungry for details about Enrique's life. She talked to Maria Isabel. She found the porch where Enrique had revealed his dreams under the stars. And she tried to understand Lourdes's decision to leave home. "When I started this journey, I was judgmental," Nazario admits. "I thought, 'What kind of mother walks away from her children?'"

Tegucigalpa gave her the answer. She watched women pick through garbage to find food for their children. The smell was so bad that she could barely breathe. "Can you imagine knowing that the only way to feed your children—to give them hope for the future—is to walk away from them?" she says.

Nazario left Tegucigalpa the way Enrique did. She rode rickety buses north through Honduras and Guatemala. After 400 miles on the road, she reached the border of Mexico.

She boarded the Train of Death in Chiapas, Mexico's southernmost state. This lawless region is so dangerous that the boys call it *la bestia,* or "the Beast." Drug gangs rule much of Chiapas. Gangsters and thieves beat up defenseless migrants and steal their meager belongings. Corrupt police officers look the other way. Sometimes the police rob the migrants before sending them back across the border.

In Chiapas, Nazario rode with 300 to 400 people crowded on top of the train cars. Many of the riders were kids, some as young as seven. She watched them jump on and off the train to avoid immigration officials. She kept an eye out for gang members and thieves.

For part of her journey, Nazario traveled with a Mexican migrants' rights group. They carried shotguns and AK-47s to fight off the gangsters. Even they protested that the journey was too dangerous for Nazario.

When she traveled alone, Nazario was particularly vulnerable. "Women [on the trains] have an almost 100 percent chance of being raped," she says.

On one occasion, a gangster chased Nazario through the train cars. She escaped by locking herself in a bathroom, crawling out a window, and climbing to the top of the train. "That was probably the scariest moment I faced," she says.

Nazario's most agonizing encounters had little to do with her own safety. She hated to watch children in danger— and always wondered whether she should intervene. As a journalist, Nazario felt her role was to observe. She didn't want to influence the story she was reporting.

Still, how could she stand by while kids begged for food or slept in the weeds? She remembered watching Enrique beg on the streets of Nuevo Laredo when she first met him. He had lost his mother's phone number. His grandmother knew the number, but Enrique couldn't afford to call her. "I could have given him my cell phone to call home," Nazario recalls. "But that would have changed their story. It was a very difficult decision. But that's not what a reporter does."

In the end, Nazario decided she would only act if a child's life was in immediate danger. That happened once in Chiapas, when she met a sobbing 12-year-old boy. He had been separated from his friends and arrested. The police were about to deport him to a lawless town. "His odds of being killed were not small," she says. Nazario lent the boy her cell phone to call an uncle for help.

As Nazario rode north from Chiapas, she realized that the dangers of the trip were only part of the story. Enrique and the other migrant kids had a support system to help protect them. On the cars, one teen often stood lookout while the others slept. Boys risked their own safety to pull new riders aboard. Poor villagers along the way chased the train with gifts of food and water.

Acts of kindness like these had kept Enrique alive on his eighth trip. By the time he reached the U.S. border, he told Nazario, he was confident he would make it. He had begun to think of the Train of Death as his "Iron Hope."

Sonia Nazario spent six months retracing Enrique's journey. She survived 16-hour days on the train with little to eat or drink. She interviewed hundreds of people. By the end of her journey, she says, "I was miserable and as exhausted as I'd ever been."

Nazario returned safely to California. She wrote a series of articles about Enrique and the other kids she met on her trip. The stories earned her a Pulitzer Prize, the highest award for a U.S. journalist. She rode the train again in 2003 to do more research. Then she expanded the articles into a book called *Enrique's Journey.*

The book included the end of Enrique's story, which was far from over when Nazario left him in Nuevo Laredo. From Nuevo Laredo, Enrique had to cross the Rio Grande into Texas. He and some other young migrants paid a smuggler to help them cross the river. They waited until dark to hide from border policemen. In a shaky inner tube, Enrique nervously floated on the murky green water. Then he slipped cautiously into the cold river. His teeth chattered as the waves washed him to shore.

The smuggler then led the group on a mad sprint—over a fence, under a pipe, across a bridge and a highway. Enrique arrived, exhausted, at a van that would take him to North Carolina.

After seven failed attempts, Enrique's dream had come true. He was reunited with his mother. "He was alone his whole life," Nazario says. "Now he could let out all the love he held inside for years."

Telling Enrique's story wasn't easy for Nazario. After coming home, she had nightmares about the Train of Death. She woke up in a sweat, feeling the tracks rumbling under her.

Eventually the nightmares faded. Today, when Nazario thinks about her journey, she tried to remember the acts of kindness she witnessed.

Most of all, she remembers a moment when the train slowed in the Mexican state of Veracruz. Crowds raced to the tracks, throwing bundles of food to the migrant children. She recalls a 100-year-old woman who had made little bags of tortillas and beans. The woman tossed them into the begging hands of the children on the trains.

"She said to me, 'If I have one tortilla left, I will give half away.'" Nazario says. "That's something I'll never forget."

12 Labels/ Blueprints

by Sara Holbrook

SUMMARY

"Labels" and "Blueprints" are two poems that begin to explore some of the most pressing questions that arise in secondary school: *Who am I? Where do I come from? What makes me . . . me?*

SOURCE: *"Labels" comes from* By Definition: Poems of Feelings. *"Blueprints" comes from* Am I Naturally This Crazy? *Sarah Holbrook has published many poetry collections for children and teenagers. She also likes to blog.*

READING SESSIONS: 2
(one session for each poem)

LANGUAGE AND VOCABULARY

Prior to reading each poem, explore the words *label* and *blueprint* by asking students to look at some sample labels and blueprints and discuss their purposes.

Labels & Blueprints	Definition	Characteristics?	Purpose?

After reading each poem, discuss the definitions and infer what Holbrook believes about using labels or blueprints when talking about people or groups.

THINK, TALK, AND WRITE ABOUT TEXT

Think about the labels we give to each other. Think about the way labels can be harmful. Make a list of all the labels you have used, or you have heard used, to describe a person or group.

Talk about the definitions for *label* and *blueprint.* A *label* is placed on something to indicate contents, ownership, origin, or other pertinent information. A *blueprint* is a detailed plan or outline that influences the ultimate design of a product. After reading each poem and discussing the definitions of the titles, use the organizer below to help you keep track of your ideas and insights about labeling individuals or groups.

Text Talk

T – Talk about it.

A – Ask questions.

L – Look at the events from another point of view.

K – Keep track of what is important.

	Talk about each poem and use information or evidence from each poem to infer the author's purpose in writing these poems.
	Question whether or not labels and blueprints serve a purpose.
◉	Look from another point of view at the practice of labeling people. How might the labeler's position on labeling be different from the position of the person or group receiving the label?
☆	What are the important thoughts or ideas that you will take away from reading and discussing these two poems?

Labels

by Sara Holbrook

This poem and the one that follows challenge us to think about who we are, where we came from, and what we will become.

People get tagged with these labels,
like African-American,
Native-American,
White,
Asian, Hispanic,
or Euro-Caucasian —
I just ask that you get my name right.
I'm part Willie,
part Ethel,
part Suzi and Scott.
Part assembly-line worker,
part barber, a lot of dancer
and salesman.
Part grocer and mailman.
Part rural, part city, part cook
and part caveman.
I'm a chunk-style vegetable soup
of cultural little bits,
my recipe's unique
and no one label fits.
Grouping folks together
is an individual waste.
You can't know me by just a look,
you have to take a taste.

Blueprints

by Sara Holbrook

Will my ears grow long as Grandpa's?
What makes us look like kin?
Tell me where'd I get long eyelashes
and where'd I get my chin?
Where'd I get my ice cream sweet tooth
and this nose that wiggles when I talk?
Where'd I get my dizzy daydreams
and my foot-rolling, side-step walk?
Did I inherit my sense of humor
and these crooked, ugly toes?
What if I balloon like Uncle Harry
and have to shave my nose?
How long after I start growing
until I start to shrink?
Am I going to lose my teeth
some day?
My hair?
My mind?
Do you think
I'll be tall or short or thin
or bursting at the seams?
Am I naturally this crazy?
Is it something in my genes?
I'm more than
who I am,
I'm also
who I'm from.
It's a scary speculation—
Who will I become?

13 LAFFF

by Lensey Namioka

SUMMARY

Lensey Namioka has crafted a short story that focuses on two main characters: Angela Tang and Peter Lu. Peter has created a time machine and uses the machine to help Angela "win" a writing contest.

SOURCE: *Lensey Namioka was born in Beijing, China, and came to America when she was 9 years old. She is the author of several popular books, including the Zenta and Matsuzo Samurai series.*

READING SESSIONS: 2

LANGUAGE AND VOCABULARY

Writers choose words carefully in order to establish the tone of a text. Tone allows readers to determine the author's attitude toward the characters and the central ideas in the text. Prior to reading, ask students to discuss and predict the tone of the story, based on the following words or phrases.

	Before Reading	After Reading
immigrated		
nerd		
mad scientist		
curiosity		
first language		
honorable mention		
suspense		

After reading, invite students to revisit the words to help them determine the tone of this text.

THINK, TALK, AND WRITE ABOUT TEXT

Talk about how you think Angela and Peter view their families as Chinese immigrants in America. What actions or attitudes do the Tangs and the Lus seem to have in common based on the information in this story?

Search online for a few pictures of Fu Manchu. Compare the pictures you found to the description of Lu Manchu (Peter). Angela thinks that Peter loses his nerd status after Halloween because of his costume. If this is true, **discuss** why you think students' attitudes toward Peter might have changed.

Fu Manchu was seen as an evil genius. **Write** a note for future readers of this story, telling them how Peter is like or unlike Fu Manchu.

LAFFF

by Lensey Namioka

When Angela discovers that Peter, also known as Dr. Lu Manchu, has invented a time machine, they think of different ways they can use it to their advantage . . . including winning a writing contest. Will it actually work?

READ-ALOUD TIP

The momentum of this story is carried by the dialogues between Angela and Peter and their parents. Change your voice to match the characters and vary the pacing— use a slower pace to indicate thought and a faster pace to indicate action.

BACKGROUND LANGUAGE

Fu Manchu is a fictional character created by British author Sax Rohmer. Show students a picture of Fu Manchu as context for Peter's costume and his interest in science. With older students, you may want to discuss archetypes and evil genius.

In movies, geniuses have frizzy white hair, right? They wear thick glasses and have names like Dr. Zweistein.

Peter Lu didn't have frizzy white hair. He had straight hair, as black as licorice. He didn't wear thick glasses, either, since his vision was normal. Peter's family, like ours, had immigrated from China, but they had settled here first. When we moved into a house just two doors down from the Lus, they gave us some good advice on how to get along in America.

I went to the same school as Peter, and we walked to the school bus together every morning. Like many Chinese parents, mine made sure that I worked very hard in school.

In spite of all I could do, my grades were nothing compared to Peter's. He was at the top in all his classes. We walked to the school bus without talking because I was a little scared of him. Besides, he was always deep in thought.

Peter didn't have any friends. Most of the kids thought he was a nerd because they saw his head always buried in books. I didn't think he even tried to join the rest of us or cared what the others thought of him.

Then he surprised us all. As I went down the block trick-or-treating, dressed as a zucchini in my green sweats, I heard a strange, deep voice behind me say, "How do you do?"

I yelped and turned around. Peter was wearing a long, black Chinese gown with slits in the sides. On his head he had a little round cap, and down each side of his mouth drooped a thin, long mustache.

"I am Dr. Lu Manchu, the mad scientist," he announced, putting his hands in his sleeves and bowing. He smiled when he saw me staring at his costume. It was a scary smile, somehow.

Some of the other kids came up, and when they saw Peter, they were impressed. "Hey, neat!" said one boy. I hadn't expected Peter to put on a costume and go trick-or-treating like a normal kid. So maybe he did want to join the others after all—at least some of the time. After that night he wasn't a nerd anymore. He was Dr. Lu Manchu. Even some of the teachers began to call him that.

When we became too old for trick-or-treating, Peter was still Dr. Lu Manchu. The rumor was that he was working on a fantastic machine in his parents' garage. But nobody had any idea what it was.

One evening, as I was coming home from a babysitting job, I cut across the Lus' backyard. Passing their garage, I saw through a little window that the light was on. My curiosity got the better of me, and I peeked in.

I saw a booth that looked like a shower stall. A stool stood in the middle of the stall, and hanging over the stool was something that looked like a great big shower head.

Suddenly a deep voice behind me said, "Good evening, Angela." Peter bowed and smiled his scary smile. He didn't have his costume on and he didn't have the long, droopy mustache. But he was Dr. Lu Manchu.

"What are you doing?" I squeaked.

Still in his strange, deep voice, Peter said, "What are *you* doing? After all, this is my garage."

"I was just cutting across your yard to get home. Your parents never complained before."

"I thought you were spying on me," said Peter. "I thought you wanted to know about my machine." He hissed when he said the word *machine*.

Honestly, he was beginning to frighten me. "What machine?" I demanded. "You mean this shower-stall thing?"

He drew himself up and narrowed his eyes, making them into thin slits. "This is my time machine!"

I goggled at him. "You mean . . . you mean . . . this machine can send you forward and backward in time?"

"Well, actually, I can only send things forward in time," admitted Peter, speaking in his normal voice again. "That's why I'm calling the machine LAFFF. It stands for Lu's Artifact For Fast Forward."

Of course Peter always won first prize at the annual statewide science fair. But that's a long way from making a time machine. Minus his mustache and long Chinese gown, he was just Peter Lu.

"I don't believe it!" I said. "I bet LAFFF is only good for a laugh."

"Okay, Angela. I'll show you!" hissed Peter.

He sat down on the stool and twisted a dial. I heard some bleeps, cheeps, and gurgles. Peter disappeared. He must have done it with mirrors. I looked around the garage. I peeked under the tool bench. There was no sign of him.

"Okay, I give up," I told him. "It's a good trick, Peter. You can come out now."

Bleep, cheep, and gurgle went the machine, and there was Peter sitting on the stool. He held a red rose in his hand. "What do you think of that?"

I blinked. "So you produced a flower. Maybe you had it under the stool."

"Roses bloom in June, right?" he demanded.

That was true. And this was December.

"I sent myself forward in time to June when the flowers were blooming," said Peter. "And I picked the rose from our yard. Convinced, Angela?"

It was too hard to swallow. "You said you couldn't send things back in time," I objected. "So how did you bring the rose back?"

But even as I spoke I saw that his hands were empty.

The rose was gone.

"That's one of the problems with the machine," said Peter. "When I send myself forward, I can't seem to stay there for long. I snap back to my own time after only a minute. Anything I bring with me snaps back to its own time, too. So my rose has gone back to this June."

I was finally convinced, and I began to see possibilities. "Wow, just think: If I don't want to do the dishes, I can send myself forward to the time when the dishes are already done."

"That won't do you much good," said Peter. "You'd soon pop back to the time when the dishes were still dirty."

Too bad. "There must be something your machine is good for," I said. Then I had another idea. "Hey, you can bring me back a piece of fudge from the future, and I can eat it twice: once now, and again in the future."

"Yes, but the fudge wouldn't stay in your stomach," said Peter. "It would go back to the future."

"That's even better!" I said. "I can enjoy eating the fudge over and over again without getting fat!"

It was late, and I had to go home before my parents started to worry. Before I left, Peter said, "Look, Angela, there's still a lot of work to do on LAFFF. Please don't tell anybody about the machine until I've got it right."

A few days later I asked him how he was doing.

"I can stay in the future time a bit longer now," he said. "Once I got it up to four minutes."

"Is that enough time to bring me back some fudge from the future?" I asked.

"We don't keep many sweets around the house," he said. "But I'll see what I can do."

A few minutes later, he came back with a spring roll for me.

"My mother was frying these in the kitchen, and I snatched one while she wasn't looking."

I bit into the hot, crunchy spring roll, but before I finished chewing, it disappeared. The taste of soy sauce, green onions, and bean sprouts stayed a little longer in my mouth, though.

It was fun to play around with LAFFF, but it wasn't really useful. I didn't know what a great help it would turn out to be.

· · · · ·

Every year our school held a writing contest, and the winning story for each grade got printed in our school magazine. I wanted desperately to win. I worked awfully hard in school, but my parents still thought I could do better.

Winning the writing contest would show my parents that I was really good in something. I love writing stories, and I have lots of ideas. But when I actually write them down, my stories never turn out as good as I thought. I just can't seem to find the right words, because English isn't my first language.

I got an honorable mention last year, but it wasn't the same as winning and showing my parents my name, Angela Tang, printed in the school magazine.

The deadline for the contest was getting close, and I had a pile of stories written, but none of them looked like a winner.

Then, the day before the deadline, *boing*, a brilliant idea hit me.

I thought of Peter and his LAFFF machine. I rushed over to the Lus' garage and, just as I had hoped, Peter was there, tinkering with his machine.

"I've got this great idea for winning the story contest," I told him breathlessly. "You see, to be certain of winning, I have to write the story that would be the winner."

"That's obvious," Peter said dryly. "In fact, you're going around in a circle."

"Wait, listen!" I said. "I want to use LAFFF and go forward to the time when the next issue of the school magazine is out. Then I can read the winning story."

After a moment Peter nodded. "I see. You plan to write down the winning story after you've read it and then send it in to the contest."

I nodded eagerly. "The story would have to win, because it's the winner!"

Peter began to look interested. "I've got LAFFF to the point where I can stay in the future for seven minutes now. Will that be long enough for you?"

"I'll just have to work quickly," I said.

Peter smiled. It wasn't his scary Lu Manchu smile, but a nice smile. He was getting as excited as I was. "Okay, Angela. Let's go for it."

He led me to the stool. "What's your destination?" he asked. "I mean, when's your destination?"

Suddenly I was nervous. I told myself that Peter had made many time trips, and he looked perfectly healthy. Why not? What have I got to lose—except time?

I took a deep breath. "I want to go forward three weeks in time." By then I'd have a copy of the new school magazine in my room.

"Ready, Angela?" asked Peter.

"As ready as I'll ever be," I whispered.

Bleep, cheep, and gurgle. Suddenly Peter disappeared. What went wrong? Did Peter get sent by mistake, instead of me?

Then I realized what had happened. Three weeks later in time Peter might be somewhere else. No wonder I don't see him.

There was no time to be lost. Rushing out of Peter's garage, I ran over to our house and entered through the back door.

Mother was in the kitchen. When she saw me, she stared.

"Angela! I thought you were upstairs taking a shower!"

"Sorry!" I panted. "No time to talk!"

I dashed up to my room. Then I suddenly had a strange idea. What if I met myself in my room? Argh! It was a spooky thought. There was nobody in my room. Where was I? I mean, where was the I of three weeks later? Wait. Mother had just said she thought I was taking a shower. Down the hall, I could hear the water running in the bathroom. Okay. That meant I wouldn't run into me for a while.

I went to the shelf above my desk and frantically pawed through the junk piled there. I found it! I found the latest issue of the school magazine, the one with the winning stories printed in it.

How much time had passed? Better hurry. The shower had stopped running. This meant the other me was out of the bathroom. Have to get out of here!

Too late. Just as I started down the stairs, I heard Mother talking again. "Angela! A minute ago you were all dressed! Now you're in your robe again and your hair's all wet! I don't understand."

I shivered. It was scary, listening to Mother talking to myself downstairs. I heard my other self answering something, then the sound of her— my—steps coming up the stairs. In a panic, I dodged into the spare room and closed the door.

I heard the steps—my steps—go past and into my room. The minute I heard the door of my room close, I rushed out and down the stairs.

Mother was standing at the foot of the stairs. When she saw me, her mouth dropped. "But . . . but . . . just a minute ago you were in your robe and your hair was all wet!"

"See you later, Mother," I panted. And I ran.

Behind me, I heard Mother muttering, "I'm going mad!"

I didn't stop and try to explain. I might go mad, too.

It would be great if I could just keep the magazine with me. But, like the spring roll, it would get carried back to its own time after a few minutes. So the next best thing was to read the magazine as fast as I could. It was hard to run and flip through the magazine at the same time. But I made it back to Peter's garage and plopped down on the stool.

At last I found the story: the story that had won the contest in our grade. I started to read. Suddenly I heard bleep, cheep, and gurgle, and Peter loomed up in front of me. I was back in my original time again. But I still had the magazine! Now I had to read the story before the magazine popped back to the future. It was hard to concentrate with Peter jumping up and down impatiently, so different from his usual calm, collected self.

I read a few paragraphs, and I was beginning to see how the story would shape up. But before I got any further, the magazine disappeared from my hand. So I didn't finish reading the story. I didn't reach the end, where the name of the winning writer was printed.

That night I stayed up very late to write down what I remembered of the story. It had a neat plot, and I could see why it was the winner.

I hadn't read the entire story, so I had to make up the ending myself. But that was okay, since I knew how it should come out. The winners of the writing contest would be announced at the school assembly on Friday.

After we had filed into the assembly hall and sat down, the principal gave a speech. I tried not to fidget while he explained about the contest.

Suddenly I was struck by a dreadful thought.

Somebody in my class had written the winning story, the one I had copied. Wouldn't that person be declared the winner, instead of me?

The principal started announcing the winners. I chewed my knuckles in an agony of suspense, as I waited to see who would be announced as the winner in my class.

Slowly, the principal began with the lowest grade. Each winner walked in slow motion to the stage, while the principal slowly explained why the story was good.

At last, at last, he came to our grade. "The winner is . . ." He stopped, slowly got out his handkerchief, and slowly blew his nose. Then he cleared his throat. "The winning story is 'Around and Around,' by Angela Tang."

I sat like a stone, unable to move. Peter nudged me.

"Go on, Angela! They're waiting for you."

I got up and walked up to the stage in a daze. The principal's voice seemed to be coming from far, far away as he told the audience that I had written a science fiction story about time travel.

The winners each got a notebook bound in imitation leather for writing more stories. Inside the cover of the notebook was a ballpoint pen. But the best prize was having my story in the school magazine with my name printed at the end.

Then why didn't I feel good about winning?

After assembly, the kids in our class crowded around to congratulate me. Peter formally shook my hand. "Good work, Angela," he said and winked at me. That didn't make me feel any better. I hadn't won the contest fairly. Instead of writing the story myself, I had copied it from the school magazine.

That meant someone in our class— one of the kids here—had actually written the story. Who was it?

My heart was knocking against my ribs as I stood there and waited for someone to complain that I had stolen his story.

Nobody did.

As we were riding the school bus home, Peter looked at me. "You don't seem very happy about winning the contest, Angela."

"No, I'm not," I mumbled. "I feel just awful."

"Tell you what," suggested Peter. "Come over to my house and we'll discuss it."

"What is there to discuss?" I asked glumly. "I won the contest because I cheated."

"Come on over, anyway. My mother bought a fresh package of *humbow* in Chinatown."

I couldn't turn down that invitation. *Humbow*, a roll stuffed with barbecued pork, is my favorite snack.

Peter's mother came into the kitchen while we were munching, and he told her about the contest.

Mrs. Lu looked pleased. "I'm very glad, Angela. You have a terrific imagination, and you deserve to win."

"I like Angela's stories," said Peter. "They're original."

It was the first compliment he had ever paid me, and I felt my face turning red.

After Mrs. Lu left us, Peter and I each had another *humbow*.

But I was still miserable. "I wish I had never started this. I feel like such a jerk."

Peter looked at me, and I swear he was enjoying himself. "If you stole another student's story, why didn't that person complain?"

"I don't know!" I wailed.

"Think!" said Peter. "You're smart, Angela. Come on, figure it out."

Me, smart? I was so overcome to hear myself called smart by a genius like Peter that I just stared at him.

He had to repeat himself. "Figure it out, Angela!"

I tried to concentrate. Why was Peter looking so amused?

The light finally dawned. "Got it," I said slowly. "I'm the one who wrote the story."

"The winning story is your own, Angela, because that's the one that won."

My head began to go around and around. "But where did the original idea for the story come from?"

"What made the plot so good?" asked Peter. His voice sounded unsteady.

"Well, in my story, my character used a time machine to go forward in time . . ."

"Okay, whose idea was it to use a time machine?"

"It was mine," I said slowly. I remembered the moment when the idea had hit me with a boing.

"So you s-stole f-from yourself!" sputtered Peter. He started to roar with laughter. I had never seen him break down like that. At this rate, he might wind up being human.

When he could talk again, he asked me to read my story to him.

I began. "In movies, geniuses have frizzy white hair, right? They wear thick glasses and have names like Dr. Zweistein . . ."

14 Licked

by Paul Jennings

SUMMARY

Andrew's dad is always on his case about manners. One day, his mom challenges his dad to refrain from reprimanding Andrew through an entire dinner with guests. However, Andrew has an idea: He comes up with every way he can to aggravate his dad, until one trick nearly pushes Andrew's dad over the edge.

SOURCE: *"Licked" comes from Unbearable! by Paul Jennings. Jennings specializes in short stories that end in a twist.*

READING SESSIONS: 2

LANGUAGE AND VOCABULARY

We usually think of words as having "a" meaning. But most words have more than one meaning, depending on the context in which the word is used. Sometimes the meaning is clearer when you see or hear the word in context. Using the chart below, and without providing the context, ask students to predict what they think each bold word in the organizer means.

Before Reading	After Reading
Licked (title)	
"**mad** about manners"	
"You'll give the boy a **complex**."	
"going **crook**"	
currants	
serviettes	

After reading, discuss how the context confirmed their predictions or whether the context helped them learn another meaning.

THINK, TALK, AND WRITE ABOUT TEXT

Think about the manners you are expected to use at your home. Are different manners expected when you have company?

Talk about the way Andrew carefully set a trap for his father. What does this say about the relationship Andrew has with his parents?

Talk about the clues in the story that show Andrew knew that the best time to teach his father a lesson would be when his father had invited his boss for dinner.

Discuss whether or not you think Andrew owes his father an apology. Include reasons he should apologize as well as reasons you think he shouldn't apologize.

Discuss whether you think Andrew should receive a punishment.

Write an apology letter you think Andrew would send to his father after the trouble he caused at dinner.

Exchange your letter with a classmate. Read each other's letters and write a letter you think Andrew's father would write in response to the apology.

Licked

by Paul Jennings

Andrew's father has a big, important dinner coming up; his boss is coming over, and the family must be on best behavior. But Andrew doesn't want to be on best behavior. In fact, Andrew wants to test his dad, to see how much he can get away with during the dinner. In this funny story, a son pushes his dad to the limit, just to see what will happen. How far will Andrew go?

READ-ALOUD TIP

This story is a family drama, so it will be important to develop distinct voices for Andrew and his parents. Use these voices to amplify the conflict: Andrew's slyness, his parents' indignation, his father's anger, and Mr. Spinks's horror with Andrew's behavior.

BACKGROUND LANGUAGE

The language in this story is relatively easy, but students may question what some words or phrases mean. Many students may not have seen a fly swatter, so you may want to show a picture of one. Jennings is an Australian author, so some of the words or phrases may be unfamiliar: *mad about manners; coming for tea; serviettes* (table napkin); and *sucking out the middle of a chicken bone.*

Tomorrow when Dad calms down, I'll own up. Tell him the truth. He might laugh. He might cry. He might strangle me. But I have to put him out of his misery.

I like my dad. He takes me fishing. He gives me arm wrestles in front of the fire on cold nights. He plays Scrabble instead of watching the news. He tries practical jokes on me. And he keeps his promise. Always.

But he has two faults. Bad faults. One is to do with flies. He can't stand them. If there's a fly in the room he has to kill it. He won't use fly spray because of the ozone layer, so he chases them with a fly swat. He races around the house swiping and swatting like a mad thing. He won't stop until the fly is flat. Squashed. Squished—sometimes squirming on the end of the fly swat.

He's a dead-eye shot. He hardly ever misses. When his old fly swat was almost worn out, I bought him a nice yellow one for his birthday. It wasn't yellow for long. It soon had bits of fly smeared all over it.

It's funny, the different colors that squashed flies have inside them. Mostly it is black or brown. But often there are streaks of runny red stuff and sometimes bits of blue. The wings flash like diamonds if you hold them up to the light. But mostly the wings fall off unless they are stuck to the swat with a bit of squashed innards.

Chasing flies is Dad's first fault. His second one is table manners. He is mad about manners.

And it is always my manners that are the matter.

"Andrew," he says. "Don't put your elbows on the table."

"Don't talk with your mouth full."

"Don't lick your fingers."

"Don't dunk your biscuit in the coffee."

This is the way he goes on every mealtime. He has a thing about flies and a thing about manners.

Anyway, to get back to the story. One day Dad is peeling the potatoes for tea. I am looking for my fifty cents that rolled under the table about a week ago. Mum is cutting up the cabbage and talking to Dad. They do not know that I am there. It is a very important meal because Dad's boss, Mr. Spinks, is coming for tea. Dad never stops going on about my manners when someone comes for tea.

"You should stop picking on Andrew at tea time," says Mum.

"I don't," says Dad.

"Yes you do," says Mum. "It's always 'don't do this, don't do that.' You'll give the boy a complex." I have never heard of a complex before but I guess that it is something awful like pimples.

"Tonight," says Mum. "I want you to go for the whole meal without telling Andrew off once."

"Easy," says Dad.

"Try hard," says Mum. "Promise me that you won't get cross with him."

Dad looks at her for a long time. "Okay," he says. "It's a deal. I won't say one thing about his manners. But you're not allowed to either. What's good for me is good for you."

"Shake," says Mum. They shake hands and laugh.

I find the fifty cents and sneak out. I take a walk down the street to spend it before tea. Dad has promised not to tell me off at tea time. I think about how I can make him crack. It should be easy. I will slurp my soup. He hates that. He will tell me off. He might even yell. I just know that he can't go for the whole meal without going crook. "This is going to be fun," I say to myself.

⬤ ⬤ ⬤ ⬤ ⬤

That night Mum sets the table with the new tablecloth. And the best knives and forks. And the plates that I am not allowed to touch. She puts out serviettes in little rings. All of this means that it is an important meal. We don't usually use serviettes.

Mr. Spinks comes in his best suit. He wears gold glasses and he frowns a lot. I can tell that he doesn't like children. You can always tell when adults don't like kids. They smile at you with their lips but not with their eyes.

Anyway, we sit down to tea. I put my secret weapon on the floor under the table. I'm sure that I can make Dad crack without using it. But it is there if all else fails.

The first course is soup and bread rolls. I make loud slurping noise with the soup. No one says anything about it. I make the slurping noises longer and louder. They go on and on and on. It sounds like someone has pulled the plug out of the bath. Dad clears his throat but doesn't say anything.

I try something different. I dip my bread in the soup and make it soggy. Then I hold it high above my head and drop it down into my mouth. I catch it with a loud slopping noise. I try again with an even bigger bit. This time I miss my mouth and the bit of soupy bread hits me in the eye.

Nothing is said. Dad looks at me. Mum looks at me. Mr. Spinks tries not to look at me. They are talking about how Dad might get a promotion at work. They are pretending that I am not revolting.

The next course is chicken. Dad will crack over the chicken. He'll say something. He hates me picking up the bones.

The chicken is served. "I've got the chicken's bottom," I say in a loud voice.

Dad glares at me but he doesn't answer. I pick up the chicken and start stuffing it into my mouth with my fingers. I grab a roast potato and break it in half. I dip my fingers into the margarine and put some on the potato. It runs all over the place.

I have never seen anyone look as mad as the way Dad looks at me. He glares. He stares. He clears his throat. But still he doesn't crack. What a man. Nothing can make him break his promise.

I snap a chicken bone in half and suck out the middle. It is hollow and I can see right through it. I suck and slurp and swallow. Dad is going red in the face. Little veins are standing out on his nose. But still he does not crack.

The last course is baked apple and custard. I will get him with that. Mr. Spinks has stopped talking about Dad's promotion. He is discussing something about discipline. About setting limits. About insisting on standards. Something like that. I put the hollow bone into the custard and use it like a straw. I suck the custard up the hollow chicken bone.

Dad clears his throat. He is very red in the face. "Andrew," he says.

"Yes," I say through a mouthful of custard.

"Nothing," he mumbles.

Dad is terrific. He is under enormous pressure but still he keeps his cool. There is only one thing left to do. I take out my secret weapon.

I place the yellow fly swat on the table next to my knife.

Everyone looks at it lying there on the white tablecloth. They stare and stare and stare. But nothing is said.

I pick up the fly swat and start to lick it. I lick it like an ice cream. A bit of chewy, brown goo comes off on my tongue. I swallow it quickly. Then I crunch a bit of crispy, black stuff.

Mr. Spinks rushes out to the kitchen. I can hear him being sick in the kitchen sink.

Dad stands up. It is too much for him. He cracks. "Aaaaaagh," he screams. He charges at me with hands held like claws.

I run for it. I run down to my room and lock the door. Dad yells and shouts. He kicks and screams. But I lie low.

Tomorrow, when he calms down, I'll own up. I'll tell him how I went down the street and bought a new fly swat for fifty cents. I'll tell him about the currants and little bits of licorice that I smeared on the fly swat.

I mean, I wouldn't really eat dead flies. Not unless it was for something important anyway.

15 A Mouthful

by Paul Jennings

SUMMARY

In this first-person account the narrator is mortified about her father's tendency to play practical jokes on her and her friends. Finally, she hatches a plan to get back at him.

SOURCE: *"A Mouthful"* comes from Uncovered! *by Paul Jennings. Jennings specializes in short stories that end in a twist.*

READING SESSION: 1

LANGUAGE AND VOCABULARY

Paul Jennings is an Australian author, so some of the terms, or the way words are used, might seem unfamiliar to us. One of the ways to keep track of words or phrases that are new or used in a new way is to create a visual word wall (see below). Combining the unknown word with a strong image that shows how the word was used in the story can make the word and the story more memorable. Create a visual for the quotes and then see if you can retell the story by using your visuals for support.

Visual Word Wall

"…he does something that **makes my face go red.**"	"Oh look, disgusting. **Foul.**"	"Anna is **pulling a terrible face.**"
"…he says through **clenched** teeth."	"Dad is a **bit taken aback** at Anna being sick."	"We also do the **washing up** after dinner."

THINK, TALK, AND WRITE ABOUT TEXT

Think about how you would feel if your father played practical jokes on you and your friends. Do you think you would try to solve the problem the same way the narrator of "A Mouthful" did?

Discuss types of jokes. Are practical jokes, gags, pranks, and wisecracks all the same? Do all jokes have victims? Brainstorm examples that illustrate when jokes are harmful and when they are harmless.

When is a joke harmful?	When is a joke harmless?

The title of the story is "A Mouthful." After reading the story, **discuss** in what way the title could have a double meaning.

One of the things making this story so funny is that the kids win by turning the tables on dad. In many of his other stories, bullies often lose and underdogs often win. **Write** a short response about reading this story and explain whether or not you would like to read more of Paul Jennings's stories and why.

A Mouthful

by Paul Jennings

Dad just loves to play practical jokes on his daughter and her friends. But he's about to get a taste of his own medicine!

READ-ALOUD TIP

As with "Licked," this family drama story, also by Paul Jennings, can be read effectively by using different voices to represent the narrator and her father. Highlight sections the author indicates as dramatic moments through word choice and punctuation: *"makes my face go red"* or *"Ooh, ooh, ooh!" she screams.*

BACKGROUND LANGUAGE

The language is generally very accessible, although some phrases may be unfamiliar to students, including: *pulling a terrible face, through clenched teeth, a bit taken aback,* and *do the washing up.*

Parents are embarrassing.

Take my dad. Every time a friend comes to stay the night he does something that makes my face go red. Now don't get me wrong. He is a terrific dad. I love him but sometimes I think he will never grow up.

He loves playing practical jokes.

This behavior first starts the night Anna comes to sleep over. Unknown to me, Dad sneaks into my room and puts Doona our cat on the spare bed. Doona loves sleeping on beds. What cat doesn't?

Next Dad unwraps a little package that he has bought at the magic shop. Do you know what is in it? Can you believe this? It is a little piece of brown plastic cat poo. Pretend cat poo. Anyway, he puts this piece of cat poo on Anna's pillow and pulls up the blankets. Then he tiptoes out and closes the door.

I do not know any of this is happening. Anna and I are sitting up late watching videos. We eat chips covered in sauce and drink two whole bottles of Diet Coke.

Finally we decide to go to bed. Anna takes ages and ages cleaning her teeth. She is one of those kids who are into health. She has a thing about germs. She always places paper on the toilet seat before she sits down. She is so clean.

Anyway, she puts on her nightclothes and gets ready for bed. Then she pulls back the blankets. Suddenly she sees the bit of plastic cat poo. "Ooh, ooh, ooh!" she screams. "Oh look, disgusting. Foul. Look what the cat's done on my pillow!"

Suddenly Dad bursts into the room. "What's up, girls?" he says with a silly grin on his face. "What's all the fuss about?"

Anna is pulling a terrible face. "Look," she says in horror as she points at the pillow.

Riveting Read-Alouds for Middle School © Janet Allen and Patrick Daley, Scholastic Inc.

Dad goes over and examines the plastic poo. "Don't let a little think like that worry you," he says. He picks up the plastic poo and pops it into his mouth. He gives a grin. "Delicious!" he says through clenched teeth.

"Aargh," screams Anna. She rushes over to the window and throws up chips and Diet Coke. Then she looks at Dad in disgust.

Dad is a bit taken aback at Anna being sick. "It's okay," he says, taking the plastic poo out of his mouth. "It's not real." Dad gives a laugh and off he goes.

And off goes Anna. She decides that she wants to go home to her own house. And I don't blame her.

"Dad," I yell after Anna is gone. "I am never speaking to you again!"

"Don't be such a drama queen," he says. "It's only a little joke."

It's always the same. Whenever a friend comes over to stay Dad plays practical jokes. We have fake hands in the rubbish, exploding drinks, pepper in the food, short-sheeted beds, and Dracula's blood seeping out of Dad's mouth. Some of the kids think it's great. They wish their Dad were like mine.

But I hate it. I just wish he were normal.

He plays tricks on Bianca.

And Yasmin.

And Nga.

None of them go home like Anna. But each time I am so embarrassed.

And now I am worried.

Cynthia is coming to stay. She is the school captain. She is beautiful. She is smart. Everyone wants to be her friend. And now she is sleeping over at our house.

"Dad," I say. "No practical jokes. Cynthia is very mature. Her father would never play practical jokes. She might not understand."

"No worries," says Dad.

Cynthia arrives, but we do not watch videos. We slave away on our English homework. We plan our speeches for the debate in the morning. We go over our parts in the school play. After all that, we go out and practice baskets because Cynthia is captain of the basketball team. Every now and then I pop into the bedroom to check for practical jokes. It is best to be on the safe side.

We also do the washing up after dinner because Cynthia offers—yes *offers*—to do it.

Finally it is time for bed. Cynthia changes into her nightclothes in the bathroom and then comes into the bedroom. "The cat's on my bed," she says. "But it doesn't matter. I like cats." She pulls back the blankets.

And screams. "Aargh! Cat poo! Filthy cat poo on my pillow!" She yells and yells and yells.

Just then Dad bursts into the room with a silly grin on his face. He goes over and looks at the brown object on the pillow. "Don't let a little thing like that worry you," he says. He picks it up and pops it into his mouth. But this time he does not give a grin. His face freezes over.

"Are you looking for this?" I say.

I hold up the bit of plastic poo that Dad had hidden under the blankets earlier that night.

Dad looks at the cat. Then he rushes over to the window and is sick. Cynthia and I laugh like mad.

We do love a good joke.

16 Lost in the Pacific

by Tod Olson

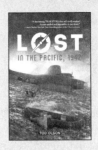

SUMMARY

Lost somewhere over the Pacific—and out of fuel—the crew of a World War II B-17 bomber fighting plane prepares for an emergency landing.

SOURCE: *Tod Olson is author of the historical fiction series How to Get Rich. He works as an editor, and lives in Vermont with his family, his mountain bike, and his electric reclining chair.*

READING SESSIONS: 2

LANGUAGE AND VOCABULARY

Share with students the concept web below. Ask them to speculate how each word might relate to the topic of Emergency Plane Landing. After reading, revisit the web. Encourage students to elaborate more on the connection between the words and the topic. Students may wish to add other words. Encourage them to explain the connections.

THINK, TALK, AND WRITE ABOUT TEXT

Reread the first three paragraphs. Ask students to describe what the author intended with his imagery:

- "unforgiving as a concrete wall" (par. 1)
- "Island eyes" (par. 2)
- "a vast tarmac of water" (par. 3)

What measures did the crew take to ready themselves for the crash?

As you heard the details of the preparations of the crash, **what were you feeling?** Can you imagine yourself in the airmen's place?

After the crash, **what** new challenge did the survivors face?

The author hints at the end that several of the men survived. **Who** do you think did or did not survive?

Lost in the Pacific

by Tod Olson

This is the true story of a plane crew on a top-secret mission across the Pacific Ocean during World War II. Lost and out of fuel, the plane prepares to crash land in the choppy waters below. Will the crew and its secret passenger survive?

READ-ALOUD TIP

As you read aloud this account, use your voice to intensify the fear the men were feeling. After the introduction, the tone of the text quickly turns to desperation. This is followed by an analytical, matter-of-fact telling of how the crew tried to save themselves, punctuated by a description of their fearfulness at the odds.

BACKGROUND LANGUAGE

Many students may not know words related to airplanes or crashes. Showing students the type of plane used at this time in WWII and pinpointing who and where each of the occupants were during this terrifying landing in the Pacific could provide language context.

October 21, 1942
Somewhere over the South Pacific

The Pacific Ocean looked calm and inviting from 5,000 feet up, with the drone of four sturdy motors in Jim Whittaker's ear. But he had no desire to land a 25-ton, 4-engine plane down there. To a B-17 bomber, plunging from the sky, the ocean is as unforgiving as a concrete wall.

Yet by 1:30 p.m. on October 21, 1942, that was the only option left. Whittaker was the B-17's copilot. He and the rest of the crew were ferrying a VIP passenger on a top-secret mission deep into the war zone. They had completely missed Canton Island, the tiny speck in the great blue where they were supposed to refuel. Now they were flying in a giant square pattern, hoping to spot land. They took turns staring out the windows at the ocean below, mistaking cloud shadows for islands. "Island eyes," the airmen called it—the surest sign that desperation had set in.

The fact was they were lost, somewhere in the middle of the Pacific. They were nearly out of fuel, and the only landing strip they had was a vast tarmac of water.

No one knew exactly how they had lost their way. Maybe the tail winds were stronger than the weathermen had predicted. Maybe the compass had taken a hit when they nearly crashed taking off in Hawaii. Either way, the navigator had finally given up trying to figure out where they were. He was a young guy named John DeAngelis who had gotten married just two days before they were called away. Now he was probably wondering if he would ever see his wife again.

"Do you fellows mind if I pray?" he shouted to the crew over the roar of the engines.

Pray? Whittaker thought. How about keeping your mind on the task at hand: surviving an impact with the Pacific Ocean.

Whittaker decided not to say a word. DeAngelis could swan dive into the ocean and it wouldn't matter. Their lives were in Bill Cherry's hands now—the 27-year-old pilot from Texas who sat next to Whittaker with the controls in his hands.

Cherry and Whittaker began to talk strategy. It had been ten and a half months since the United States was drawn into World War II. In that time, plenty of bomber crews had ditched in the Pacific. Not one, as far as they could remember, had escaped without casualties.

If the surface of the ocean were flat, it would be one thing. But today, the water rose and fell in treacherous swells. If you came in across the current you had to time it exactly right. Scrape the crest of a swell and the nose would dip, sending the plane plummeting to the depths. Avoid one crest and you could ram the plane into the next one, shattering the entire craft into pieces in an instant.

There was only one way to do it, Whittaker and Cherry agreed. Come in parallel to the swells and set the plane down in a trough. That, of course, was easier said than done. The troughs were a moving target, and the wind blew across your flight path, making it hard to hold a line. Hitting a landing spot just right would still take perfect timing, expert piloting skills, and a whole lot of luck.

While Cherry and Whittaker worked out a strategy, their top-secret passenger took charge of the crew behind them. And if luck really had anything to do with their fate, maybe he would tip the scales in their favor. He wasn't some desk-bound politician or stuffy diplomat. The VIP on board was none other than Eddie Rickenbacker.

For anyone who cared about flying—and for most everyone else—that was all the introduction he needed. Aside from Charles Lindbergh, he was the world's most famous pilot. He hadn't flown in combat since 1918, when World War I ended. But to millions of Americans, his heroics against the Germans were unforgettable. He had shot down more enemy aircraft than any other American pilot.

Now, Rickenbacker was a businessman—president of Eastern Airlines. But he had a well-known reputation for surviving close scrapes. He had first become famous as an auto racer, driving primitive cars at breakneck speeds. As a fighter pilot, he nearly had his plane shredded by German bullets several times. Then, in the spring of 1941, he had been a passenger on one of his own airliners when it crashed in a Georgia forest. Trapped in the wreckage, he managed to direct rescue efforts with broken ribs, a shattered elbow, a fractured skull, and an eyeball torn loose from its socket. He was in such bad shape that the famous radio commentator Walter Winchell reported his death on the air. When Rickenbacker heard it from his hospital bed, he picked up a water pitcher and threw it at the radio.

A year and a half later, Rickenbacker still looked frail from the crash and walked with a cane. But with another crash looming, he seemed determined to survive one more time. Rickenbacker grabbed the young sergeant, Alex Kaczmarczyk, and pried open the bottom hatch in the B-17's tail. Then he and Kaczmarczyk lightened the plane's load to save fuel and lessen the impact when they went down. Out went the cots, the tool kit, blankets, empty thermos bottles, and the luggage. Sacks full of high-priority mail sailed into the wind, soon to be a soggy, unreadable mess of good wishes that would never make it to the soldiers on the front lines.

Cherry announced he was starting his descent, and the water outside Whittaker's window looked more distinct by the second. Back in the radio compartment, the men piled essential provisions by the hatch: a few bottles filled with water and coffee; emergency rations in a small metal box; a two-man raft rolled into a tight package. Once they landed, they could have as little as thirty seconds to get out before the plane went under—assuming they were still alive.

• • • • •

The men stacked mattresses in position, padding the aft, or rear, side of the walls that separated the compartments of the plane. They all took their positions. Three men—Kaczmarczyk, DeAngelis, and Rickenbacker's military escort, Colonel Hans Adamson—lay on the floor, braced against the mattresses. Rickenbacker sat near them, belted into a seat near a window. Johnny Bartek, the engineer, sat just behind the cockpit. The plane had two inflatable rafts packed into compartments on the outside of the nose. It would be Bartek's job to release them just after they ditched. Jim Reynolds, the radio operator, sat at his desk in the center of the plane. He tapped out SOS

after SOS, hoping that someone out there would register their location before they hit the water. There was nothing but silence from the other end.

"How much longer?" someone asked.

"Not yet," Rickenbacker answered, peering out the window.

In the cockpit, the altimeter showed they were 500 feet above the sea. Cherry cut two of the engines to save fuel. Whittaker grabbed cushions from the seats behind them and stuffed them under their safety harnesses.

"It's sure been swell knowing you, Bill," he said, offering his hand.

Cherry gripped his co-pilot's hand for a second and then said in his Texas drawl, "You're going to know me a long time yet, Jim."

In the back, someone asked again, "How much longer?"

"Fifty feet!" said Rickenbacker. Then right away, "Thirty feet!"

Cherry was staring into the waves, trying to pick a trough to aim for. The swells looked towering—twice the height of a man.

"Twenty feet!"

They were coming in at 90 miles an hour, but to Whittaker the plane seemed strangely still—the roar of the engines muffled, the whoosh of the wind against the fuselage fainter than it should have been. And then there was the radio, whining its lonely signal into the sky.

"Ten feet!"

Bartek reached above them and loosened a set of bolts. The wind snatched the door of the cockpit escape hatch and sent it hurtling to the sea. A rush of air howled through the opening.

"Cut it!" yelled Cherry.

Whittaker pulled a switch, and all electrical power on the plane went dead.

Cherry pulled back hard on the wheel, lifting the nose and ramming the tail into the water.

Back in the radio compartment, the noise was deafening. Pieces of equipment that had been bolted down a moment ago flew through the cabin like shrapnel from a bomb.

And then the belly of the plane hit the water.

Whittaker exploded forward, and the safety belt tried to slice him in half. Pressure filled his head. His eyes strained against their sockets. He couldn't see a thing. He began to lose consciousness.

And then, just as suddenly as it had begun, the pressure released. The belt went slack against his chest. His vision returned.

They had gone from 90 miles an hour to a dead stop in less than 50 feet. He couldn't be sure who had survived and who had not. The Pacific Ocean was pouring fast into the plane. And no one in the big, broad world knew where they were.

Exactly six minutes later, the eight men sat jammed into three inflatable rafts no bigger than bathtubs. In the distance, the nose of their plane lingered above the waves, as if taking a final gasp of air. Then it disappeared.

The B-17 crew and their famous passenger were on their own—three tiny specks in an ocean that covered 68 million square miles. They were convinced they would be rescued in a day or two, if not before nightfall. But one scorching day turned into another, and their secret mission became a fierce battle for survival.

The odds were not in their favor. They had fish hooks and lines but no bait. They were surrounded by water, all of it too salty to drink. The sun tormented them during the day. At night, they huddled in the bilge at the bottom of the rafts, trying to stay warm.

Back at home, news of the B-17's disappearance took its place next to headlines from bloody battles in Africa, in Eastern Europe, in the western Pacific. Eventually, word traveled halfway around the world that somehow, several emaciated and sunburned men had made it to safety. Not all of them survived. But those who did had a story—of desperation and endurance and ingenuity. That story would become one of the most told and retold tales of hope in a war where millions of victims would never find their way home.

17 On the Bridge

by Todd Strasser

SUMMARY

Seth and Adam appear to be opposites. At the beginning, Seth sees himself as a fraud and Adam as an authentically cool guy. They are still opposites at the end, but how have the roles changed?

SOURCE: *Todd Strasser loves to write stories from his own experiences, and from learned experiences. He often visits schools to talk about being a writer and learn about being a kid.*

READING SESSION: 1

(If you need to divide the story into two sessions because of time, stop after the 7th paragraph on page 96, which starts with "Seth smirked.")

LANGUAGE AND VOCABULARY

Discuss the definitions of the words *fraud* and *authentic*. Using the chart below, prompt students to find examples in the text that illuminate the meaning of each word and how it applies to each of the two characters. By the end of the story, does the same word apply to the same character as in the beginning of the story? Why or why not?

	Context	At the beginning . . .	In the end . . .
fraud	". . . he (Seth) felt like a fraud. Like a kid trying to imitate someone truly cool."	Seth's jacket looked new.	
authentic	". . . Adam's leather jacket looked authentically old and worn."	Adam's jacket looked like it had been in fights.	

THINK, TALK, AND WRITE ABOUT TEXT

Think about times in your life when you have wished you could be like someone else. Seth says he is "awestruck" by Adam and his behavior. What makes being around Adam so important to Seth?

Discuss the ways people get to be popular. What makes one person a leader while others remain followers? Use the organizer below to list the characters' actions, showing what makes each a leader or a follower.

Seth (follower)	Adam (leader)
Seth (leader)	**Adam (follower)**

Explore the article about peer pressure at http://kidshealth.org/en/teens/peer-pressure.html. How does information in the article help explain Seth's behavior in this story?

Do a search for articles about teens throwing things down onto traffic. Use details from this story to write a news article that might have appeared after the incidents in "On the Bridge."

On the Bridge

by Todd Strasser

What makes a person "cool"? To Seth, Adam was the very definition of *cool*. He would have given anything to be like Adam. That is, until Adam reveals his true colors.

READ-ALOUD TIP

This story is told essentially through the dialogue between Adam and Seth. Read the story prior to your read-aloud to develop a personality for each: Seth as unsure, groveling, and feeling less than Adam, who is arrogant and filled with disdain. Change your voice to illuminate each character.

BACKGROUND LANGUAGE

The language in this story is very accessible, but you could explore how *cool* was described and whether being *cool* today is the same as when this story was written.

I beat the crap out of this guy at the mall yesterday," Adam Lockwood said. He was leaning on the stone wall of the bridge, smoking a cigarette and watching the cars speed by on the highway beneath him. His black hair fell down into his eyes.

"How come?" Seth Dawson asked, leaning on the stone wall next to him.

Adam shrugged. The turned-up collar of his leather jacket rose and fell along his neck. "He just bugged me, that's all. He was bigger, probably a senior. I guess he thought he could take me 'cause I was smaller. But I don't let anyone push me around."

"What'd you do to him?" Seth asked. He too was smoking a cigarette. It was his first ever, and he wasn't really inhaling. Just holding the smoke in his mouth for a while and then blowing it out.

"I'm pretty sure I broke his nose," Adam said. "I couldn't hang around to find out because the guy in the pizza place called the cops. I'm already in enough trouble with them."

"What for?" Seth asked. He noticed that when Adam took a drag, he seemed to hold the smoke in his mouth and then blow it out his nose. But it was probably just a different way of inhaling. Adam definitely inhaled.

"They just don't like me," Adam said. "You know how it is."

Seth nodded. Actually, he didn't know how it was. But there was no way he'd admit that. It was just pretty cool to think that the cops didn't like you. Seth was pretty sure the cops didn't even know who he was.

The two boys looked back down at the highway. It was a warm spring afternoon, and instead of taking the bus home after school they'd decided to walk to the diner. There Adam had instructed Seth on how to feed quarters into the cigarette machine and get a pack of Marlboros. Seth had been really nervous about getting caught, but Adam had told him it was no sweat. If the owner came out, you'd just tell him you were picking them up for your mother.

Now the pack of Marlboros was sticking out of the breast pocket of Seth's new denim jacket. It wasn't supposed to look new, because he'd ripped the sleeves off and had washed it in the washing machine a hundred times to make it look old and worn. But somehow it had come out looking new and worn. Seth had decided to wear it anyway, but he felt like a fraud. Like a kid trying to imitate someone truly cool. On the other hand, Adam's leather jacket looked authentically old and worn. The right sleeve was ripped and the leather was creased and pliant. It looked like he'd been in a hundred fights with it. Seth had never been in a fight in his life. Not a serious punching fight, at least.

The other thing about Adam was, he wore the leather jacket to school every day. Adam wasn't one of these kids who kept their cool clothes in their lockers and only wore them in school because their parents wouldn't let them wear them at home. Seth had parents like that. His mother would have had a fit if she ever saw him wearing his sleeveless denim jacket, so he had to hide it in the garage every day before he went into the house. Then in the morning when he left for school he'd go through the garage and pick it up.

Seth leaned forward and felt the smooth cold granite of the bridge with his fingers. The bridge was old and made of large granite blocks. Its heavy stone abutments stood close to the cars that sped past on the highway beneath it. Newer bridges were made of steel. Their spans were longer and the abutments were farther from the road.

On the highway, a red convertible approached with two girls riding in the front seats. Adam waved, and one of the girls waved back. A second later the car shot under the bridge and disappeared. He turned to Seth and grinned. "Maybe they'll get off on the exit ramp and come back," he said.

"You think?" Seth asked. Actually, the thought made him nervous. "They must be old enough at least to drive."

"So?" Adam asked. "I go out with older girls all the time."

"Really?" Seth asked.

"Sure." Adam took another drag off his cigarette and blew the smoke out of his nose. Seth wanted to try that, but he was afraid he'd start to cough or do something else equally uncool.

"What do you do with them?" Seth asked.

Adam glanced at him with a sly smile. "What do you think I do with them?"

"I mean, do you go out?"

"Sure, if they want to take me out, we go out. Otherwise sometimes we just hang around and make out."

Seth was awestruck. At a party once he'd played spin the bottle and pass the orange and had kissed a few girls in the process. But he'd never seriously made out.

In the distance a big semi-trailer appeared on the highway. Adam raised his arm in the air and pumped his fist up and down. The driver responded with three loud blasts of his air horns. A moment later the semi rumbled under them and disappeared.

"Let me try that," Seth said. Another truck was coming and he leaned over the stone ledge and jerked his arm up and down. But the trucker ignored him.

Adam laughed.

"How come it didn't work?" Seth asked.

"You gotta do it a special way," Adam told him.

"Show me," Seth said.

"Can't, man," Adam said. "You just have to have the right touch. It's something you're born with."

Seth smirked. It figured. It was just his luck to be born without the touch that made truckers blow their horns.

The traffic was gradually getting thicker as the afternoon rush hour approached. Many of the drivers and passengers in the cars seemed unaware of the two boys on the overpass. But a few others stared up through their windshields at them.

"Bet they're wondering if we're gonna drop something on them," Adam said. He lifted his hand in the air as if he was holding an imaginary rock. Down on the highway more of the people in the cars were looking up at him now. Suddenly Adam whipped his arm forward. Even though there was nothing in his hand, a woman driving a blue sedan put her hands up in fear. Her car swerved momentarily out of its lane.

Seth felt his jaw drop. He couldn't believe Adam had done that. If the car had been going faster it might have gone out of control and crashed into the stone abutment next to the highway.

Meanwhile Adam grinned at him. "Scared the crap out of her."

"Maybe we ought to go," Seth said, suddenly worried that they were going to get into trouble. What if a cop had seen them? Or what if the woman was really mad?

"Why?" Adam asked.

"She could get off and come back here."

Adam shrugged. "Let her," he said. 'The last person in the world I'd be afraid of is some old lady." He took a drag off his cigarette and turned away to watch the cars again.

Seth kept glancing toward the exit ramp to see if the woman in the blue car had gotten off. He was really tempted to leave but he stayed because he liked being with Adam. It made him feel good that a cool guy like Adam let him hang around.

A few minutes passed and the blue car did not appear on the exit ramp. Seth relaxed a little. He had smoked his Marlboro almost all the way down to the filter and his mouth tasted awful. Smoke kept getting in his eyes and making them water. He dropped the cigarette to the sidewalk and crushed it under his sneaker, relieved to be finished with it.

"Here's the way to do it," Adam said. He held the butt of his cigarette between his thumb and middle finger and flicked it over the side of the bridge and down into the traffic. With a burst of red sparks it hit the windshield of a black car passing below. Adam turned and grinned. Seth smiled back uncomfortably. He was beginning to wonder just how far Adam would go.

Neither of them saw the black car pull off onto the exit ramp and come up behind them on the bridge. Seth didn't notice it until he heard a door slam. He turned and saw three big guys getting out of the car. They were all wearing tight shirts which outlined their muscles. Seth suddenly decided it was time to go, but he quickly realized that the three guys had spread out, cutting off any way to escape. He and Adam were surrounded.

"Uh, Adam." Seth nudged him with his elbow.

"Wha—?" Adam turned around and his mouth fell open. In the meantime the three big guys came closer. Seth and Adam backed against the bridge wall. Seth felt his stomach tighten painfully. His heart began to beat like a machine gun. Adam looked pale and pretty scared too. Was it Seth's imagination, or was his friend trembling?

"Which one of you geeks flicked that butt on my car?" The question came from the husky guy with a black moustache and long black hair that curled behind his ears.

Seth and Adam glanced at each other. Seth was determined not to tell. He didn't believe in squealing on his friends. But suddenly he noticed that all three guys were staring at him. He quickly looked at Adam and saw why. Adam was pointing at him.

Before Seth could say anything, the husky guy grabbed him by the collar of his jacket and lifted him off the ground. Seth's feet kicked uselessly in the air for a second and then he was thrown against the front fender of the black car. He hit with a thud and lost his breath. Before he had a chance to recover, the guy grabbed him by the hair and forced his face toward the windshield.

"Lick it off," he growled.

Seth didn't know what he was talking about. He tried to raise his head, but the husky guy pushed his face closer to the windshield. Lord, he was strong.

"I said, lick it."

Lick what? Seth wanted to ask. Then he looked down at the glass and saw the spot of gray ash where Adam's cigarette had hit. Oh, no. He stiffened. The thought made him sick. He tried to twist his head around, but the guy leaned his weight against Seth and pushed his face down again.

"Till it's clean," the guy said, pressing Seth's face down until it was only an inch from the smooth, tinted glass. Seth stared at the little spot of ash. With the husky guy's weight on him, he could hardly breathe. The car's fender was digging into his ribs. Where was Adam?

The husky guy leaned harder against him, squeezing Seth painfully against the car. He pushed Seth's face down until it actually pressed against the cool glass. Seth could feel a spasm in his chest as his lungs cried for air. But he clamped his mouth closed. No way was he going to give that guy the satisfaction of seeing him lick that spot.

The husky guy must have known it. Suddenly he pulled Seth's head up, then slammed it back down against the windshield. Wham!

Seth reeled backwards, his hands covering his nose and mouth. Everything felt numb, and he was certain his nose and some teeth were broken. He slipped and landed on the ground in a sitting position, bending forward, his throbbing nose and mouth covered by his hands.

He heard someone laugh. Looking up he saw the three guys get back into the black car. A second passed and the car lurched away, leaving rubber.

"You're bleeding." Adam was standing over him. Seth took his hands away from his mouth and saw that they were covered with bright red blood. Blood dripped down from his nose and chin onto his denim jacket, leaving slowly darkening red spots. He tilted his head back, trying to stop the bleeding. At the same time he squeezed the bridge of his nose. It hurt, but somehow he knew it was not broken after all. He touched his front teeth with his tongue. They were all still there, and none felt loose.

"You want a hand?" Adam asked.

Seth nodded and Adam helped him up. He was shaky on his feet and worried that his nose was going to start bleeding again. He looked down and saw that his denim jacket was covered with blood.

"I tried to help you," Adam said, "but one of them held a knife on me."

Seth glanced at him.

"It was a small knife," Adam said. "I guess he didn't want anyone to see it."

Seth felt his nose again. It was swollen and throbbed painfully. "Why'd you point at me?" he asked.

"I figured I could jump them if they made a move on you," Adam said. "How could I know they had knives?"

Seth shook his head. He didn't believe Adam. He started to walk toward home.

"You gonna make it okay?" Adam asked.

Seth nodded. He just wanted to be alone.

"I'll get those guys for you, man," Adam said. "I think I once saw one of them at the diner. I'm gonna go back there and see."

Seth nodded again. He didn't even turn to watch Adam go.

On the way to his house, Seth stopped near some garbage cans a neighbor had left at the curb for collection. He looked down at his denim jacket. The spots of blood had turned dark. If he took it home and washed it now, the stains would probably make it look pretty cool. Like a jacket that had been worn in tons of fights. Seth smirked. He took it off and threw it in the garbage can.

Riveting Read-Alouds for Middle School © Janet Allen and Patrick Daley, Scholastic Inc.

18 Attack of the Man-Eaters

by Lauren Tarshis

SUMMARY

A British engineer arrived in present-day Kenya in 1898. His job—with the help of 9,000 workers—was to build a railroad. But when they arrived in Tsavo, something terrible started happening: two lions were killing men in the middle of the night. Over nine months, the lions killed 135 people. Why did the lions do this? Many years later, scientists have studied the conditions in Tsavo in 1898 and understand more about the lions' terrifying behavior.

SOURCE: *Scholastic* SCOPE *is an ELA magazine for secondary school that features engaging, multigenre content, and rich skill-building support material.*

READING SESSION: 1
(If you need to divide the story into two sessions because of time, stop before the subhead "Surely my luck will change.")

LANGUAGE AND VOCABULARY

Students are sure to find this informational text engaging because of its content—two lions stalk and kill more than a hundred men over several months. Use the chart below to preview some related words from the text. Before reading, ask students to predict how the words will be used. Confirm, reject, or revise their predictions after reading.

Words from the text	How we think these words will be used . . .	How they were used in text . . .
stalking		
terrified		
cunning		
preyed		
vulnerable		
lurking		
rogue		
aggressive		

THINK, TALK, AND WRITE ABOUT TEXT

In 1898, Colonel Patterson went to Mombasa to build a 500-mile railroad. **Think** about how that would change the landscape and the access for those living in the area.

Why do you think some workers thought the lions were supernatural spirits?

Discuss whether you think Colonel Patterson should have been considered a hero for killing the two lions that terrorized the men working on the railroad.

After research, scientists have discovered several factors that led to the tragic loss of life. List those factors for the workers and for the lions' behavior. Use the information from your cause-and-effect organizer to write an opinion piece related to the impact of growth in populated areas.

Attack of the Man-Eaters

by Lauren Tarshis

Imagine: A man travels to a new country for work, and many of his coworkers are killed by lions. One by one, night after night. That is exactly what happened to Colonel J. H. Patterson, who arrived in Kenya in 1898 to build a railroad. Listen carefully to learn more about the terrible "man-eaters of Tsavo." What made these beasts so savage?

READ-ALOUD TIP

Since this is informational text, help students remember the details by stopping briefly after each section (before the subheads) and review what they have heard so far. Using RPM (recall, predict, move on), have students *recall* important details from the section, use the next heading to *predict* what will happen in the next section, and *move on* to continue reading. Repeat several times during the read-aloud.

BACKGROUND LANGUAGE

The rich details in this text will help students make solid predictions about many of the words previously unknown to them. A category of words that will be used throughout relates to animal behaviors: *cunning, prey, stalking, lurking, aggressive,* and *rogue*. You may want to clarify the meaning of these words as you encounter them in the read-aloud.

Colonel J. H. Patterson was dazzled when he first arrived in the African city of Mombasa in March of 1898. The city, in present-day Kenya, was "enchanting," he wrote, "fresh and green and bathed in brilliant sunshine." Patterson was a British engineer who had gone to Africa to complete an important job—the construction of the 500-mile-long Uganda Railroad.

The job was challenging, to be sure. He led a small army of workers—9,000 men. And they cut a path through a punishing African desert and snake-infested jungle. It was backbreaking work, and there were constant food and water shortages.

But by the middle of April, it seemed that the worst was behind them. They had arrived in the Tsavo forest, where there were cooling breezes and clear river water to drink. As Patterson wrote, "the noise of our hammers echoed merrily through the district."

Within days, another sound echoed through the Tsavo forest—screams of terrified men. "Our work was interrupted in a rude and startling manner," Patterson wrote. Two male lions were stalking and eating the men, night after night. Over the next nine months, the lions would kill 135 men. The lions behaved with such cunning that some of the workmen could not believe they were animals. "Some were firmly convinced they were spirits," Patterson wrote, "devils in lions' shape."

Gruesome Attack

The first hint of trouble had been the disappearance of two workers in the middle of the night. A witness swore

Riveting Read-Alouds for Middle School © Janet Allen and Patrick Daley, Scholastic Inc.

he saw two lions storm into the open tent and drag the men away into the darkness. Patterson was skeptical. Lions sometimes attacked humans, of course. But usually they preyed on people who seemed vulnerable—a woman gathering water, a lone hunter tramping through the forest. Patterson found it hard to believe that two lions would barge into a noisy camp crowded with strong men. He searched the area and found no lion prints or human remains. He decided the two men had simply gotten tired of the backbreaking work and left camp on their own.

But just two nights later, the quiet night was shattered by screams once again. One of the most popular workers, an Indian named Inghan Singh, was gone. This time there was no doubt about his fate. Three of his tent-mates had witnessed a gruesome lion attack. The lion had thrust his head through the open tent door and grabbed Singh with its mouth. Singh had wrapped his arms around the lion's head and shouted "*Choro!*" (Hindi for "let go"). He struggled wildly as the lion dragged him out of the tent. His friends had huddled in their beds, listening in shock to the sound of their friend's hopeless struggle.

Patterson and another man followed a trail of fresh blood and enormous paw prints that led toward a thicket of thorny trees. "A dreadful spectacle presented itself," Patterson wrote. What little remained of Singh lay in the pool of blood. "It was the most gruesome sight I have ever seen. I vowed then and there that I would spare no pains to rid the neighborhood of the brutes."

Patterson went after the lions with single-minded focus. Each night, he stationed himself in the branches of a different tree, where he would scan the darkness for hours at a time. He used live goats or donkey carcasses as bait. But the lions seemed to be purposefully avoiding him. They were not tempted by the bleating goats or the scent of fresh donkey meat. "They seemed to have developed a preference for human flesh." Patterson wrote. Night after night, the lions attacked, always in different areas of the camp.

The men became so terrified that they refused to work. Hundreds fled the camps. All work on the railroad stopped.

"Surely my luck will change..."

Patterson nearly went mad from fear and sleeplessness. But he did not give up. Weeks went by. Months. Finally, one December night, Patterson was perched on a shooting platform he constructed out of four poles and a slab of wood. Around midnight, he heard the snapping of a twig and the sound of a large animal pushing its body through the dense brush. "The man-eater," Patterson thought. "Surely tonight my luck will change and I will bag one of the brutes."

But it soon became clear that the lion wasn't simply lurking in the bush. "He was stalking me," Patterson realized. The animal was circling, getting closer and closer, "growling in a sinister manner." For hours, Patterson stood motionless as the lion circled below, its eyes glistening. At one point, something struck Patterson on the back of his head and he thought the lion had somehow attacked him from behind. It turned out to be an owl, looking for a comfortable branch. Patterson's heart raced with fear. "I was so frightened I nearly fell from my perch."

By this time the lion was crouched directly beneath him. Patterson's shooting platform was so flimsy that the lion could topple it with one good charge at the tree. "I was for a moment rather certain that I was to be its next victim."

So he gathered his courage and took hold of his rifle. The night was so dark he could barely make out the burly shape beneath him. Steadying his shaking arms, he took aim and pulled the trigger. His shot exploded in the darkness, and was followed by "the most terrific roar." He could see the lion stagger into the bush and then heard a loud thud. And then, silence.

Patterson waited anxiously, convinced that the "devil" remained alive. As dawn broke, he climbed down from his platform and followed a blood trail through the bush. "And there, I was startled to a see a huge lion right in front of me, seemingly alive and crouching for a spring. On looking closer, however, I satisfied myself that he was really and truly stone-dead."

Workers rushed over to Patterson and lifted him high into the air. They paraded him around camp, shouting with joy. Telegrams of congratulations came from around country. The celebration became even more jubilant the next week, when Patterson managed to kill the second lion, and the terror of the lions finally ended.

Modern Answers

For more than a century, the story of the man-eaters of Tsavo has captivated scientists. What made those two lions behave so ferociously? Most experts agreed that those beasts were "rogues"—individual lions that behaved more savagely than normal lions.

Over the past decade, scientists at Chicago's Field Museum have been studying this episode with particular intensity. Since 1928, the year Patterson sold the lions' skins to the museum for $5,000, scientists have been studying the lions for clues to their behavior. One interesting find is that both lions suffered from injuries to their teeth and jaws, which would have made hunting large animals more difficult.

The scientists also traveled to Tsavo forest and spent months observing the lions that prowl there. They were surprised to learn that these lions are naturally more aggressive than other African lions. Each year they kill people from the surrounding villages.

Finally, the scientists pored over historical records from 1898. They learned there was a drought in the area, which would have killed many animals. More importantly, there was an outbreak of a disease called rindepest, which killed cattle as well as large wild animals like wildebeests and antelopes. This was a crisis for the area's lions, which preyed on these animals.

All this information came together like pieces in a puzzle. It has enabled the scientists to understand the terrifying events of 1898 more clearly. The lions of Tsavo, they believe, were not rogues. They were naturally aggressive animals suffering from a variety of problems—tooth injuries, drought, and disease that killed their natural prey. Patterson and his men had arrived in Tsavo at this inopportune moment. Perhaps the man-eaters weren't so savage after all. Perhaps they hunted the railroad workers for a simpler reason: They were hungry.

Today, these animals are preserved and on display at the Field Museum. You can stand within a few feet of them. When you stare into their mysterious faces, it's easy to imagine the terror Patterson's men must have felt on those dark African nights a century ago.

One also sees that these events of 1898 were tragic not only for the human victims, but for the lions as well.

19 Ain't I a Woman?

by Sojourner Truth

SOURCE: *Sojourner Truth was born into slavery in New York, but escaped to her freedom in 1826. She later became an outspoken abolitionist.*

READING SESSION: 1

SUMMARY

Sojourner Truth, a former slave, gave this speech at a Women's Convention in Akron, Ohio, in 1851. After Truth spoke, several versions were transcribed by attendees who heard her speak that day. Although there is controversy over its accuracy, the most common version, included here, was provided by Frances Gage, the president of the convention.

LANGUAGE AND VOCABULARY

Before reading, ask students to define *colloquial language.* Colloquial speech or writing is defined as ordinary or informal language as opposed to formal speech or writing. Ask students to predict the meaning of the colloquial language in the chart.

Interpreting Colloquial Language

	Prediction Before Reading Speech	Definition After Reading Speech
kilter		
'twixt		
ain't		
bear the lash		

After reading, discuss the meanings of the words based on the context.

THINK, TALK, AND WRITE ABOUT TEXT

Think about the courage it took for Sojourner Truth to speak her truth at this Women's Convention in 1851.

Discuss the context in which this speech was given. The Civil War would not begin for another 10 years and the women's suffrage movement would not lead to a constitutional amendment until 1920. Given these social and legal constraints, why might a black woman be reluctant to deliver this speech?

Sojourner Truth's language is simple, yet powerful. She uses her language to communicate her deeply-held beliefs. **Discuss** how each of the lines below reveals Sojourner Truth's beliefs.

- "But what's all this here talking about?"
- "Ain't I a woman?"
- "What's that [intellect] got to do with women's rights or negro's rights?"
- "If the first woman God ever made was strong enough to turn the world upside down all alone, these women together ought to be able to turn it back . . . "

If you were writing Sojourner Truth's biography, what words would you use to describe her?

Ain't I a Woman?

Sojourner Truth, Women's Convention, Akron, Ohio, May 28–29, 1851

In 1851, many women gathered at a "Women's Convention" in Ohio, where they discussed women's rights. One of the speakers, a former slave known as Sojourner Truth, gave the most notable speech of the convention. Transcribed some years after the convention, the speech now known as "Ain't I a Woman?" challenges her audience to think about women's rights from Truth's unique perspective as both a woman and an African American former slave. Consider Truth's question, "ain't I a woman?" and whether the repetition of that phrase helps her make her case.

READ-ALOUD TIP

This speech by Sojourner Truth is short and powerful. The punctuation will indicate to you the emphasis Sojourner Truth placed on her demands and questions. Your voice will need to be powerful and challenging in order for students to grasp the magnitude of Sojourner Truth's attitude and actions.

BACKGROUND LANGUAGE

Sojourner Truth emphasizes the question, "And ain't I a woman?" Introduce students to the women's suffrage movement to help them understand Truth's question and the context for her speech.

Well, children, where there is so much racket there must be something out of kilter. I think that 'twixt the negroes of the South and the women of the North, all talking about rights, the white men will be in a fix pretty soon. But what's all this here talking about?

That man over there says that women need to be helped into carriages and lifted over ditches, and to have the best place everywhere. Nobody ever helps me into carriages, or over mud-puddles, or gives me any best place! And ain't I a woman? Look at me! Look at my arm! I could have ploughed and planted, and gathered into barns, and no man could head me! Ain't I a woman? I could work as much and eat as a man—when I could get it—and bear the lash as well! And ain't I a woman? I have borne thirteen children, and seen them most all sold to slavery, and when I cried out with my mother's grief, none but Jesus heard me! And ain't I a woman?

Then they talk about this thing in the head; what's this they call it? [Intellect, somebody whispers] That's it, honey. What's that got to do with women's rights or negro's rights? If my cup won't hold but a pint, and yours holds a quart, wouldn't you be mean not to let me have my little half measure–full?

Then that little man in black there, he says women can't have as much rights as men, 'cause Christ wasn't a woman! Where did your Christ come from? Where did your Christ come from? From God and a woman! Man had nothing to do with Him.

If the first woman God ever made was strong enough to turn the world upside down all alone, these women together ought to be able to turn it back, and get it right side up again! And now they is asking to do it, the men better let them.

Obliged to you for hearing me, and now old Sojourner ain't got nothing more to say."

20 How Slavery Really Ended in America

by Adam Goodheart

SOURCE: *"How Slavery Really Ended in America" is from The New York Times UpFront, a Scholastic classroom magazine that delivers compelling, current news for high school students.*

READING SESSIONS: 2

SUMMARY

At the start of the Civil War in 1861, three confederate slaves escaped to a Union camp. Although not an abolitionist, it was Major General Benjamin Butler's response to this event that set in motion the liberation of southern slaves. The Emancipation Proclamation is often thought to have been the single event that set free slaves in the American south. But abolition actually came about after a series of smaller events preceding Lincoln's famous address.

LANGUAGE AND VOCABULARY

Defining a word is only one aspect of learning a new word. Use this organizer before reading to explore what students know about the word *contraband* from background and word parts. After reading, ask students to use information about the word to make connections and expand the definition.

"Defining" a Word

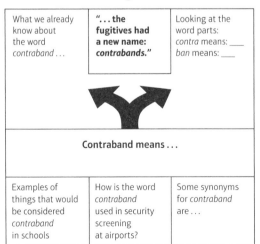

What we already know about the word *contraband* ...	*"... the* **fugitives had a new name: contrabands."**	Looking at the word parts: *contra* means: ___ *ban* means: ___
Contraband means ...		
Examples of things that would be considered *contraband* in schools	How is the word *contraband* used in security screening at airports?	Some synonyms for *contraband* are ...

THINK, TALK, AND WRITE ABOUT TEXT

Before reading, ask students what they know about the Civil War. After reading, ask students to **think about and discuss** why most Americans believe that the Civil War was fought to free all slaves.

When a controversial event happens, there are almost always many points of view. Often the debate over who is right or what is legal is fought until the highest power has to step in and make a decision. **Identify** the points of argument from each side (the slaves seeking asylum at the Union camp, Colonel Mallory from the Confederacy, and General Butler from the Union) and how the conflict was eventually resolved.

Have students work in groups to evaluate the arguments, choose a position, and **write** a letter of recommendation to President Lincoln prior to his decision to end slavery.

How Slavery Really Ended in America

by Adam Goodheart

You've probably heard of the Emancipation Proclamation, the speech that President Lincoln gave in 1863 declaring all southern slaves to be free. But what you might not know about is a series of events in 1861 that paved the way for the Emancipation Proclamation. As you read "how slavery really ended in America," think about whether it changes your view of what you already knew about the Emancipation Proclamation.

READ-ALOUD TIP

This informative text uses a narrative structure that will carry listeners as you read aloud. The challenge may be students' lack of knowledge about the Civil War, the Emancipation Proclamation, the Fugitive Slave Law, and "laws" related to slavery. Reading this text in two or three sessions will give students time to absorb the important details.

BACKGROUND LANGUAGE

Understanding the meaning of *secession* and *contraband* are critical as the ruling about the fugitives was related to how these two words were defined by the military leaders.

On May 23, 1861, a little more than a month after the Civil War had begun at Fort Sumter, three young black men rowed across the James River in Virginia and asked for asylum at a Union-held citadel called Fort Monroe.

Frank Baker, Shepard Mallory, and James Townsend were field hands who—like hundreds of other slaves— had been pressed into service by the Confederates and compelled by their master, Colonel Charles Mallory, to build an artillery emplacement amid the dunes across the harbor.

After a week or so, the three slaves decided to try their luck, just across the water, with the Union.

When they made it to the fort, they were summoned to see the commanding general. He began asking them questions: Who was their master? Was he a rebel or a Union man? Could they tell him anything about the Confederate fortifications they had been working on? Their response to this last question— that the battery was still far from completion—seemed to please.

For Major General Benjamin Butler, who wasn't an abolitionist, the three slaves presented a problem. The laws of the United States were clear: In 1850, Congress had passed the Fugitive Slave Act, which said all fugitive slaves must be returned to their masters. It was still the law of the land—including in the states of the Confederacy, which, as the federal government was concerned, were still part of the United States.

More important, no interference with slavery was the cornerstone of the Union's war policy. President Abraham Lincoln made this clear in his inaugural address: "I have no purpose, directly or indirectly, to interfere with the institution of slavery in the states where it exists," he said.

Butler's Response

Yet to Fort Monroe's commander, the fugitives seemed like a novel case. The enemy had been using them to construct a battery aimed directly at his fort—and no doubt would put them right back to work if he returned them. They had offered him some highly useful military intelligence. And Virginia was officially in rebellion against the federal government, having seceded along with several other Southern states—a total of 11 by that summer.

General Butler, who had been a lawyer in Massachusetts, could not have known that his response that day would change the course of American history.

Butler had barely begun writing a report before he was interrupted by another message: A Confederate officer, under flag of truce, had approached the causeway of Fort Monroe. The Virginians wanted their slaves back. Butler rode out to meet Major John Baytop Cary of the Virginia Militia.

"I am informed," Cary said, "that three Negroes belonging to Colonel Mallory have escaped within your lines . . . What do you mean to do with those Negroes?"

"I intend to hold them," Butler said.

"Do you mean, then, to set aside your constitutional obligation to return them?"

Butler had prepared what he thought was a fairly clever answer. "I mean to take Virginia at her word," he said. "I am under no constitutional obligations to a foreign country, which Virginia now claims to be."

"But you say we cannot secede," Cary retorted, "and so you cannot consistently detain the Negroes."

"But you say you have seceded," Butler said, "so you cannot consistently claim them. I shall hold these Negroes as contraband of war, since they are engaged in the construction of your battery and are claimed as your property."

Butler had been reading up on military law. In time of war, he knew, a commander had a right to seize any enemy property that was being used for hostile purposes. The three fugitive slaves, before their escape, had been helping to build a Confederate gun emplacement. If the Southerners insisted on treating blacks as property, this Yankee lawyer would treat them as property too.

Cary, frustrated, rode back to the Confederate lines. Butler returned to Fort Monroe feeling rather pleased with himself. Still, he knew that it would be a short-lived victory if his superiors in Washington didn't like what he had done.

But before Butler's report could reach Washington, things got even more complicated. The next day, eight more fugitives turned up outside the fort. The day after, there were 47—and not just young men, but women, old people, entire families. Two days later, a Massachusetts soldier wrote home: "Slaves are brought in here hourly."

· · · · ·

Lincoln's Reaction

Within days of the three fugitive slaves crossing the river, their exploits— and their fate—were being discussed throughout the nation. President Lincoln realized he might now be forced to make a decision about matters he had been previously trying to avoid: slavery, emancipation, and race.

Lincoln and his cabinet gathered to discuss Butler's handling of the situation. In the end, they allowed the general to decide what to do with fugitive slaves—including whether to continue declaring them contraband of war.

By early June, some 500 fugitives were within the Union lines at Fort Monroe. One newspaper estimated that "this species of property under Gen. Butler's protection [is] worth $500,000, at a fair average of $1,000 apiece in the Southern human flesh market."

Journalists throughout the Union joked incessantly about the "shipments of contraband goods" and within a few weeks, the fugitives had a new name: contrabands.

It was a perfect bit of slang: Were these blacks people or property? Free or slave? Such questions were, as yet, unanswerable—for answering them would have raised a lot of other questions that few white Americans were ready to address. Calling them "contrabands" let the speaker or writer off the hook by letting the escapees be all those things at once. The term also mocked slavery and federal laws that, for nearly a century, had acknowledged no meaningful difference between a bushel of corn and a human being with black skin.

Each morning at Fort Monroe, dozens of fugitives lined up to pitch in with manual labor. Soon they seemed almost like members of the garrison. A *New York Times* correspondent wrote: "I have no doubt they would make fair or even excellent soldiers."

Many of the Union soldiers had never really spoken with a black person before; the farm boys from Vermont had probably never even seen one before leaving home. Now they were talking with real men and women who had been (and perhaps still were) slaves.

Some of the slaves shared horrific accounts of their lives. One man described "bucking," a practice in which a slave had his wrists and ankles tied and slipped over a wooden stake before being beaten. Almost all spoke of loved ones sold away; the most chilling thing was that they would say it matter-of-factly, as if their wives or children had simply died.

No Bloodbath

Perhaps most surprising of all for Northerners accustomed to Southern tales of contented slaves was this, in the words of one Union soldier: "There is a universal desire among the slaves to be free . . . even old men and women, with crooked backs, who could hardly walk or see."

Within weeks of the first contrabands' arrival at Fort Monroe, slaves reported to be flocking to Union lines in Northern Virginia, on the Mississippi, and in Florida. It is unclear how many of these escapees knew of Butler's decision, but quite a few probably did since news of this kind usually traveled fast among slaves.

Army regiments needed labor—extra hands to cook meals, wash clothes, and dig latrines. With black men and women willing to do these things, whites were happy not to ask inconvenient questions. It was not the first time, nor would it be the last, that the allure of cheap labor would trump political principles in America.

Just as important was what did not happen: the terrible moment—long feared among whites—when slaves would rise up and slaughter their masters. It soon became apparent from the behavior of the contrabands that the vast majority of slaves did not want vengeance: They simply wanted to be free.

Many were even ready to share in the hardships and dangers of the war. Millions of whites realized they did not have to fear a bloodbath. This new awareness in itself was a revolution.

Most important, though, was the resolution in the minds of the slaves themselves. Within about a year, the stream of a few hundred contrabands arriving at Fort Monroe became a river of tens—probably even hundreds—of thousands. They "flocked in vast numbers—an army in themselves—to the camps of the Yankees," a Union chaplain wrote.

Emancipation Proclamation

By July 1861, General Butler began pressing the Lincoln administration to admit that the contrabands were not really contraband, that they had become free. Indeed, that they were—in a legal sense—no longer things but people.

It would take until January 1863—and tens of thousands more Union casualties—before the Lincoln administration was ready to endorse that view with its Emancipation Proclamation, which declared all slaves in Confederate states free. Though hugely significant, the proclamation actually had limited effect: It did not apply to slaves in border states that had remained loyal to the Union and there was no way for the government in Washington to enforce the Emancipation Proclamation in the Confederacy.

But clearly, the momentum was gathering that ultimately led to slavery's demise.

It's amazing how earthshaking events are sometimes set in motion by small decisions. Who knew in 1955 that when Rosa Parks boarded a segregated bus in Montgomery, Alabama, and refused to give up her seat to a white man, she would spark the civil rights movement of the 1950s and '60s? More recently, who could have predicted that a Tunisian fruit vendor's refusal to pay a bribe would set off a revolution that continues to sweep across the Arab world?

And who knew, back in 1861, that three slaves rowing across the James River seeking their own freedom would—as much as anything else in the Civil War—set in motion events that ultimately destroyed the institution of slavery itself?

21 It Came From the Swamp!

by N. B. Grace

SUMMARY

In the small village of Tollund, Denmark, workers make a grisly discovery as they dig in the peat bog nearby—the body of a murdered man. The police, with the help of scientists, determine that the well-preserved body is more than 2,000 years old. Even as scientists are learning more about the Tollund Man, they still have many questions left unanswered.

SOURCE: *"It Came From the Swamp!" is from XBOOKS, an informational text program by Scholastic.* www.scholastic.com/xbooks

READING SESSION: 1

LANGUAGE AND VOCABULARY

Students will probably not know much, if anything, about peat bogs. Building some background, especially with an image, will help students generate words related to peat bogs. Prior to reading, display a photo of a peat bog (search online) use the "3-2-1 Admit Slip" below to provide students with an image that will guide their generation of words, ideas, and questions.

3-2-1 ADMIT SLIP: *Peat Bog*

3. List **three** words or details you think of when you look at this picture.

2. Write **two** ideas you have, based on the picture and your words. If possible, use your words as you write your ideas.

   a. I think …

   b. I think …

1. Write **one** question you have.

THINK, TALK, AND WRITE ABOUT TEXT

This article begins with the line that the brothers had a really dirty job. Look at the picture on the Admit Slip you completed and make some predictions about dirty jobs that would be related to the peat bog photo. As you listen to this article, **think** about whether you would want to do this work.

Peat bogs are described as "dark and eerie," and some people believed the bogs were inhabited by trolls and spirits. **Discuss** how finding a human face while digging in the bog would add to the legends.

The police were called when the body was discovered, but the museum experts were also called. **Why** do you think both organizations were involved?

Visit the website http://www.tollundman.dk/fischers-historie.asp to read museum curator Christian Fischer's brief account of what probably happened to the Tollund Man over 2,300 years ago. How does this account compare to the details you heard when we read "It Came From the Swamp"?

Write a brief summary comparing the Tollund Man and the Elling Woman. Then, explain why the discovery of the Elling Woman did not draw as much attention as the discovery of the Tollund Man. If you need more information about the Elling Woman, visit http://www.tollundman.dk/ellingkvinden.asp to help you compare the two discoveries.

It Came From the Swamp!

by N. B. Grace

Workers digging in a peat bog uncover a gruesome sight—the well-preserved body of a man who was obviously murdered. But this body was extra special. It belonged to a man who lived about 2,400 years ago. Find out what else scientists have learned about him.

READ-ALOUD TIP

When reading informational text, you may need to stop for brief check-ins to see if students are getting the most important information. Informational text won't flow the way a story does, so you will need to use your voice to emphasize the text features, such as bulleted information.

BACKGROUND LANGUAGE

Students will definitely need to know what a peat bog is. Explain that a peat bog is a type of wetland filled with decaying plant material, usually moss.

It was just another day of work . . . until something unexpected came up.

Brothers Emil and Viggo Hojgaard had a really dirty job. And on one day in 1950, digging in a bog would turn up something really shocking.

Early in the morning, the two men and Viggo's wife, Grethe, headed out to work in a bog near the village of Tollund, Denmark. Bogs, like swamps, are soft, wet areas of ground. They can be dark and eerie. Many legends have been written about them. People used to believe that trolls and spirits lurked in bogs, waiting to prey on innocent travelers.

In fact, bogs can be dangerous. People can lose their footing, get sucked into the ooze, and drown. And long ago, people were sometimes killed and then thrown in the muck!

On this particular day, the Hojgaards were cutting peat. That's a type of dense soil made of rotted plants. They dug into the ground with shovels and then cut the peat into bricks. The bricks would later be dried and burned for fuel.

Suddenly, Grethe noticed something in the muck. It was a human face!

Digging up a gruesome mystery

Had the Hojgaards uncovered a murder victim? They called the police.

When the police heard that a body had been found in a bog, they contacted a local museum. The police weren't sure whether the man had been murdered. But they suspected that if he had been, it wasn't recently. Two ancient bodies had been found in the bog years earlier.

The police and the museum experts joined the Hojgaards at the bog. The experts from the museum would take over the investigation.

They carefully uncovered the body of a small man. He had a well-preserved face. And he looked as if he were sleeping. But as the experts brushed away bits of dirt from the man's body, they discovered something shocking. He had a rope tied around his neck!

Workers gently removed the body, placed it in a box, and took it to the museum. Scientists there confirmed that the body had been mummified, or preserved, in the bog. The Tollund Man, as he is now called, had been killed about 2,400 years before. Now they had to figure out why.

Scientists try to find out more about the Tollund Man.

The Tollund Man is in good company. Over the past few centuries, mummified human remains have been found in bogs all over northern Europe. Most of these remains were found by people who were cutting peat—just like the Hojgaards had been.

Some bog bodies are in better shape than others. Sometimes only body parts are uncovered. Other bog bodies are whole but very decayed.

The Tollund Man is one of the best-preserved bog bodies ever discovered. Archaeologists—scientists who study past ways of life—were eager to get their hands on him. He was examined first in 1950 and then again 2002.

Here's what scientists learned when they examined the Tollund Man.

- He died around 350 BCE.
- His wisdom teeth had come in, so he was least 20 years old. Scientists think that he was probably closer to 40.
- He was at least 5'3" tall.
- He had scars on his feet that showed he walked barefoot some of the time.
- His last meal was soup. The soup contained barley with a fungus on it. Why was this fungus in the soup? Scientists think that it might have been added to the meal to make him unconscious before he was killed.

Was this murder part of a religious ritual?

Archaeologists had learned a lot about the Tollund Man. But one question continued to haunt them. Why had he been killed? Scientists agreed that he'd been murdered. He had been hanged by the rope that was found around his neck. But why?

It wasn't the first time this question had come up. Many of the bog bodies that have been found over the centuries showed signs of violent deaths. Some, like the Tollund Man, had been hanged. Others had been strangled. Many had their throats cut. Some had been clubbed or stabbed. Several bodies were cut into parts.

There were other surprising things about the bodies. Some were wearing clothes, but others were naked. One was blindfolded. Numerous bodies were found weighed down with boulders. And a few had been tied down or pinned by branches so they couldn't get away.

One of these bodies is now known as the Elling Woman. She was the Tollund Man's neighbor. The Elling Woman was found 12 years before Tollund Man. She was buried just 260 feet away from where he was discovered. A farmer had been digging for peat in the bog when his shovel struck her body.

Elling Woman's body was not as well preserved as the Tollund Man's. Still, experts could tell that she too had been hanged. And she had been buried with care. She had been placed on her side in a grave in the peat. And a blanket had been wrapped around her feet.

How did all these bodies end up in bogs? It wasn't by accident. Some scientists think that the bodies might have been placed in bogs after they were executed for being criminals or outcasts.

Had the Tollund Man committed a crime thousands of years ago—and paid with his life? Maybe.

Or perhaps there's another explanation for his murder.

Some experts believe that the Tollund Man may have been killed as part of a religious ritual. In some religions, animals are sacrificed in the hope of pleasing a god or goddess. Some ancient religions even sacrificed humans. Is this what happened to the Tollund Man?

Unfortunately, it's impossible to say whether the Tollund Man was sacrificed in a religious ritual or punished for a crime. People who lived in the area at the time of his death didn't leave written records.

But there are some clues. One clue come from ancient Romans who traveled to these lands. They wrote down what they learned during their travels.

According to the Romans, people in northern Europe would offer human sacrifices to their gods. Perhaps the people who killed Tollund Man wanted the gods to bring them a good harvest or warm weather.

Another clue is the way the Tollund Man was placed in the bog.

Experts point out that his body was handled carefully. It was not treated like a criminal's would have been. His corpse wasn't carelessly thrown into the bog. Instead, the Tollund Man had been placed gently in a grave dug into the peat. He was laid on his side, with his legs bent against his stomach. Scientists also think that his eyelids and mouth were closed after he died.

Did this careful treatment indicate something special about the Tollund Man?

Scientists don't know for certain. But they do know that a man who walked barefoot and was about 5'3" was murdered over 2,000 years ago. And his body was placed in a bog. He ate soup before he died.

But why was he killed? That's still a mystery.

22 The Cesspool

by Allan Zullo

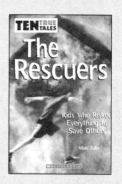

SUMMARY

Eleven-year-old Kevin has a fear of dark, tight spaces. But when his young neighbor, Kisho, falls into a hole and is trapped in a noxious cesspool, only Kevin is small enough to go down the hole and rescue the toddler. Can Kevin overcome his fear to save little Kisho?

SOURCE: *"The Cesspool" comes from* The Rescuers: Kids Who Risked Everything to Save Others. *The author, Allan Zullo, has written many books for children about history, sports, animals, and, of course, heroes!*

READING SESSIONS: 2

LANGUAGE AND VOCABULARY

Choosing the right words is especially important when writing. Writers of informational texts have to use **specialized language** that will make the information accessible to readers. Discuss the words in the word box below and use them to predict information you might learn from reading "The Cesspool."

cesspool	underground	container
suffocation	fumes	oxygen
air tank	debris	drilling
poisonous	gases	shaft
noxious	repeat	sling
paramedics	stench	sewage

Based on the words above, ask students what information they think they will learn from this article.

THINK, TALK, AND WRITE ABOUT TEXT

Some people are afraid of spiders, others are afraid of flying, and others fear leaving their homes. **Think** about fears you have and what may have caused you to have these fears.

At the beginning of this article, Kevin is bullied into riding his bike into a dark culvert. Search online for an image of a culvert. **Discuss** why riding your bike through a culvert might be frightening for anyone. Why was it particularly scary for Kevin? In what ways might this be dangerous?

When Kisho falls into the abandoned cesspool, **what** are the complicating factors in rescuing him? Once Kevin gets Kisho and starts being pulled out, what further complications do they discover? How do these factors make it even more fearful for Kevin?

Mrs. Matsui says Kevin is an angel. Would you agree? If you had been his mother, would you have allowed Kevin to go down into the cesspool for the rescue?

Use the specialized words from the language word box to **write about** this experience from Kevin's point of view.

The Cesspool

by Allan Zullo

Sometimes you're in the right place at the right time; sometimes you're at the wrong place at the wrong time—it depends on how you look at it. One day, Kevin finds himself the only person who can save a toddler who has fallen into a sewer. The job is scary, stinky, and disgusting. Will Kevin be able to save the day?

The five boys wheeled their bicycles up to the construction site of a highway interchange. Pointing to a large culvert—a cement tube that went under the road—the group's leader, Billy Burton, exclaimed, "Wow, look at that. It's big enough for us to ride through. Let's do it!"

"I'm not sure that's a good idea," said Kevin "Bones" Manoa. "What if there's a downpour and it fills up with . . . "

"Look at the sky, Bones. It's mostly blue. No big rain clouds," Billy said. Peering inside the culvert, he added, "It probably goes off at an angle, because I can't see any light at the other end. This is going to be fun. Bones, you go first."

"Me? Why me?" asked the 11-year-old who was tagged with the nickname for being so skinny.

"Because you're the only one who has a light on his bike."

"Well, I, um . . . "

"What's the matter, Bones? Are you afraid of the dark?"

"No, of course not!"

"Then go ahead and lead the way."

As the youngest and smallest of the group, Kevin had never been asked to lead anything with the group. The other four boys were older and in sixth or seventh grade. The fifth grader couldn't pass up the opportunity to go first, even though he hated confined, dark spaces. They gave him the willies ever since he and his mother were trapped in an elevator at an office building in downtown Honolulu after a power outage. Kevin, who was five at the time, and his mom had to sit in the pitch black for more than four hours. Kevin had kept a night-light on in his bedroom ever since.

Now he had to be the first one to enter a dark tunnel in front of his pals. He couldn't let them down. After all, when you wear glasses and braces and are underweight and short for your age, you need all the friends you can get. The last thing you want to do is prove that you're a weenie.

"Hey, Bones, are you chicken or what?" Billy snorted.

"Bawk! Bawk! Cluck! Cluck!" the other boys cracked, flapping their arms like chicken wings.

Kevin turned red, hopped on his bike, flicked on the headlamp and pedaled into the darkness. "Follow me—unless you're too scared!" he shouted over his shoulder. He got no more than twenty yards in when his heart began to race. His palms dripped with sweat and his body trembled, causing his bike to wobble just enough for the handlebars to scrape against the insides of the culvert.

The boys behind him were making scary sounds, and laughing as their voices echoed off the culvert's curved walls.

It's awfully dark in here, Kevin told himself. *Where does it end? You can't chicken out now.* He had reached a turn in the culvert and suddenly his body relaxed. *Light! I see light at the end of the tunnel!* He pedaled faster and soon emerged at the other side.

When the others caught up with him, he said, "Whew! That was fun!" It really wasn't for him, although he felt a sense of accomplishment, having faced one of his fears and conquered it—at least for one day.

But Kevin would soon face this same fear again—only this time, it would be a matter of life or death.

Going back through the culvert wasn't as hard for Kevin. "Hey, guys, I have to go home now," he said after they came out. "I have to help my mom set up her booth at the Na Hula Festival." His mother, Lana, a native Polynesian, was proud of her culture and had passed down that appreciation to her son.

"Make sure to say hi to all the hula dancers," said Billy. Shaking his hips and moving his hands like a hula girl, Billy made the other boys laugh.

Kevin gave a fake grin and rode off along the north shore of Hawaii's Pearl Harbor toward his home in Pearl City. The harbor was the scene of the fierce Japanese attack in 1941 that had forced the United States to enter World War II. His route took him along streets shaded in palm trees and dotted with colorful bungalows.

On his way home, Kevin was thinking about all the desserts his mother was preparing to sell at the festival. He couldn't wait to get a bite of his favorite, Honolulu Lulu, made with crushed pineapple, whipped cream, shredded coconut, and cooked rice.

He snapped out of his mouthwatering daydream after hearing someone shout, "Suzu! Get back here!" Kevin looked to his right and saw a young Asian woman in a kimono chasing after a Yorkshire terrier. It was scampering across the front yard toward the street, where a speeding pickup truck was approaching. Looking at the dog and then at the truck, Kevin estimated the paths of the animal and vehicle would likely meet a few feet in front of him—unless he tried to stop it.

Kevin pulled to the curb, leaped off his bike and, with his arms outstretched, jumped up and down, trying to scare the dog away from the street. His actions worked. Without slowing down, the terrier made a sharp left and dashed into the neighbor's yard as the truck roared past.

"Suzu! Come here!" demanded the woman. "Suzu!"

The little dog wasn't paying any attention to her and instead was sniffing the neighbor's flowers. Kevin crawled up behind Suzu, then sprang on her, and caught her. The dog yelped in protest as Kevin brought the pet to its grateful owner.

"Oh, thank you so much," she said, cuddling Suzu. "You saved her life."

"I'm glad I could help," Kevin replied.

She bowed to Kevin. "I'm Mrs. Matsui, and you've already met Suzu." Coaxing a little boy, about two years old, who had been hiding behind her, she added, "And this is my son, Kisho. Suzu is not supposed to go outside, but Kisho opened the door and she bolted. I don't know who I should be mad at most— Kisho or Suzu."

Kisho waddled over to Kevin and held out his hand. In his fist was a partially eaten Tootsie Roll. "Toots," the toddler said. "Toots."

"Oh, isn't that sweet?" said Mrs. Matsui. "Kisho wants to share his Tootsie Roll with you."

I don't want to share it with him, Kevin thought. *He's got slobber all over it. What am I going to do?* "No, thank you."

Kisho frowned. "Toots for you." He thrust out his hand again, so Kevin pretended to take a bite. "Mmm, good. Thank you."

But the toddler wasn't fooled and began to cry.

"Okay, okay," said Kevin. He took a bite and then choked it down. "Thank you, Kisho." *I hope I don't get sick from the kid's germs.* "Well, I better get home. I'm glad your dog is safe.

Bye, Mrs. Matsui. Bye, Kisho." *You better not have any cooties.*

When Kevin returned home, he mentioned the Suzu incident to his mother. He didn't see the dog or Kisho or Mrs. Matsui for several months even though they lived only three blocks away from his house.

But they met again in a crisis that no one could have ever imagined.

• • • • •

It happened on the day when Kevin had helped his mother carry several plantings of tuberose bulbs to the home of Mrs. Ferguson, an elderly family friend and neighbor. While walking back, they watched an ambulance, two police squad cars, and three fire trucks pull up to a house at the end of the block. A crowd was gathering in the backyard. "Let's see what's going on," Kevin said.

When they reached the house, Kevin told his mother, "Hey, I know the people who live here—the Matsuis. You know, the ones whose dog I helped save." Kevin went up to a police officer who was marking off the area with yellow tape and asked, "What's going on?"

"A little boy fell into a cesspool and he's stuck down there," the officer replied.

Kevin had heard his mother talk about cesspools recently after the local newspaper, the *Honolulu Advertiser*, ran a series on the dangers of these abandoned underground containers that are used for the disposal of human waste from toilets. One of the articles mentioned that although Hawaii was arguably the prettiest state in the union, it also was the cesspool capital of the nation. At the time, more abandoned cesspools existed in the Aloha State than anywhere else in the country.

And now a little boy was trapped at the bottom of one.

"No one can figure out how to get him out," a bystander said to the gathering crowd. "If they don't rescue him soon, he'll die from suffocation either from all the poisonous gases down there or lack of oxygen."

Firefighters, police, and paramedics were hustling back and forth. Kneeling next to the hole was Mrs. Matsui, wringing her hands close to her chest, her face a picture of agony. "My baby! My baby!" she wailed. Her grief-stricken husband was holding her for support.

From talking to the neighbors, Kevin learned that Kisho had been playing in the backyard with his parents and Suzu. He stood on top of the abandoned cesspool, which had been covered with wooden planks and nailed shut. When Kisho began jumping up and down on the boards, they snapped in two from rot. The boy plunged feet-first down a narrow 15-foot-deep shaft and into a tank that contained a layer of disgusting human waste up to his chest. The only good news was that Kisho wasn't seriously injured from the fall. He was standing up in the foul muck and crying for his parents.

When the firefighters arrived, they ripped the rotten wood from the top of the cesspool. The shaft was only 12 inches by 16 inches—much too small for any rescuer to enter. Emergency workers had taken a hose and connected it to an air tank. Then they dropped the hose down the shaft so the boy could breathe fresh air, and at least be kept alive, although no one knew for how long.

Kevin overheard officials discussing strategy. They decided against digging to make the shaft larger, fearing it would collapse and bury Kisho in debris. "We can get the drilling rig from the road construction crew at the new interchange and burrow a hole parallel to the shaft," said one of the rescuers. "Then we can dig a tunnel to the cesspool tank and bring him out that way."

"But that could take more than a day," said another rescuer. "The boy could die in the meantime from all the fumes."

"We'll keep pumping air down to him while we drill and hope for the best. There's no other way."

"Maybe we could lower someone in there and snatch the boy."

"We're all too big to fit in that shaft."

Maybe they're all too big, but I'm not, Kevin told himself. As he walked over to his mother, his heart began racing at the thought of what he was about to propose. *Should I really suggest it? Will they even let me? And if they do, can I really pull it off?*

"Mom," said Kevin, "Kisho could be stuck down there for over a day, and he might not survive. The best way to get him out is if someone small—someone like me—is lowered into the cesspool and pulls him out."

"Kevin, you can't be serious. It's much too dangerous."

"What if that were me down there, Mom, and some older boy offered to rescue me. Wouldn't you want his mother to give him permission?"

"Well, I guess so . . . "

"Thanks, Mom." He took her hand and led her to the front of the cordoned-off area where he caught the attention of the fire captain who was in charge of the rescue operation.

"Excuse me, sir," Kevin said. "I'm Kevin Manoa and this is my mother, Lana. Before you drill, let me try to get Kisho. I'm small and skinny—my friends call me Bones—so I should be able to fit in the shaft."

The captain shook his head. "Son, thanks for the offer. But there's no way I'm going to risk your life. It's very hazardous. The noxious fumes in there could knock you out. The only reason the little boy is alive is because we're pumping air down in the cesspool."

"But I heard you say that Kisho could die—that the fumes will eventually get to him. And drilling will take another day to complete. Let me at least try."

The captain squinted at Kevin's mother. "And you approve of this?"

"I'm really worried for my son's safety," she replied. "But if there's a chance that he can help save that little boy's life, then I give my permission."

The captain studied Kevin's slender frame and bony arms. "Are you sure you're up to it, son?"

No, not really, Kevin thought. *What am I thinking?* "Y-y-yes s-s-sir."

The captain put an arm around Kevin, hustled him over to the opening, and announced to the rescuers, "We're going to lower this young man in the hole and see if he can bring out Kisho."

Kevin glanced at the men and saw in their eyes a mix of respect for what he was about to do and doubt that he could actually rescue Kisho.

Mrs. Matsui, who was still at the edge of the opening, stood up and stared at Kevin. "I know you from somewhere."

"Yes, when your dog escaped."

"Of course!" She clasped his hand and bowed. "You're an angel sent here once again in a time of need."

The firefighters fitted Kevin with a rope sling that wrapped around the back of his thighs. Although it was an extremely warm day, Kevin felt a sudden chill. The thought of entering a dark, tight shaft made him shiver.

One worker who was adjusting the sling noticed Kevin's body shaking. "There's still time to back out," he whispered to Kevin.

"I'll be fine. I'm just a little scared, that's all."

"I understand. Keep in mind that you'll be in control while we're lowering you. If you feel like you can't go any farther because the shaft is too tight or the fumes are making you sick, just holler and we'll pull you right up."

Kevin nodded.

Mrs. Matsui dropped to her knees and yelled down in the hold, "Kisho, be brave. We're sending an angel down to get you!"

Kisho gave a little whimper.

"It's time," said the captain. "Are you ready, Kevin?"

No, I'll never be ready for this. "Let's do it." Kevin sat on the edge of the hole and peered into the smelly darkness. "Uh, would you mind shining a light down there?" he asked. When the workers moved in a powerful work lamp, he clutched the rope, and slid in feet-first. It was an extremely tight fit. Even though he had to scrunch his scrawny shoulders, they still rubbed against the rough walls of the shaft.

As he was lowered, the stench from the cesspool grew stronger. And so did his fear of dark, tight spaces. He was shuddering and sweating, fighting off frightening thoughts of a cave-in that would bury him alive.

Oh, God, what am I doing in here, he thought. *Why did I volunteer for this?* His breathing came faster, but the more he inhaled, the more sick to his stomach he became from the nauseating fumes. *I want out of here! I can't stand the stench. I can't stand being here.* He closed his eyes but only for a moment.

"How are you doing, Kevin?" the captain shouted.

Kevin wanted to shout, "Pull me up, now!" But he didn't. "Okay, I guess." The fumes were making him woozy and he began to gag and cough. He felt like he was suffocating. "I-I don't know if I can make it. The fumes."

"Do you want us to pull you up?"

Yes! Yes! Yes! Just then, Kevin heard Kisho whine. *That poor little kid, I've gone this far. I've got to try.* "I'm so close, Captain. I can see Kisho. Keep lowering me."

A few seconds later, Kevin reached the foul-smelling muck and sank in up to his knees. For a moment, he thought he was going to pass out, but he grabbed the air hose and inhaled some of the fresh, pumped air. When he gained control of his senses, he saw how terrified Kisho was.

"Kisho, do you remember me? I was playing with your dog. You gave me a bite of your Tootsie Roll."

The boy nodded. "I want my mommy."

"I've come to take you out of here." Kevin looked up. The light at the top of the shaft seemed so far away. *Hurry up! No more talking.* Kevin gave the toddler a bear hug and said, "Hold on to me and I'll hold on to you." Then he shouted to the workers above, "We're ready! Take us up!"

Inch by inch they were raised out of the muck. Each held on tightly to the other. "Hurry up, hurry up," he muttered to the workers. About halfway to the top, where the shaft narrowed, they became lodged. "Stop! Stop!" he shouted. The rope was cutting into his thigh. "We're stuck!"

This was his worst nightmare. Fighting panic, Kevin squirmed and wiggled. So did Kisho until Kevin lost his grip on the boy and the toddler plunged back into the muck. "Oh, no! I lost him!" Looking down, Kevin shouted, "Kisho, say something."

The toddler responded by letting out a loud wail.

Kevin shouted to the workers, "Pull me up! Now!" Free from holding onto Kisho, Kevin was hauled up the shaft. Once he was lifted out of the hole, he collapsed on the ground and took several deep breaths of fresh air.

"Where's my baby?" screamed Mrs. Matsui. "Where's my baby?"

"He slipped out of my hands when we got stuck," Kevin replied.

Throwing her hands to sides of her head, she buried her face in husband's chest and sobbed. Her husband cried, too.

The captain came over to Kevin. "Can you try one more time?"

I really don't want to go down there, thought Kevin. But he looked over at the devastated parents and knew he had to try again. "I guess so, but the shaft is too narrow for the both of us."

"I have an idea that might work," said the captain. He tied a second rope around Kevin's waist. At the other end was a loop. "Put this loop under his armpits. Then, hold on to the rope so that when we pull you up, he will come up, too, right below you." The captain cocked his ear. "I don't hear Kisho crying anymore." He rushed over to the opening and shouted down, "Kisho! Kisho! Can you hear me?"

There was no answer.

Turning to Kevin, the captain said, "We have no time to lose. The boy might have passed out or slipped under the muck."

Oh, God, here we go again, thought Kevin. He was quickly lowered into the cesspool. It wasn't any easier the second time. In fact, it was worse and he began gagging. When he reached the muck, he found Kisho alive and standing up. But the toddler was in a daze.

Kevin quickly slipped the loop over the toddler's head until it was secured under his armpits. Then he held on to the rope. "Okay!" he shouted. "Get us out of here!"

The workers pulled on the sling and began lifting Kevin and Kisho out of the filth. It took less than a minute, much too slow for Kevin.

When they were lifted out, Kevin crawled a few feet away from the opening and threw up. Covered in mud and raw sewage, he reeked of a smell so horrible that no one wanted to get near him.

"Hose him down," the captain ordered a rescuer.

"Please," Kevin said. "I can't stand myself." He stood up while he was sprayed with a garden hose. Firefighters wrapped him in a blanket and took him to the hospital for observation. Kevin was released later that evening.

Meanwhile, paramedics gave Kisho oxygen before they stripped off his filthy, stinky clothes and gave him a quick bath. Kisho spent the night in the hospital and was sent home the next day with no health problem or injuries.

A day later, Kevin and his mother walked over to the Matsuis' to see how Kisho was feeling.

"You are an angel who saved my baby's life," aid Mrs. Matsui, hugging Kevin.

"I'm glad things worked out," he said. "Sometimes it pays to be skinny like me."

23 The Olympian Chronicles

adapted from Mythlopedia

SUMMARY

These humorous retellings of classic Greek myths recount the stories of how Aphrodite started the Trojan War and how Odysseus took forever to return home from the war—using "their own words."

SOURCE: *"The Olympian Chronicles"* is adapted from Mythlopedia. Published by Scholastic, Mythlopedia tells some tales as old as time . . . in new and exciting ways!

READING SESSIONS: 2

LANGUAGE AND VOCABULARY

Mythology is a part of all cultures and societies. We see mythological characters and events in literature, advertising, and traditional events. As we read the retelling of Odysseus's travels, take time to discuss how mythology affects our lives. Use the Knowledge Ladder below to help guide your discussion of myths.

Knowledge Ladder: *Myth*

Myth (mythology)

L: Look at the words at the top and list what you know about myths.

A: Ask why mythology is so important to cultures/societies.

D: Define *myth*.

D: Demonstrate your knowledge of myth by listing the characteristics of myth.

E: Explain what you know about the difference between a myth and other types of stories.

R: Read a retelling, "The Olympian Chronicles," and discuss the differences between this retelling and the original version.

THINK, TALK, AND WRITE ABOUT TEXT

Think about myths for a moment. We all know how a story that is passed around becomes more exaggerated with each retelling. Finally, even the person involved in the story might not recognize it. Now, think about how those same kinds of stories and people become exaggerated over hundreds of years. Why do you think it is important to a culture or society to keep these myths alive?

The author of "The Olympian Chronicles" uses humor to help engage us in the lives of famous mythological beings. **Discuss** how it helps us as readers to hear the story being told with humorous comments and contemporary connections.

The author says that ". . . reality TV is tame compared to Greek mythology." Based on the two stories you read, would you say this is true?

What we just read was a retelling. How would Odysseus's story be told differently if the author were writing a summary? **Use the organizer** to help you note the differences in retelling, summary, and response.

Almost, But Not Quite the Same: *Characteristics of an Effective Retelling, Summary, and Response*

	Definition	Characteristics	Usually Includes	Does Not Include
Retelling				
Summary				
Response				

The Olympian Chronicles

adapted from Mythlopedia

Long before reality TV came along, there was Greek mythology—filled with drama and suspense as the gods and goddesses quarreled among themselves and wreaked havoc with mortals' lives. Just listen to these two retellings by Aphrodite, goddess of love, and Trojan War hero Odysseus.

READ-ALOUD TIP

This retelling of mythological events provides an opportunity for a humorous recounting of the lives of gods and goddesses. If the pronunciation of these mythological beings is unfamiliar or challenging, use a reference source such as the one found at Encyclopedia Mythica: http://www.pantheon.org/miscellaneous/pronunciations.html.

BACKGROUND LANGUAGE

This story should provide students with background knowledge for mythology as well as motivate them to read more myths. The names will be the most challenging. Highlighting the names and keeping track of them, as shown in this organizer, will help students with the language.

Greek Name	Roman Name	God/Goddess of . . .
Hephaestus	Vulcan	Blacksmiths, fire, volcanoes

Holy Hades! Have you noticed that references to Greek and Roman mythology are everywhere these days? Take space, for instance. Most of the constellations and planets in our solar system get their names from mythology. The planet Mars (in Greek, it's Ares) is named for the god of war. The constellation Pegasus is named for a famous flying horse. Another one, Orion the hunter, . . . well, if you believe the story, the mighty god Zeus placed him in the stars to keep him from killing all the animals on Earth.

Back on the ground, lots of well-known products are named for the gods, goddesses, and heroes of Greek mythology. You know the famous sportswear company with the swoosh logo? It gets its name from Nike, the goddess of victory! Even Paris, France, is named for a mythological character who caused big, big trouble between the Greeks and the Trojans.

And what about the myths themselves? Let's just say that reality TV is tame compared to Greek mythology. These stories are filled with revenge, love, jealousy, war, and adventure. And monsters. Lots and lots of monsters.

In the following stories, we'll meet two of the most famous characters in all of mythology: Aphrodite, the goddess of love, and the clever hero Odysseus. Aphrodite was involved in a contest that started a war. Odysseus fought in that war, then took the long way home in a trip that became known as the Odyssey. But you know what? Don't take my word for it. Let's let the superstars of Greek mythology speak for themselves.

Aphrodite, we'll start with you.

Thank you, dear. Don't you just love me? Well, of course you do. I am the goddess of love! Since I stepped out of the sea foam, it's been Hel-*lo* Romance! The gods on Olympus are too good to be true! Except for Zeus! I'm not a fan. He ordered me to marry that loser Hephaestus! You know him. He's the one the Romans call Vulcan. He's so ugly that when he was born his mother threw him off Mount Olympus. But he is quite crafty. And he loves to make me presents. In fact, he wove me a magical golden belt that makes me even *more* irresistible than I was before.

Now Ares and Adonis totally love me. But who wouldn't? You know what I'm saying?

Here's a story I just love to tell. It's about the time I won a beauty contest . . . and might have *accidentally* started a war. Oops.

One day all the gods and goddesses of Olympus were gathered at a wedding. All, that is, except for Eris, the goddess of discord. She was furious that she hadn't been invited. So she started discord of her own by tossing a golden apple marked "For the Most Beautiful" into the reception.

Hera, Athena, and yours truly—Aphrodite—each claimed that the apple was intended for her. Then we began to argue. The mighty god Zeus decided that Paris, Prince of Troy, should settle the argument by judging us in a beauty contest.

Each goddess in the contest offered Paris a bribe, hoping that he would choose her as the most beautiful. Of course, Paris couldn't resist *my* offer.

I promised to make him irresistible to Helen, the most beautiful woman in the whole world (they don't call me the goddess of love for nothing!).

Helen was already married to Menelaus, the king of Sparta. But that didn't stop Paris. Oh no, not at all. The prince kidnapped Helen and took her to the city of Troy.

What happened next is epic! The Greek hero Agamemnon led an expedition of Greek soldiers to rescue Helen. The next thing you know, it was war.

I suppose the best person to tell you what happened next is the great Greek hero of the Trojan War, Odysseus.

* * * * *

Odysseus

Truth time: I have no idea where I am. Don't tell the crew, okay? Not that they'd care. Ever since we landed on that island and they ate what they call "crazy fruit," they've forgotten everything. Seriously, the islands have been nothing but trouble. I'll never forget being trapped on that creepy island with those one-eyed weirdos. We're lucky any of us got out alive! And now my crew is pigging out at that strange Circe's house. At this rate, we'll never get home!

As long as I'm lost, I might as well tell you my story. At least part of it. The whole story would take years—just like this trip!

When the Trojan War began, a very wise person—an oracle—told me that if I went to Troy, it would be many years before I returned home. Well, I'm no *fool*. But I pretended to be a really big one when the Greek soldiers came for me. Unfortunately, they didn't fall for my act. So off I went to war. I even persuaded the great Greek warrior Achilles to join me.

But that's another story. (Check that one out sometime. You'll like it.)

After a long period of fighting, the goddess of wisdom, Athena, gave me the idea for a brilliant plan to end the war. The Trojan horse! We built a huge wooden horse on wheels, and loaded it with soldiers. Then we rolled it up to the gates of Troy and knocked on the door. We told the Trojans that we had a gift for them. When they opened the gates and rolled the horse into the city, Greek soldiers jumped out. And before you know it Troy was destroyed! The war was over. We were going right home. Or so I thought.

You see, however, during the war, we had angered several other gods and goddesses. They got back at us by making our journey home a complete nightmare.

Poseidon, the god of the sea, stirred up a terrible storm, blowing our ship off course. The crew and I landed on an island. While we were searching for food and shelter, we entered a cave. Little did we suspect that the cozy cavern was the home of the Cyclops Polyphemus. The gigantic shepherd also happened to be a son of Poseidon. In fact, the entire island was inhabited by one-eyed, man-eating Cyclopes! This was no cute little Airbnb!

That evening, Polyphemus—the shepherd—returned to his cave with a flock of sheep. He found us eating his food and making ourselves at home. So he rolled a boulder across the entrance, trapping us inside. Then he set about making a feast . . . of us! That night, he ate two men for dinner. The next morning, he ate two more for breakfast. And guess what the Cyclops had for lunch? Two more men!

With time *and men* running out, I came up with a plan. I offered Polyphemus some tea and we struck up a conversation. When he asked me my name, I answered, "No Man." As I continued to talk slowly and softly, Polyphemus fell sound asleep.

While the Cyclops snored, I, and the remaining men—who had not been part of the day's feeding— sharpened an olive branch into a spear. Then we jabbed it sharply into the giant's one eye. Polyphemus screamed. Hearing the scream, the other Cyclopes on the island came running to the entrance of the cave. When they asked Polyphemus who was hurting him, he screamed, "No Man!" "What?" they shouted. "Didn't you hear me? No man is hurting me," answered Polyphemus. Certain that Polyphemus was losing his mind, the other Cyclopes went away.

The next morning, when Polyphemus let his big sheep out of the cave, my men and I held onto the undersides of the sheep and escaped to our ship. Furious, Polyphemus hurled boulders at the ship, but missed because he couldn't see. (Remember? Olive branch in the one big eye he had.) The frustrated Cyclops begged his father, Poseidon, to prevent me from getting home, or at least to make sure that my men died along the way. That way, I'd have no other choice but to get home aboard a stranger's ship. Poseidon vowed to fulfill part of his son's wish.

When we reached the island of Aeaea, we had to deal with the sorceress Circe. I was immune to her magic but not to her charms. I confess, I fell in love with Circe. Despite what common sense would tell you, I stayed on Aeaea for a year.

Next, we had to get past the Sirens. Do you know about them? They're a group of sea nymphs whose haunting songs lure sailors to their deaths. While the crew plugged their ears with beeswax, I lashed myself to the mast so I wouldn't be tempted to sail toward the sirens' song.

Then, at Thrinacia, my men had a cookout. Unfortunately, they had stolen the beef for the barbeque from the sun god Helios's herd of sacred cattle. Hot with rage, Helios asked Zeus for help. So Zeus struck our ship with a thunderbolt, wrecking the boat and killing everyone but me.

Poseidon's vow came about. There was no way for me to continue this journey—unless I boarded another ship.

Fortunately, I was rescued by the Phaeacians. They took me on board one of their ships and sailed me home to Ithaca.

For the ten years that I had been trying to get home from the war, my wife, Penelope, didn't know whether I was alive or dead. During that time, other men had their eyes on my empty throne.

They crowded around Penelope, urging her to give up on me. Penelope did her best to fend them off. But they hung around the palace, ate her food, drank her wine, and generally made pests of themselves. Let's face it . . . ten years is ten years. But Penelope stayed strong—"gods love her"—as they say.

Finally I reached my home on Ithaca. With the help of the goddess Athena, who had come to admire me for my cleverness, I disguised myself as a beggar. Penelope did not recognize me when I entered the great hall. She announced to all the men who had gathered in the hall that enough was enough and that her *next* husband would be the man who could string Odysseus's bow and shoot an arrow through twelve axe handles. None of the men was strong enough to string the bow.

Then I, disguised as a beggar, humbly stepped forward. I strung the bow, lifted it, and shot an arrow through all twelve axe handles. As the other men looked on in amazement, I threw off my disguise! My son, Telemachus, rushed to my side. Together, he and I battled the men until every last one was gone. Finally, I was home.

Odysseus's odyssey was indeed over.

24 The Totally Sad Story of Romeo & Juliet

by Jack Silbert

SOURCE: *Jack Silbert is a writer and editor based in Hoboken, NJ. He is the author of several books for children and adults, and his writing has appeared in* The New York Times *and* New Jersey Monthly, *on AOL, and elsewhere.*

READING SESSION: 1

SUMMARY

This is a humorous retelling of the classic love story by William Shakespeare about a young man and woman, Romeo and Juliet, who—despite their families' hatred for each other—fall in love. They marry. And then a misunderstanding brings their love to a tragic end.

LANGUAGE AND VOCABULARY

Dig into students' background knowledge of the play *Romeo and Juliet*. Fill in the chart below, encouraging students to share all that they know, have heard, or have read about *Romeo and Juliet*. Ask clarifying questions to keep the discussion going: Who? Why? What? Then what? The more they can tell about the story, the more fun the retelling will be to listen to.

What I Know About "Romeo and Juliet"
Who?
Why?
What?

THINK, TALK, AND WRITE ABOUT TEXT

How good a job did the kid from the mall do in his retelling? Did the story make sense? For those students who know the play, did the retelling help them better understand it?

How might this old play (written between 1591 and 1595) still be relevant today? How realistic is it to base a story on "feuding families"?

Challenge students to summarize the story of Romeo and Juliet in three to five sentences. Have students share their summaries.

The Totally Sad Story of Romeo & Juliet

by Jack Silbert

Imagine that you're sitting at the mall food court. Your friends are way late. Your cell is practically dead so you put that away. To kill some time you lean back and listen to two high school kids. They're talking about an English assignment. The older kid is telling the younger one not to sweat it. The assignment? Read *Romeo and Juliet* by William Shakespeare. Listen to his retelling of this classic play—made easy.

READ-ALOUD TIP

This modernized retelling of *Romeo and Juliet* should be read fairly quickly to highlight the humor and the language. Punctuation in this retelling helps guide the reader into changing the narrator's tone to match the action of the drama. You may want to note the places in the text where the narrator seems to use asides to emphasize his point.

BACKGROUND LANGUAGE

The purpose of this read-aloud is to establish background with informal text prior to reading the actual play. Many students will know the *Romeo and Juliet* story line, and the contemporary language is a support for readers.

So, this is like a totally sad story. This Shakespeare dude must've really wanted to get the ladies—and even the bros—crying at the end. Because, trust me, there is no happy ending here.

There's this dude Romeo—he's all fit and stuff. You would not want to mess with him. And then there's this hot girl, Juliet. They had names like that in the really old days. So no one had normal names, like Kylie, Miley, Jaden, or Malala. They all had names like Benvolio and Tybalt and Mercutio. What were their parents thinking, right?!

Romeo and Juliet come from these two huge families with, like, tons of cousins and second cousins. One family is the Montagues and the other is the Capulets. And man, they totally hate each other. No friendly barbecues, no "hey, what's up?" at softball games, I mean, they can't stand each other. Know what I'm saying?

So, this dude Sampson, who works for old man Capulet, sees this other dude Abraham, who hangs with a Montague, and he bites his thumb. Like, he bites his own thumb, not Abraham's thumb, which in the old days was like saying, "What you looking at? You wanna fight?"

And Abraham says something like, "I'm not looking at you. Do *you* wanna fight?" And they basically start beating on each other. But the fight gets broken up before anybody gets seriously messed up. And the Prince—he's like the principal of this whole town—he says, "Yo, next time you dudes get in each other's face, I'll go medieval on both of you, and you don't want that."

Okay, so back to the story. Remember Juliet, the cute girl? Well, her old man decides he's going to throw this amazing party. But he's going to have to send a servant out to tell everybody, 'cause, like, they didn't have texting or Facebook or evites back then. But this servant is maybe a little slow or something, and he can't make out the names on the list, so he stops someone to help him read it. And check this out—the guy he asks is Romeo. Uh-oh, right?

So Romeo looks at the invite list, and there are all these names of people he doesn't really like. But then he sees Rosaline's name. Rosaline is, like, really, really hot, and Romeo has always wanted to date her. So he decides to crash the party, which will be totally easy, because it's a costume party.

Meanwhile, Juliet's mom is trying to fix her up with this guy named Paris. Whatever.

Anyway—Romeo's kind of bummed because he is totally into Rosaline but he thinks she, like, isn't into him. But one of Romeo's best buds, Mercutio, tells him, "Chill, Ro-yo. Just go to the party and hang out. There's going to be a lot more girls there, I promise."

So Romeo goes to the party. He starts checking out the girls. Nobody really makes him look twice, to tell the truth. That is, until, BAM, he sees Juliet. He is, like, stunned. Instant crush. And at the same time, Juliet is saying to herself, "Who is that hot guy?" Which seems good but it is bad, because in the very beginning of the story, Shakespeare wrote that Romeo and Juliet were "star-cross'd lovers," which probably means that this relationship is doomed. Oh yeah, big trouble ahead. Count on it.

Of course Romeo and Juliet don't know this tale is going to come to a real nasty end.

So Romeo goes up to Juliet, dances around real smooth, and they hold hands for a while. Then he works up some nerve and goes, "O, then, dear saint, let lips do what hands do." Then he kisses her, and it's like, *Wow!* I mean, it was awesome for both of them. But then Juliet's nurse pulls her away. No, she wasn't sick; in those days a nurse was like a nanny for older girls. And nurses were always freaking out over nothing—but especially kissing.

Juliet's cousin, Tybalt, sees that Romeo is trying to move in on Juliet. And since she is a Capulet and Romeo is a Montague, well there is no way he's going to let this happen. So he says to Juliet's father, "Yo, hand me that sword." But Juliet's dad says, "Chill, Tybalt. Don't wreck the party."

Then it's curfew time or something, 'cause everyone has to leave. But when Romeo is heading for his part of town, he stops, and jumps over this big fence into Juliet's yard. He's, like, climbing up trees to get near Juliet's room. At the same time, Juliet goes out to her balcony and kind of stares up at the moon. She gets all goofy and says, "O, Romeo, Romeo, wherefore art thou, Romeo?" And it's like, duh, HELLO!, he's sitting on a branch right under your balcony. But maybe, like, she took out her contacts before bed?

But she figures it out, and suddenly Romeo's climbing up the wall 'cause he wants to hang with his babe on the balcony. He's not there more than a minute when, *boom!*, they fall in love, hard. I mean, they have it so bad for each other that Romeo goes, "Do you want to get married?" And Juliet goes, "Yes, that would be excellent!" No control, right?

Long story short—they figure out a way to run off and get married! Except they get married in secret because, remember, their families hate each other. No posting. No selfies. Nothing. The wedding was all done in secret.

A little while later, Juliet's hot-tempered cousin Tybalt runs into Romeo and Mercutio hanging out in the square, which is kind of like an outdoor mall. Tybalt starts getting all up in Romeo's face. All he wants to do is fight Romeo. But Romeo won't fight him, so Tybalt jumps in Mercutio's face, and he and Mercutio start beating on each other. Then things get out of control! Mercutio gets killed by Tybalt. So Romeo kills Tybalt, which is dumb because, well, now he and Juliet are going to have a real hard time explaining to the families that they are married.

When news of this deadly brawl reaches the Prince he exiles Romeo, which is like getting expelled from school, but you've got to move to a whole other state or something. So Romeo and Juliet have to split up for a while. Juliet goes, "O, think'st though we shall ever meet again?" 'cause she's really in love and is afraid that her husband, Romeo, won't be able to come back. And then Juliet gets even more depressed 'cause now her old man wants her to marry Paris. Um, EXCUSE ME, she's, like already married. But her parents are clueless about that and are still planning a wedding.

Drama. Drama. Drama.

Juliet is super depressed so she goes to this priest. Feeling bad for her, the priest comes up with this crazy plan. He gives Juliet this stuff to drink so that everyone will think she's dead, until Romeo can get back from being grounded. But this stuff is so strong that everybody thinks she really is dead, and they put her in this tomb thing.

The priest told Juliet that he'll send Romeo a letter explaining everything. But you know how the mail is . . . really slow. That night Romeo—who's exiled out of town—dreams that Juliet has found him dead. He thinks the dream is a sign. So he says, "I'm outta here." He takes off to see Juliet, but he stops, like at a drugstore, for some over-the-counter poison or something—for what reason I don't know but he's depressed, too. Yikes. So he misses this letter that the priest sent that says, "Hey Romeo, heads up! Juliet isn't dead. She's just sleeping." Oops.

But then Romeo sees Juliet and he goes, "Ah, dear Juliet, why art though yet so fair?" 'Cause, you know, if she was dead she ought to be green and starting to smell funny—she wouldn't be all fair and that. And that makes Romeo totally bummed out, so guess what he does? Yup. He drinks the poison. *Duh!* I mean, like, *Duhh!* Oh, then you'll never guess this part. She wakes up and sees Romeo and goes "O happy dagger!" and kills herself.

I mean, what is *wrong* with these people? Seriously, right?

And that is Shakespeare's most famous love story.

Wanna go check out the mall now?

25 The Freedom Writers Diary #16

The Freedom Writers With Erin Gruwell

SUMMARY

Diary entry #16 is one of several entries written by Erin Gruwell's students. This personal narrative was written by a young woman involved in a real-life "Romeo and Juliet" situation. However, the situation has a very different ending from the original Shakespearean drama.

SOURCE: The Freedom Writers Diary *is a collection of anonymous diary entries from the students in Erin Gruwell's class.*

READING SESSION: 1

LANGUAGE AND VOCABULARY

Newton's Third Law states: *For every action, there is an equal (in size) and opposite (in direction) reaction.* The writer of this diary entry wonders about Juliet's parents' reactions to her actions as she experiences her own parents' reactions to her actions. Discuss how Newton's Third Law applies to this writer's actions.

THINK, TALK, AND WRITE ABOUT TEXT

Restriction can mean many things. **Talk** about why you might be put on restriction. If your parents put you on restriction, what would you lose? What do you think they hope you will gain during the time you are on restriction? How effective was it for this writer?

The author of this diary refers to a tradition in her culture known as the *Quinceañera*. Work in groups to explore this tradition. **Use the following organizer** to keep track of your findings.

Origin	Purpose	Changes Over Time	Today's Quinceañera

Discuss the impact of waiting until the writer turned 15 to see her boyfriend again.

Imagine that 20 years have passed and you are a parent. Write a note to your future self about what you think a parent should know and do that would be effective when their children seem to be in trouble.

The Freedom Writers Diary #16

The Freedom Writers With Erin Gruwell

A young girl compares her storybook romance to the romance of the title characters in Shakespeare's *Romeo and Juliet*. Except, luckily for her, their stories don't end the same way.

Dear Diary,

We just finished reading *Romeo and Juliet*; I couldn't believe that Juliet stabbed herself over a guy that she only knew for a few days. I guess I wasn't as in love as I thought I was, because I'd never do something that crazy for my boyfriend.

At first when we started reading this story, I compared myself with Juliet. We are both young and in love with a guy that we couldn't last a day without seeing, only Juliet fell in love at first sight and it took me two months to supposedly be in love. Running away seemed like an easy way for us to rebel against my parents' disapproval of my boyfriend. Yet it didn't come out the way we had planned.

Juliet's parents found her dead next to her boyfriend. Unfortunately, my parents found me alive next to my boyfriend. Lucky for Juliet, she died and she didn't see the reaction of her parents, nor did she have to go through punishments. I survived, and unlike Juliet's parents, my parents didn't welcome me with tears falling down from their faces. Instead, when my parents arrived at my boyfriend's house, my mother was the first to get out of the car. As she looked into my eyes, I felt the shame I had caused her. She headed toward my boyfriend and started screaming and lecturing him. My dad came toward me cussing and screaming.

When we arrived home, my mother kept screaming at me, *"Eres tan estúpida por irte con un muchacho que ni siquieras conoces!"* (You are so stupid for running away with a guy that you don't even know!) I wonder how Juliet's parents would have reacted to their daughter's actions and how Juliet would have responded. I just went into my room, not saying a word. My parents followed me. They kept telling me that I couldn't see my boyfriend ever again. They put me on restriction. I wasn't allowed to use the phone, have any company, or go out with anybody. That's why I'm here in Ms. G's class right now.

My mother thought it would be best for me to attend a school near her work and in a different school district that was at least one hour away from home. She thought that driving me to and picking me up from school would prevent me from contacting my boyfriend and that I'd forget about him. It didn't work.

Just like Juliet, I found a way to see my boyfriend. I ditched my classes and would call him from the public phones on campus. My mother didn't have an idea of what was going on until I got caught by one of my relatives. My aunt was on the same bus that my boyfriend and I were riding.

My mom was ashamed to hear that her own relative saw me kissing my boyfriend on a bus. She didn't know what to do. Finally, my parents decided that I could be with my boyfriend under one condition. That my boyfriend and I waited until I turned fifteen (this is a tradition from my culture, indicating that when a girl turns fifteen, she is a woman and mature enough to take serious responsibilities). Since I thought I was so in love and would do anything to be with my boyfriend without sneaking behind my parents' back, we both agreed to wait. So, we stopped seeing each other, just before my class got to the end of the story.

I hate to admit that my parents were right all along. How can we both believe that we were so in love with each other if we didn't even take the time to really know each other? I was too young and stupid, like Juliet, to fall in love. Luckily, I didn't kill myself and have a tragic ending like Romeo and Juliet did. I guess I wasn't that desperate.

26 The Escape

by J. B. Stamper

SUMMARY

Boris committed a terrible crime and is serving a life sentence in prison. When he tries to escape, things get worse, and he lands in solitary. But a loose stone in his cell reveals a secret passageway and one more chance to escape. In order to do so, Boris must confront some of his greatest fears. Will he make it out alive or be trapped forever?

SOURCE: *J. B. Stamper is known as the scariest woman in her neighborhood. Her stories can be found in many collections, including* Tales for the Midnight Hour.

READING SESSION: 1

LANGUAGE AND VOCABULARY

When describing a setting, person, or event, authors choose each word carefully in order to make an emotional impact on the reader. Encourage students to begin collecting descriptive words used in "The Escape" so they have a word bank for the writing they will do.

Collecting Descriptive Language for Writing

Words Describing Boris's Fears (Phobias)	Words Describing Boris	Words Describing the Prison *Long, dark hallways*
Words Describing Solitary Confinement *It was the worst place in the worst place in the world.*	Words Describing Boris's Feelings or Emotions	Words Describing Boris's Escape

THINK, TALK, AND WRITE ABOUT TEXT

Phobia is defined as a persistent, irrational fear. Boris's phobias focused on fear of rats and fear of tight, small, cramped spaces. **Think** about your life. Do you have phobias? Do you know others who have phobias?

How does the sentence, "It was the worst place in the worst place in the world" help you **visualize** the setting?

Discuss why you think the author chose not to tell the readers Boris's crime. What do you know about the crime from details in the text?

When Boris is locked up in solitary, he yells after the guard, "You'll be sorry!" **Think:** Is this an example of foreshadowing?

What techniques did the author use to generate tension in this story? **Discuss** what you think happens at the end. Who is "the voice" who has come to find Boris?

Work in groups to **write** a description, story, poem, or script for a person with a different phobia.

1. Before writing, visit http://kidshealth.org/en/teens/phobias.html to learn more about phobias.
2. Search online for phobias to find an interesting phobia to highlight in your writing.
3. Modify and use your descriptive language chart to generate descriptive words for your writing.
4. Don't forget to add tension for the reader!

The Escape

by J. B. Stamper

Do you know what a phobia is? A *phobia* is a fear of something. Some people are afraid of heights. Some are afraid of spiders. Others are even afraid of the dark. In this story you are going to meet a man named Boris. Boris is in prison, and he has a couple of phobias. He's deathly afraid of rats. And he really hates tight, small, cramped spaces. Nothing bothers him more. As you listen to this tale, can you identify with Boris and his phobias?

READ-ALOUD TIP

Change your voice to represent the conflict between the guard and Boris. The author uses short sentences and paragraphs to increase the intensity of Boris's escape. Adjust your pacing by emphasizing the beginning of each paragraph so your voice matches the increasing anxiety about Boris's fate.

BACKGROUND LANGUAGE

Understanding what a phobia is will help students understand Boris's motivation for trying to escape and the terror he is feeling.

Boris looked down the long, dark hallway of the prison. It looked endless—as endless as the life sentence he was in for.

Boris was being taken to a place that few people had seen, but everyone feared. Solitary—solitary confinement. The other prisoners said the word with a shudder. It was the worst place in the worst place in the world.

Behind him, the guard laughed and shoved Boris in the back. "This'll teach you a lesson, won't it," he said. "Once you've been in solitary, there'll be no more bad behavior from you. Solitary will break you, just like it does everyone else."

Boris wanted to turn around and scream at the guard. But he forced his feet to move down the hall. He knew that it was over for him. He had no hope left.

Seven years ago, he had committed a crime. It was a crime so terrible that he couldn't believe that he'd done it. Did he regret it? Every second of his life. But it was done. And now he was in prison until he died. He was trapped like an animal in a cage. He couldn't face it any longer!

That's why he had tried to escape.

It happened just after sunset. He was all alone in the prison courtyard. The guard who was supposed to be there had made a mistake. He'd left Boris alone.

Boris had seen his chance. He'd run for the wall like a wild animal. He had climbed up and was almost over. Then he'd heard the words, "Freeze, prisoner!"

And he had frozen.

That was yesterday. And, now, he was headed to an even worse cage.

"You don't have to put me in solitary," Boris said to the guard in a scared voice. "I'll never try that again, I promise!"

The guard just laughed. "You'll learn your lesson," he said again. "Maybe they'll let you out after a few months. But you're a tough one. I know what you did to get inside. You don't deserve anybody's pity."

Boris felt a wave of despair wash over him. There was no way he could get out of this. He would just have to deal with it—somehow.

They were coming to the end of the hallway. Boris saw a rusting iron door at the end. He saw the thick bars across the small window in the door.

He knew that this was it—solitary. The others had told him what it would be like inside.

They were right. The guard unlocked three locks. Then he swung open the door. He pushed Boris inside.

The room was like a pen. It was long and narrow with one bed. High up there was a small window with bars across it.

The walls were of old, rough stone. To Boris, it felt as if they were closing in on him.

His breath started to come in short gasps. His heart pounded. Boris turned to the guard.

"No," he begged. "I can't take it here. Let me go back to where I was. I'll never do anything wrong again."

"You should have thought of that earlier," the guard said. Then he slammed the heavy door in Boris's face.

Boris reached for the door. He grabbed the bars in his hands and tried to shake them. His mind flew into a panic.

"You'll be sorry!" he yelled after the guard.

The guard just looked back and laughed.

Boris's legs were shaking so badly that he had to sit down on the bed. He shut his eyes. He didn't want to look around the cell. He was afraid that he would lose his mind. Slowly, he sank down onto the dirty cot and fell into a troubled sleep.

Thunder woke Boris from a terrible nightmare. In the nightmare, rats were running at him, screeching. There was nothing that scared him more than rats.

Reluctantly, he opened his eyes. What if the rats were really there? It was his biggest worry . . . that there might be rats in solitary.

Boris looked around at the shadowy walls of the cell. It was almost dark, and the walls seemed to be closing in on him. Then a flash of lightning lit up the room from the small window over his bed. The light fell on the moldy stone walls of the cell.

It was only a few seconds of light. But Boris thought he saw something— something that lit a small candle of hope in his mind. One of the stones in the wall looked different. There was a thin crack in the cement around it.

Boris tried to fight off the feeling of hope. But he couldn't help himself. Maybe another prisoner had dug around the stone. No one could see the crack unless they were lying on the bed. He had only seen it because of the lightning. He waited, full of terror that he might be wrong. A flash of jagged lightning cut through the sky again.

Boris pushed himself off the bed. His hands were shaking as he reached down and grabbed the large stone. Slowly and methodically, he moved it back and forth.

Then, suddenly, it came loose! Boris pulled harder, and the rock fell forward into his hands.

As Boris stared into the hole left by the rock, a flash of lightning lit up the cell again. Through the hole in the wall, he saw a tunnel stretching out before him . . . and a rat hurrying down into it.

Boris jumped back in horror. No, he couldn't stand seeing the rat. He started to put the stone back in place.

Then another flash of lightning cut through the darkness. The tunnel lit up in front of Boris. It seemed to beckon him to freedom.

With his eyes, Boris measured the size of the tunnel. It was narrow at the beginning—but not so narrow that he couldn't squeeze his body through. He saw that it became wider in a few feet. It was wide enough to let him escape—wide enough to take him to freedom.

Another flash of lightning lit up the tunnel. Boris searched for any sign of the rat, but the tunnel seemed empty.

"Maybe I didn't see the rat at all," Boris whispered to himself. "Maybe it was just a shadow of my nightmare."

Boris peered deeper into the tunnel. Then his eyes fell on something strange. There was a scrap piece of paper lying on the tunnel floor, near the entrance.

He reached in his hand and pulled out the note. He felt its dry surface. The paper was wrinkled with age.

He waited impatiently for the lightning to strike again. When it did, he quickly read the message on the paper.

'To the next prisoner who finds this paper," Boris read. "I escaped the horror of this cell by this passage. May you share my good luck."

The light faded away before Boris could finish reading the message. He sat in the darkness, shaking with fear and hope.

The message seemed to be written in a dark red liquid. Boris guessed that it was the blood of the person who had written it.

At last, the lightning came again. He read on, "This is the only way out!" The message was signed with two initials, "N.G."

Just then, Boris heard the guard's footsteps outside his cell. He threw himself over the stone and hole. He pressed his body against the wall.

He waited as the footsteps came to a stop outside his cell. He thought he would scream from the horrible tension.

Then the footsteps moved away. They slowly drifted down the hallway. Finally, they faded into the night.

Suddenly, Boris knew he couldn't wait any longer. He stuck his head into the tunnel and pushed the rest of his body through.

He tried to look back, but the tunnel was too narrow. There was no turning back now.

Boris squirmed deeper and deeper into the tunnel. Crawling on his stomach, he felt like a snake slithering into its hole. He felt the tunnel grow damper and colder.

Just as the tunnel began to grow slimy, it opened up and became wider.

Boris stood up on his trembling legs. He tried to see into the darkness ahead. He put his hands out in front of him and walked slowly through the black tunnel.

The rocky walls were sharp and tore at his hands. He wiped the sweat from his forehead with one hand and felt warm blood oozing from it.

Suddenly, Boris felt sick. His legs became weak with fear. He dropped to his knees and fell forward onto his hands. Then he felt tiny, clawed feet run over his fingers.

Boris dug his fist in his mouth to keep himself from screaming. Then,

 Riveting Read-Alouds for Middle School © Janet Allen and Patrick Daley, Scholastic Inc.

once again, the sharp claws of a rat dug into his hand. Boris jumped to his feet, hitting his head on the low ceiling of the tunnel.

Then he felt them all around him. The rats were running over his shoes. They were crawling at his legs. All Boris could do was force himself to move forward into the tunnel. All he could hope for was that the rats wouldn't climb up his leg. If they did, he knew he would lose his mind.

Suddenly, the tunnel sloped down at sharp angle. Boris's feet slipped forward. He landed on his back. He slid deeper and deeper into the tunnel. He no longer felt the rats around him. He no longer heard their claws scratching the rock.

Boris came to a stop where the floor of the tunnel suddenly became flat. His breath was coming in short gasps that tore at his lungs.

He picked himself up. He reached for the slimy walls of the tunnel that he had just fallen down. Then the truth hit him like a blow. He could never go back. The walls of the tunnel behind him were too steep and slippery.

He had only one chance. He had to push on. He had to push on . . . and hope that there was an end to the tunnel.

Boris forced himself forward. He clawed at the walls with his hands, trying to hurry.

Now the tunnel was beginning to feel more and more narrow. His breath was coming in shorter and shorter gasps. Then the tunnel made a sharp turn to the left. Suddenly Boris saw something that made him cry in relief. Through an opening in the distance, he could see the pale rays of the moon.

He was almost there. He could smell the night air. Boris struggled toward the patch of moonlight ahead of him.

The tunnel was turning upward. Boris had to grab both sides of the wall and dig his feet into cracks for footholds. Slowly, he pulled himself up.

Boris felt the blood from his cuts running down into his sleeves. But the pain didn't matter. All that mattered was the patch of light ahead. Boris felt the night air against his face. He was close now. Close to freedom.

Then a sound behind him terrified him. It was the sound of those clawed feet. They were following him.

Boris scrambled up to the top of the tunnel even faster. The moonlight was so bright now that he could see his hands in front of him. He felt a rat brush against his neck. But he had only a few yards to go.

With his last bit of strength, Boris scrambled toward the moonlight. Suddenly, he felt his head crash into something hard and cold. He fell back, stunned.

Slowly, his head stopped swimming and he opened his eyes. He saw the thick bars of a heavy gate. It closed off any chance of escape. And lying on the ground in front of it were the cold, white bones . . . of a skeleton.

Boris felt a scream of despair rise up in his throat. He choked back the scream and stared at the skeleton. Was it the body of N.G.? Or was it another prisoner who had tried, and failed, to escape?

In desperation, Boris lifted the bones of the skeleton. It rattled apart into a gruesome heap. Boris pushed the bones away from the gate and fell to his knees.

He had only one hope left—that he could tunnel under the gate.

Boris picked up a bone and began to scratch away at the ground in front of the gate. Digging down, he uncovered something that had been hidden there. It was a key, an old iron key.

With trembling hands, Boris picked up the key. Then he felt through the bars of the gate for a lock. It was there! A rat began to nibble at his foot, but now Boris didn't care. He fit the key into the lock and turned it.

As the gate swung open, Boris breathed in the air of freedom and pushed his body out of the tunnel. He lay on the ground and kissed it.

Standing up, Boris looked up at the stars and swore on them that he would never commit a crime again. His thoughts were interrupted by a harsh voice.

"Boris," the voice said, "I've come to find you."

Boris didn't look back. He ran and ran until he found a place to hide for the rest of the night. He had made his escape.

And, he told himself, he would never, ever, be caught again.

27 Us and Them

by David Sedaris

SUMMARY

On November 1st, David Sedaris and his family are visited by their neighbors the Tomkeys, who are trick-or-treating a day late in strange costumes. Worse yet, the Sedaris kids must share their candy with the Tomkeys. The children refuse, and their mother steps in, only to find David in his room, trying to quickly eat all his chocolate . . . with hilarious results.

SOURCE: *David Sedaris is a humor writer who has published often-autobiographical stories as both books and articles.*

READING SESSION: 1

(If you need to divide the story into two sessions because of time, stop after the 2nd paragraph in the 2nd column on page 143, ending with ". . . I chalked it up to tension.")

LANGUAGE AND VOCABULARY

The word *attribute* means to see behavior or events as resulting from a specific, identifiable cause. For example, the narrator attributes the Tomkeys lack of knowledge about Halloween etiquette to not having a TV. After reading "Us and Them," ask students to what would they attribute the narrator's behavior. Share the words in the concept circle below to help them explain his behavior.

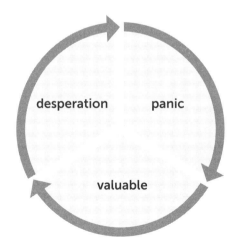

desperation   panic

valuable

THINK, TALK, AND WRITE ABOUT TEXT

Think about your Halloween experiences. What were the unwritten rules related to the Halloween candy you received? Were you allowed to keep all of the candy or did your parents get involved in how much candy you were allowed to keep?

Talk about the "rules" of Halloween. When are you too old to trick-or-treat? Do you have to have a costume? Are there rules of etiquette for trick-or-treating? In what ways did the Tomkeys break some of these unwritten rules?

What passage in the text most clearly shows the narrator's **point of view** about the Tomkeys and their lifestyle?

The narrator's mother says, "You should look at yourself. I mean, really look at yourself." **Why** did she repeat that line? What impact do you think this had on the narrator?

Write an opinion statement about this childhood event from the point of view of the narrator. Then, write another opinion statement from the point of view of the narrator as an older, more mature person looking back at this event.

Us and Them

by David Sedaris

Who celebrates Halloween on November 1st? In this hilarious story from humor writer David Sedaris, you'll hear about how one family handles unexpected, unwelcome trick-or-treaters who show up a day late.

READ-ALOUD TIP

Many adult readers are familiar with David Sedaris's witty writing, but most students probably won't know his work. This is a family drama with a powerful message about looking at ourselves and our behaviors toward others, examined through a humorous lens. Emphasize the comedy and imagery throughout the text, and then use a more reflective, quiet tone for the last paragraph, which is the narrator's reflection.

BACKGROUND LANGUAGE

The language in the story is very accessible for listeners, so few words should need explanation. Two words you might wish to discuss if extending the read-aloud are *attribute* and *indiscriminately*. Both are related to the narrator's response to the Tomkeys.

The night after Halloween, we were sitting around watching TV when the doorbell rang. Visitors were infrequent at our house, so, while my father stayed behind, my mother, sisters and I ran downstairs in a group, opening the door to discover the entire Tomkey family on our front stoop. The parents looked as they always had, but the son and daughter were dressed in costumes— she as a ballerina and he as some kind of rodent with terry-cloth ears and a tail made from what looked to be an extension cord. It seemed they had spent the previous evening isolated at the lake, and had missed the opportunity to observe Halloween. "So, well, I guess we're trick-or-treating now, if that's OK," Mr. Tomkey said.

I attributed their behavior to the fact that they didn't have a TV, but television didn't teach you everything. Asking for candy on Halloween was called trick-or-treating, but asking for candy on November 1st was called begging, and it made people uncomfortable. This was one of the things you were supposed to learn simply by being alive, and it angered me that the Tomkeys did not understand it.

"Why, of course it's not too late," my mother said. "Kids, why don't you . . . run and get . . . the candy."

"But the candy is gone," my sister Grechen said. "You gave it away last night."

"Not that candy," my mother said. "The other candy. Why don't you run and go get it?"

"You mean our candy?" Lisa said. "The candy that we earned?"

This was exactly what our mother was talking about, but she didn't want to say this in front of the Tomkeys. In order to spare their feelings, she wanted them to believe that we always kept a bucket of candy lying around the house, just waiting for someone to knock on the door and ask for it. "Go on, now," she said. "Hurry up."

My room was situated right off the foyer, and if the Tomkeys had looked in that direction they could have seen my bed, and the brown paper bag marked "My Candy. Keep Out." I didn't want them to know how much I had, and so I went into my room and shut the door behind me. Then I closed the curtains and emptied my bag onto the bed, searching for whatever was the crummiest. All my life, chocolate has made me ill. I don't know if I'm allergic or what, but even the smallest amount leaves me with a blinding headache. Eventually, I learned to stay away from it, but as a child I refused to be left out. The brownies were always eaten, and when the pounding began I would blame the grape juice or my mother's cigarette smoke or the tightness of my glasses—anything but the chocolate. My candy bars were poison but they were name brand, and so I put them in pile No. 1, which definitely would not go to the Tomkeys.

Out in the hallway I could hear my mother straining for something to talk about. "A boat!" she said. "That sounds marvelous. Can you just drive it right into the water?"

"Actually, we have a trailer," Mr. Tomkey said. "So what we do is back it into the lake."

"Oh, a trailer. What kind is it?"

"Well, it's a boat trailer," Mr. Tomkey said.

"Right, but is it wooden or you know . . . I guess what I'm asking is what style trailer do you have?"

Behind my mother's words were two messages. The first message and most obvious was, "Yes, I am talking about boat trailers, but also I am dying." The second, meant only for my sisters and me, was, "If you do not immediately step forward with that candy you will never again experience freedom, happiness, or the possibility of my warm embrace."

I knew that it was just a matter of time before she came into my room and started collecting the candy herself, grabbing indiscriminately, with no regard for my rating system. Had I been thinking straight, I would have hidden the most valuable items in my dresser drawer, but instead, panicked by the thought of her hand on my doorknob, I tore off the wrappers and began cramming the candy bars into my mouth, desperately, like someone in a contest. Most were miniature, which made them easier to accommodate, but still there was only so much room, and it was hard to chew and fit more in at the same time. The headache began immediately, and I chalked it up to tension.

My mother told the Tomkeys that she needed to check on something, and then she opened the door and stuck her head inside my room. "What the hell are you doing?" she whispered, but my mouth was too full to answer. "I'll be just a moment," she called, and as she closed the door behind her and moved toward my bed I began breaking the wax lips and candy necklaces pulled from pile No. 2. These were the second-best things I had received, and while it hurt to destroy them it would have hurt even more to give them away. I had just started to mutilate a miniature box of Red Hots when my mother pried them from my hands, accidentally finishing the job for me.

BB-sized pellets clattered onto the floor, and as I followed them with my eyes she snatched up a roll of Necco Wafers.

"Not those," I pleaded, but, rather than words, my mouth expelled chocolate, chewed chocolate, which fell onto the sleeve of her sweater. "Not those, not those."

She shook her arm, and the mound of chocolate dropped onto my bedspread. "You should look at yourself," she said. "I mean, really look at yourself."

Along with the Necco Wafers she took several Tootsie Pops and a half dozen caramels wrapped in cellophane. I heard her apologize to the Tomkeys for her absence, and then I heard my candy hitting the bottom of their bags.

"What do you say?" Mrs. Tomkey asked.

And the children answered, "Thank you."

While I was in trouble for not bringing my candy sooner, my sisters were in more trouble for not bringing it at all. We spent the early part of the evening in our rooms, then one by one we eased our way back upstairs, and joined our parents in front of the TV. I was the last to arrive, and took a seat on the floor beside the sofa. The show was a Western, and even if my head had not been throbbing I doubt I would have had the wherewithal to follow it. A posse of outlaws crested a rocky hilltop, squinting at a flurry of dust advancing from the horizon, and I thought again of the Tomkeys, and of how alone and out of place they had looked in their dopey costumes. "What was up with that kid's tail?" I asked.

"S-h-h," my family said.

For months I had protected and watched over these people, and now, with one stupid act, they had turned my pity into something hard and ugly. The shift wasn't gradual but immediate, and it provoked an uncomfortable feeling of loss. We hadn't been friends, the Tomkeys and I, but still I had given them the gift of my curiosity. Wondering about the Tomkey family had made me feel generous, but now I would have to shift gears, and find pleasure in hating them. The only alternative was to do as my mother had instructed, and take a good look at myself. This was an old trick, designed to turn one's hatred inward, and while I was determined not to fall for it, it was hard to shake the mental picture snapped by her suggestion: Here is a boy sitting on a bed, his mouth smeared with chocolate. He's a human being, but also he's a pig, surrounded by trash and gorging himself so that others may be denied. Were this the only image in the world, you'd be forced to give it your full attention, but fortunately there were others. This stagecoach, for instance, coming round the bend with a cargo of gold. This shiny new Mustang convertible. This teenage girl, her hair a beautiful mane, sipping Pepsi through a straw, one picture after another, on and on until the news, and whatever came on after the news.

28 Soup's New Shoes

by Robert Newton Peck

SUMMARY

Soup and Rob are best friends. They live during a time when hand-me-downs and frugal living are how families get by. Soup has just returned from a shopping trip to Burlington—the biggest city in the entire state of Vermont. His purchase of a new pair of sturdy orange shoes briefly tests the strength of the boys' friendship.

SOURCE: Soup *is the first in a touching and hilarious series by Robert Newton Peck. Peck credits his teachers, friends, and family for inspiring his work.*

READING SESSION: 1

(If you need to divide the story into two sessions because of time, stop after the 5th paragraph on page 148, ending with "... or if I went to his.")

LANGUAGE AND VOCABULARY

Discuss with students how friendship can be full of both competition and compassion. Share the following diagram with students. Have them discuss examples of how friends compete and how friends can show each other compassion.

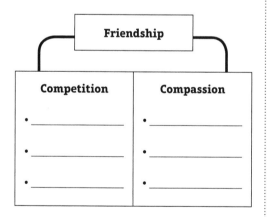

THINK, TALK, AND WRITE ABOUT TEXT

How would you describe Rob and Soup's friendship? What are some examples to support your thinking?

What does Soup mean when he says, "it's like having birds between your toes"?

Why do you think Soup gave Rob his shoes?

What was it that caused Rob to break down and cry? Was it more than the shoes? What do you think was going on with him?

Has there ever been a time when you thought life wasn't fair? **How** did you cope?

How do you think Soup felt as he gave his shoes to Rob? Might there have been mixed feelings? What do you think they were?

Reread the five paragraphs beginning with "Soup has a way of taking his time . . . " Ask students what clues do these paragraphs give us about Soup, Rob, and Miss Kelly.

Though this story takes place many years ago, the pain of poverty resonates today. The deep themes of this story may affect some students. **Focus** the discussion on these kinds of feelings as well as the healing power of friendship—and of helping others.

Soup's New Shoes

by Robert Newton Peck

Rob and Soup—whose real name is Luther Vinson—are best friends. They live in a very small town in a corner of Vermont, a very small New England state. Times are tough and money is tight. Most families live on very little. But there is one thing Rob and Soup have in abundance, and it doesn't cost a penny—it's friendship. In this story, their friendship gets tested a bit when Soup comes back from a shopping trip to Burlington, the biggest city in the state.

READ-ALOUD TIP

The power of this read-aloud comes from capturing the dialogue of the boys. Pay attention to the earnest wonder and amazement over Soup's trip. Then try to capture Rob's pain and anguish as well as Soup's compassion and steady comments.

BACKGROUND LANGUAGE

The book is set in rural Vermont in the 1920s, so you will encounter words that are part of the vernacular of people living in a rural setting. Practice reading this excerpt aloud to help familiarize yourself with words that may be dated or location-specific, such as *a trait of his nature* and *farther uproad.*

Hey, I'm back," said Soup. It was Saturday evening, and he'd been gone all day. But now he was standing at the kitchen door in his store clothes and his hair was still combed. Not actually so slicked as to have a part, but it wasn't all mussed up and curly like usual. For Soup, that was combed.

"How was it?" I said, as he came in.

"Great."

"Was it as big as they say?"

"Bigger," said Soup.

"Honest?"

"It's my guess that Burlington has got to be about the biggest place in the whole world."

"How many people did you see, Soup?"

"Oh," said Soup, leaning back in the kitchen chair and looking at the ceiling for guidance, "I must of seen a thousand or a million."

"Gosh, you must have been so busy saying hello to all those folks, you didn't have time to get new shoes."

"Oh, no?"

Soup unbuttoned his coat and took off his hat (the plain one he always wore in winter with the red ear lapper). Then he slowly unbuckled his left overshoe.

"Wait'll you see, Rob. They cost almost three dollars."

"Hurry up. I want to see 'em both."

Soup had a way of taking his time, especially if he knew you wanted him to hurry. It was a trait of his nature that could drive those who waited half crazy. Everybody except Miss Kelly. There was a lady that you'd hardly list as one of your favorite friends. But give Miss Kelly this—she sure could handle Luther Vinson.

A day or so ago, she'd sent some of us up to the blackboard to do a sum.

The rest of the kids merely erased the computations left by the previous scholar. But not Soup. He pulled out a wet rag from his pocket and *washed* his section of the blackboard until it was all black and shiny clean. He then had to let it dry. I wasn't up at the blackboard but in my seat where I could see Miss Kelly's foot under her desk. The way her foot was going tap-tap-tap, I knew that she was not as amused at Soup's standards of cleanliness as I was.

Miss Kelly kept Soup after school. She made him erase every square of the blackboard and dust the erasers. Then he had to wipe out the chalk tray; and on top of all that, wash every single square of blackboard all around the room. After that he had to empty the waste basket.

I'll say this much for Miss Kelly—she wasn't mean. Her role in life was not an easy one, with Soup and me around. So afterward, when the waste basket was empty, Miss Kelly told Soup what a good job he did. She said that she liked him a lot. Then she said that when she liked somebody, she called him Soup. But if she didn't like someone, he got called Luther *no matter who was listening!*

I know all this happened, as I was listening right outside the door. I'd sneaked back inside after we marched out, so I could watch Soup work or maybe get the ruler. But no such luck. There were no yelps of pain. Soup said, "Good night, Miss Kelly." And she said, "Good night, Soup. And you may wish the same to Robert."

Anyhow, getting back to Soup's trip to Burlington, this was what I was thinking about while Soup took his own sweet time to unbuckle both his overshoes. Then he put a toe on a heel and kicked off one, then the other.

"Wow!" I said. "Orange shoes."

"They're supposed to be tan," said Soup, "but I'm glad they look a bit orange."

"They sure do," I said.

"That's not all. Wait'll you hear the music they make."

"They make music?"

"Listen," said Soup.

He got up from the chair and walked around the kitchen. Every step he took in his new orange shoes made notes in sort of a squeaky melody. The left shoe played one tune and the right another. And when he stood stock-still on the floor and moved both, it sounded like some sort of an all-leather orchestra.

"It's like having birds between your toes," said Soup.

"Boy!" I said.

"The best part," said Soup, "is how you *buy* shoes like this. You get to look at your own feet down through an x-ray machine."

"What's an x-ray machine?"

"A machine that lets you look at your own bones."

"For real?"

"Honest," said Soup. "When you try on a new pair, the man at the shoe store takes you over to this machine. You climb up on a platform and put your feet into a little place inside the machine. Then you look down and see your own feet, and they're all green."

"Green?"

"Yeah. There's two other places lower down for the shoe man to look into and also one for your mother to look in. Then the shoe man points at the bones of your feet with a black pointing stick that's inside the x-ray machine."

"What's he do that for?"

"He does that while he tells your mother to see how much room your toes have to grow inside the shoes"

"What's it look like, Soup?"

"You can see all the bones of your toes. They look like a bunch of twigs. And when you wiggle your foot, the bones wiggle too."

Soup took a few more turns around the kitchen in his new orange footwear, making squeaky music with every step. It made me look down at my old shoes, which I'd had a long time. So long they hurt a bit to walk in. My feet were almost as big as Soup's.

We went upstairs to my room and fooled around with Tam, my dog. Then we played lotto, which was something like bingo, until my mother came in and told us how late it was getting. It was almost eight o'clock. So I got on my coat and boots and walked halfway home with Soup. At the halfway point, we said good night. It was real dark. Soup ran for his house and I ran for mine. We always did this for each other, whenever he came to my house or if I went to his.

On Sunday, the next day, we had a thaw. A real hot March day that chased away much of the snow. Above our farm, the hillside that faced south had big round spots of brown earth that got bigger as the day wore on until the meadow was a giant brown-and-white cheese. Holes all over. And all the gray rocks were bare and dry. They looked like sleeping sheep.

Monday morning was warm, too. Seeing as the road to town was dry and not muddy and the sky was clear, Soup and I got packed off to school in just our coats and hats. No mittens, no boots. I had my old shoes, and Soup sported his new orange pair.

"I'll race ya," I said.

We ran down the road. For a while, I was ahead of Soup. Looking back over my shoulder to see how close he was getting, I didn't see the root. It caught the toe of my shoe, and I turned around just as I pitched forward onto the still-frozen gravel of the dirt road. Both my hands were burning, as that's how I broke my fall. Just as Soup caught up to me, I turned my hands over to see all the gritty blood. Trying to get up, I saw that my right shoe was torn. It was damaged so badly that half the rotten old sole was flapping around like the mouth of an alligator we saw in a Tarzan movie. And I could look down and see almost all of my red sock.

Maybe it was because I didn't outrun Soup or because my hands hurt too much to even wipe off the bloody dirt, I started to cry. And seeing Soup's new shoe—standing next to my old one that got all torn up—didn't help. I just sat there in the dirt and bawled.

"Hey," said Soup, squatting down beside me as I blubbered away, "don't cry. Don't cry, Rob. I got a clean hanky."

Soup dried off my eyes and cheeks. I tried to talk, but all that came out of my heaving chest was sob after sob.

I couldn't say anything. Soup was about as careful as he ever could have been as he blotted the blood off my hands. He didn't even rub. He just did it the way my mother would, as light as an angel.

"Why did you have to go and get new shoes, Soup? Why did ya?"

"Don't cry, Rob. Please don't cry. It wasn't my idea to get new shoes. My cousins just took me to Burlington."

"You always get everything," I said between sobs, covering my face with my burning hands. "I don't get nothing, I just get hurt."

"No, you don't," said Soup.

"Yes, I do. If we play baseball, you always get to be batter. And then when we're prize-fighters, I always wind up with the bloody lip." I was ashamed that I was crying so hard, but I just couldn't stop.

"Don't cry."

"I hate you, Soup. I don't want to go to school with you anymore, and I won't play with you anymore."

"Hey, Rob. What's the matter?"

"Look at my shoe. I'm going home. I can't go to school with this old shoe on my foot."

"Sure, you can."

"No, I can't. I can't. I can't."

Now I was really crying and couldn't quit. It was like somebody was shaking me all over, and I couldn't see or talk or even walk. It would have been all right with me to just lie there in the road forever.

"Well," said Soup, taking off his new orange shoes, "maybe you can't wear your old shoes to school, but I sure can."

Soup gave a good yank to the heel of both his shoes, and off they came. Then he took off my old ones and put them on his feet and put his new orange pair on me.

"Get up and walk," said Soup, "or we'll be late for school. You know how Miss Kelly takes on when we're not on time."

"We're always on time, Soup. You and me, we're almost always the first ones there."

"Yeah," said Soup, "and we live farther uproad than just about anybody else."

"We better hurry," I said.

"How do you feel?"

"Okay. Your shoes are a little bit big for me. How do mine feel?"

"Well," said Soup, "one is awful tight, and one is awful loose."

"You didn't have to swap shoes with me, Soup."

"Maybe I just wanted to."

"Yes, but you were looking forward to wearing your new shoes to school and telling everybody about Burlington."

"I know. Hurry up, Rob. Why are you walking so careful?"

"So's I don't scrape your new shoes. I'd feel terrible if I knocked some of the orange off."

"I suppose the orange will come off sometime. Don't matter who does it."

"Gee, Soup. I can't believe it."

"Can't believe what?"

"I can't believe I really got your new shoes on my feet. Boy, are they ever big."

"Won't be long before I outgrow 'em, Rob. I'll even tell my mother ahead of time that they pinch my toe. While they're still orange."

"You will?"

"Sure I will, Rob. And as soon as I outgrow 'em, you know who gets 'em next."

"Me? You mean *me*, Soup?"

"'Course I do. That's what pals are for."

"We're pals, Soup. I'll always be *your* pal."

I don't know how it happened. We were just about to go up the step into the school, when I started to cry again. So we had to stop while Soup wiped my face into a smile. Then he looked me over to see if I was presentable enough to confront Miss Kelly.

"You look fine," said Soup. "Real fine. Your red socks go real good with my orange shoes."

"Thanks, Soup. Thanks a lot."

We ran into the schoolhouse and to our places. I felt like the whole world was looking at my feet. Miss Kelly noticed and smiled at me. And I was one of the very first that she sent up to write. All the way up to the blackboard, the shoes squeaked away like they were as happy as I was. I just felt orange all over.

Soup was right. It was just like having birds between your toes.

29 In My Closet, on the Top Shelf, There Is a Silver Box

by Kwame Alexander

SOURCE: *Kwame Alexander is the author of 18 books and the winner of several awards, including the 2015 John Newbery Medal.*

READING SESSION: 1

SUMMARY

One harmless date night—and, in particular, one heartbreaking moment—is captured in this poem.

LANGUAGE AND VOCABULARY

Explain that as a poet, Kwame Alexander has mastered the power of the words he chooses to tell a vivid story. Kwame Alexander uses two-word lines in this poem. As a warm-up for listening to this poem, share with students the pairs of words from the chart below. Then have them discuss the images, the implications (good and bad), and the feelings that could come from these word pairs.

Word Pairs	Images/Implications/Feelings
clouds, moving	
text, sent	
mother, crying	
clock, ticking	
me, "Let's go."	

THINK, TALK, AND WRITE ABOUT TEXT

What were you feeling at the beginning of the poem?

How did your feelings change during the middle and then at the end of the poem?

Using just a few sentences, **retell** this poem in your own words.

Listen again as I read this poem one more time. Listen for the word pairs that you find the most interesting—the most powerful.

Using Kwame's powerful poem as a model, **write** a poem around an event in your life.

In My Closet, on the Top Shelf, There Is a Silver Box

by Kwame Alexander

This powerful poem recounts a single moment that changed the lives of two people in love.

READ-ALOUD TIP

You'll want to start this poem slowly. Students will not know what's happening—at first. Then increase the pace during the middle. Then toward the end, slow the reading down. Pause at the end of the reading as the poem sinks in. One option is to read the poem one more time before the discussion begins.

Journal, filled
Candy bar, unwrapped
Picture, Kevin
Flower, Kevin
Poems, Kevin
Library card, mine
Naomi Shihab's *What Have You Lost?*, overdue
Saturday, late
Us, movies
Laughing, loving
Later, strolling
Me, "I want chocolate"
Kevin, "You already sweet enough, baby"
Store, closing
We, hurrying
Colliding, customer
Accident, sorry
Guy, angry
Me, craving
Kevin, Hershey
We, pay
Turn, leave
Surprise, a rose,
Pink, favorite
Me, "thanks"
Outside, "Hey!"
Guy, earlier
Kevin, ignore
Hands, holding

Walking, fast
Giant, steps
Me, turn
Guy, points
aims, fires
rips, back
Kevin, drops
candy, sidewalk
Rose, falls
Guy, runs
Blood, runs
Kevin, "you alright?"
Me, "Kevin!"
Eyes, closing
Me, "I Love You"
Kevin, "More than a Kit Kat?"
We, laugh
Sirens, scream
Heart, pierced
Love, bleeds
Hope, dies
Hands, empty
Sweetness of life, gone
What, remains
picture, Kevin
flower, Kevin
candy bar, unopened
locked, away
inside, silver box
top shelf, in my closet

30 Flesh Wound!

by Shea Phillips

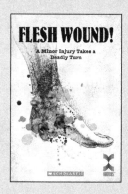

SUMMARY

Bo Salisbury enjoyed playing indoor soccer with friends from church, until one day when he got kicked during a game. What began as a small bruise soon became a life-threatening bacterial infection. Finally, after eight skin grafts and ten days in a coma, Bo Salisbury returned from the brink of death. Today he can run and even play soccer. But doctors still do not know how he got the infection or why it made him so sick.

SOURCE: Flesh Wound! *is a selection from XBOOKS, an informational text program by Scholastic.*

READING SESSIONS: 3

LANGUAGE AND VOCABULARY

Before reading, ask students to work with a partner to list as many types of infections as they can. Then, tell them to listen for the characteristics of the type of infection that is described in "Flesh Wound!"

After reading, use the "Alike But Different" organizer below to help students summarize what they have learned.

Alike But Different: *Bacteria*

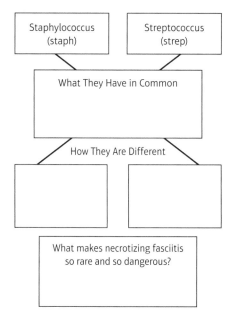

THINK, TALK, AND WRITE ABOUT TEXT

Dr. Murin says, "There are so many mysteries in medicine that we still don't understand." **Think** about the medical mysteries you know that still need to be researched and cured.

Use information from the text to **create a chart** to recount the sequence of events from when Bo Salisbury was injured while playing soccer to the end result you heard at the end of this text. As you do this, talk about each event and how that event led to the next one.

Look back at the sequence-of-events chart you created. Pick one event and **write** a journal entry from Bo Salisbury's point of view.

Flesh Wound!

by Shea Phillips

While playing soccer, Bo Salisbury gets kicked in the ankle, where a bruise quickly forms. But this is no ordinary bruise. Soon, Bo is fighting for his life. Find out what happens to him.

READ-ALOUD TIP

This informational text has an episodic format. The reader needs to find a way to keep students engaged while they are processing and retaining information. When you read the text prior to doing the class read-aloud, decide where you will stop to do RPM—recall, predict, move on. Stop after the first episode and ask students to *recall* something important in what was just read; *predict* what they think will happen next; and, *move on*. The very brief check-in will help students stay engaged.

BACKGROUND LANGUAGE

Students will likely find all the medical or scientific terminology challenging. Highlight and define the terms that are absolutely critical to understanding the text: *strep bacteria, necrotizing fasciitis* (NF), *skin grafts.*

On Saturdays, Bo Salisbury played indoor soccer with teenagers from his church.

Salisbury was a 43-year-old postmaster in Nevada City, California. He usually played goalkeeper. In that position, he was used to getting bumped and bruised.

Salisbury was in goal on May 9, 1998. It was a typical Saturday. He had a cold, but that wasn't going to slow him down. At one point during the game, players crowded around the goal, fighting for the ball. Salisbury blocked a shot. But on his follow-through, the shooter accidentally kicked Salisbury on the left ankle. Salisbury limped off the field with a stinging bruise.

The next day, the pain was worse. Salisbury took some aspirin. Then he had lunch at a local Chinese restaurant. By 2:00 P.M., his ankle was killing him. Salisbury went to the emergency room at a nearby hospital. A doctor examined Salisbury's ankle, which was turning red. The doctor decided it was just a nasty contusion, or bruise. He gave Salisbury some painkillers and sent him home.

By Monday morning, Salisbury was in terrible pain. He was sweating and felt sick to his stomach. His leg throbbed. He went to see his doctor, who sent him straight to the hospital. He told the doctors there that he felt like he was dying.

Doctors at the hospital were concerned. It was clear that Bo Salisbury had more than a bruise. But what was causing his terrible symptoms? The doctors needed a diagnosis—and fast.

They took Salisbury's blood pressure. It was dropping quickly.

They examined his leg. A blue-gray bruise had begun to spread out from his ankle. Doctors took a blood sample to test for a bacterial infection. While they waited for the results, they gave Salisbury an antibiotic drug to fight the infection.

· · · · ·

Salisbury continued to get worse. He slipped in and out of consciousness. He prepared himself to die. He told his teenage daughter not to cry and made her promise to study for her final exams. "There's nothing anyone can do for me now," he said.

Salisbury's doctors didn't know what to do. But they knew someone who might.

Salisbury would have to go to another hospital. The weather was too stormy for a helicopter, so Salisbury was wheeled to an ambulance. It raced to the University of California (UC) Davis Medical Center.

Meanwhile, like in a scene from a horror movie, the bruise continued to creep up Salisbury's leg.

When he arrived at UC Davis Medical Center, Bo Salisbury was met by Dr. Susan Murin. She heads a team of doctors at the center's intensive care unit (ICU). That's the part of the hospital that treats the sickest patients. When they arrive, most of Murin's patients are close to death. But four out five of them get better and walk out alive.

"Working in the ICU is never boring," says Dr. Murin. "You see everything down here. You're more than a specialist. You have to be able to treat everything. You never know who is going to come through that door."

Minutes after Salisbury arrived at the hospital, Murin and a team of doctors were at his bedside. One of the doctors was infectious-disease specialist Dr. Jeff Jones.

Salisbury was given oxygen and fluids. He could still talk, but he was failing fast.

Salisbury's case was confusing, even for Murin and Jones. Salisbury had kept in great shape. He had no history of illness. But in two days, he had gone from perfect health to the verge of death. What was wrong?"

Murin carefully examined Salisbury's leg. The dark bruise was spreading slowly up his leg. To Murin, the leg looked like "rotten meat." The flesh felt cold to the touch. A normal infection would be red and warm. This leg wasn't getting blood. That led Martin to suspect that Salisbury had a blood clot. Perhaps the clot was keeping blood from flowing to his leg.

Murin ordered an ultrasound. This is a test that uses sound waves to create a picture of a person's insides. The image showed no blood clot. Then a call came from the hospital Salisbury had visited first. Salisbury's blood test results were in. They showed traces of a bacteria called *Streptococcus pyogenes*.

Murin had her diagnosis. Inside Salisbury's body, a strep infection was eating his flesh.

The test results proved to Dr. Murin and Dr. Jones that Salisbury had a life-threatening disease called necrotizing fasciitis (NF). NF is usually caused by the strep bacteria.

About 15 to 30 percent of all people carry strep in their bodies. In most people, strep is relatively harmless. It can cause common illnesses like strep throat or impetigo. Those diseases are easily cured with antibiotics. But in extremely rare cases, strep can lead to NF, which is far more deadly. Only 500 to 1,500 Americans get NF every year. But more than one in five of them die from it.

People call NF the "flesh-eating disease" for good reason. Strep can consume human flesh.

Murin had seen NF only once before. But she knew how it killed. The strep bacteria produce toxins— poisons—in a patient's body. The toxins kill the soft tissue, or fascia, below the skin. The bacteria spread fast—about an inch (2.5 centimeters) an hour. And they kill tissue as they grow. If left untreated, NF can kill the patient.

Salisbury was already close to death. The antibiotics weren't working. His blood pressure kept dropping. He needed more and more oxygen. Murin was in a race against time.

"This thing travels fast," Salisbury said later. "In 72 hours, you kill it—or it kills you."

• • • • •

Bo Salisbury had been in Dr. Murin's care for just two hours. She could see that he was getting sicker by the minute.

Salisbury was given antibiotics. But the drugs couldn't stop the infection that was racing through his body. Murin knew the infected flesh would have to be cut out on Salisbury's body. She called a surgeon and pleaded with him to operate of Salisbury.

The surgeon agreed. Still, Murin thought Salisbury's chances for recovery were poor. "I honestly thought

he wasn't going to make it," she says. "He's such a nice guy. I was pulling for him. At the very least, I thought they'd have to amputate his leg."

Using special drugs, doctors put Salisbury into a coma. That's a state of deep unconsciousness. In a coma, his body could handle the shock of what was coming next.

Surgeons raced against the bacteria as it spread up Salisbury's leg. The doctors cut into Salisbury's skin and began to slice off the infected tissue. In some places, they had to cut all the way down to the bone.

Finally, they were sure they had removed all of the bacteria. They'd also had to remove most of the flesh from Salisbury's toes to his hip. But when Salisbury left the operating room, he still had his leg—and his life.

Bo Salisbury woke up from the coma ten days later. Doctors had spent a week replacing the flesh on his leg with skin grafts. They'd peeled flesh from other parts of Salisbury's body. They sewed the flesh onto his leg. Salisbury felt like he had been skinned alive. "I'm all striped now," he jokes. "People stare at me when I wear shorts."

In all, Salisbury underwent eight skin grafts. The treatments left him weak and depressed.

But little by little, Salisbury recovered. He started rehabilitation to strengthen his body. He had to re-learn how to do everyday activities. After five months, Salisbury was finally able to go home from the hospital.

Eventually, Salisbury was able to run a few miles a day. He even competed in a five-kilometer (3.11 miles) race. Some Saturdays, you can still find him playing goalie for his church soccer team.

Bo Salisbury sometimes wonders how he got such a rare disease. Strep has no effect on some people, but it can be deadly for others. Even Dr. Murin can't explain exactly why. "There are so many mysteries in medicine that we still don't understand," she says.

31 The Day of the Hunter

by Edward M. Holmes

SUMMARY

This small town has rules when it comes to hunting—rules that are often broken by Lyle Hanscom. One day, the local game warden decides to visit Hanscom at home to see what he's been up to. But when he gets there, the warden does not find what he expected.

SOURCE: *"The Day of the Hunter" was published in* Maine Speaks: An Anthology of Maine Literature, *a fascinating collection of stories all related to the state of Maine.*

READING SESSION: 1

LANGUAGE AND VOCABULARY

"The Day of the Hunter" is set in rural Maine, so the author uses colloquial language to give readers a sense of the society represented in this story. Use the guide below to discuss colloquial language used in "The Day of the Hunter." How does the use of this language affect your understanding of this community?

Colloquialism	Means
dump truck	
ayeah	
bedchamber	
"No, I guess you won't neither."	
mite of trouble	

The author notes that Lyle Hanscom has "unparalleled gall." Discuss what *unparalleled gall* is and whether the author proves Lyle has it.

THINK, TALK, AND WRITE ABOUT TEXT

Think about how the townspeople describe Lyle and his actions. Were his responses to the warden what you would expect from someone with Lyle's reputation? If not, why do you think he was acting this way?

The title of the story is "The Day of the Hunter." **Discuss** who was actually "caught" in this hunting story.

In a story where the character influences the plot, it can be interesting to **examine** what the main character says and what impact that has on you as a reader. Use the "Character Conversations" organizer below to help guide your group in making inferences about Lyle based on things he says.

Character Conversations: Characters, and their thoughts, actions, and words, are an interesting part of any story. Note the words and actions that helped you get to know Lyle Hanscom when reading "The Day of the Hunter." After you highlight something Lyle said, explain the context (event) for what was said, and write in the "In my view" column what this made you think of Lyle.

Said ...	Context (Event)	In my view ...
"Don't mind a bit, Joey. Look at what you want."	Lyle says this to the warden when he comes to see if Lyle has poached a deer.	This made me think that maybe the townspeople were wrong about Lyle because he seemed polite to the warden.
"Oh, I know that. I just ask that you don't upset her none. Might bring on another attack."		
"No, I guess you won't neither."		
"Call it a freak notion if you want, but I ain't giving no man permission to snoop in my cellar."		
"I ain't crawled underneath lately looking for no cellar, but of course you might find one."		

Write the entry you think the warden would have made in his police log after his encounter with Lyle.

The Day of the Hunter

by Edward M. Holmes

When a deer was killed out of season, everyone knew it had to be Lyle Hanscom who did it. So the game warden decides to pay him a visit and search his house for the deer. What will the warden find?

READ-ALOUD TIP

When reading aloud a story where the setting influences all other elements, it helps to practice beforehand in order to capture the setting's rich language. In this story, there are Maine terms ("ayeah") as well as rural language ("mite of trouble"). Practice the colloquial language until you are comfortable reading it with the pronunciation and cadence that frames this story. Listening to a Down East humorist or watching an episode of *Murder, She Wrote* might help with the pronunciation.

BACKGROUND LANGUAGE

Show students a map of Maine to help them establish this rural setting. The key vocabulary word is *gall*. Understanding Lyle Hanscom's "unparalleled gall" will help them think about whether Lyle's real target was the warden.

Everyone in his hometown somewhere east of the Penobscot River knew that, in or out of season, Lyle Hanscom and deer hunting were inseparable. Yet for years no one had been able to garner enough evidence to convict him. Once several casual spectators, stopping along the highway to watch three deer at the other side of a wide field, not only heard the shot that felled one of the animals, but saw a man run from a spruce grove and drag the game back into the woods.

No one could quite recognize the man in the strange, drooping overcoat he was wearing, nor was anyone able to track him with success. Still, the town's rumor mill, talk of someone's cooperative dump truck—which circled the town for an hour or two with a dead deer lying in the back—and public confidence in Lyle Hanscom's unparalleled gall unofficially pinned the deed on him.

Small wonder, then, that the nearest game warden kept a sharp watch, as often as he could, on Hanscom. The time came when the officer felt he had something on his man. Somehow word had leaked to him that Lyle had sneaked home with fresh-killed meat. When the warden drove up to Hanscom's, he could see the suspect watching him from one of the front windows. Hanscom met the law at the door and admitted him without a search warrant.

"I'd like to have a look around, if you don't mind, Lyle."

"Don't mind a bit, Joey. Look at what you want," Hanscom said. "There's just one thing I want to ask of you."

"Ayeah."

"My mother in there in the bedchamber is sick. She had a heart attack."

"Is that so? I'm sorry to hear that."

"Well, you can understand I don't want nothing done that would upset her. You can see that, can't you, Joey?"

"I got to look in that room same as any other, Lyle."

"Oh, I know that. I just ask that you don't upset her none. Might bring on another attack."

"I'll be careful," Joey said, and began making his search of the kitchen, the three small rooms, and the attic. He apologized to Mrs. Hanscom for intruding upon her, looked under the bed, and would have searched the closets if he could have found any. Back in the kitchen, Lyle sat in a rocking chair, smoking his pipe. "Guess I'll have to take a look in the cellar," the warden said.

"No, I guess you won't neither," Lyle said.

"How's that?"

"I let you in here nice as could be, Joey, and give you a chance to look around. You know as well as I do, I didn't have to. I even let you look in the room where my mother was laying sick, but I draw a line at the cellar. I don't want no game wardens or nobody else poking around in no cellar of mine."

"You know I don't have to go above two miles, " Joey said, "to get me a warrant."

"Then you'll just have to do it that way," Lyle said. "Call it a freak notion if you want, but I ain't giving no man permission to snoop in my cellar."

So Joey did it that way. When he came back, he presented Lyle with the warrant, and Lyle read it, every word as slow as he could. "All right, warden. I see I'll have to let you look in the cellar if you're bound and determined to do it. You may have a mite of trouble, though, so far as I know, this house is built on cedar posts. I ain't crawled underneath lately looking for no cellar, but of course you might find one."

It was built on cedar posts, too, about a foot off the ground, and that was the end of that, except, of course, that Lyle Hanscom's mother has given him notice, if he ever puts a fresh-killed deer in bed with her again, heart attack or no heart attack, she will turn him over to the warden herself.

32 The Hangman

by Maurice Ogden

SUMMARY

In this lengthy poem, divided into four sections, a Hangman terrorizes a town, executing its citizens one by one. At first, the townspeople try to protest against the unfair treatment, but fear soon silences them. Finally, only the narrator is left, and there's no one around to defend him.

SOURCE: *"The Hangman" first appeared in Masses and Mainstream magazine in 1951. It was written by Maurice Ogden, and has often been used to teach students about the importance of standing up for others.*

READING SESSION: 1

LANGUAGE AND VOCABULARY

Authors choose their words carefully. Highlight all the words or phrases used to describe the Hangman.

Appearance Words
buckshot eye

Attitude Words
diffident air

Discuss how the words help the reader create an image of the Hangman that is consistent with the central theme of the poem.

THINK, TALK, AND WRITE ABOUT TEXT

As you listen to each section read aloud, **write notes** in your Triple Entry Journal to help you remember the details of each section of the poem.

I noticed …	This made me think/ wonder about …	After more reading and talking, I now think …

Use the details you have noted to discuss the following prompts.

- How does the poet's repetition of these lines help lead the reader to the central theme of the text?

   "So we gave him way, and no one spoke,

   Out of _____ for his Hangman's cloak."

- In what ways do the individual sections of the poem contribute to the central theme of the whole poem?

- How does the structure of the poem influence the mood of the poem?

- Edmund Burke said, "The only thing necessary for the triumph of evil is for good men to do nothing." How does this quote connect to the theme of "The Hangman"?

Compare an animated version from YouTube to the written text. Is the impact different?

Write a one-paragraph summary that states the author or narrator's point of view and explains how the author of "The Hangman" makes that point of view clear to the reader.

The Hangman

by Maurice Ogden

A Hangman comes into town and builds his gallows next to the courthouse. At first, the townspeople question his motives, but as he hangs various people day by day, they soon cower away in fear. Will no one stand up for their own rights or the rights of their fellow man?

READ-ALOUD TIP

Because of the poem's length, you will probably need to pause after each section and give students time to write a quick reflection. Reading this poem invites you to take on the voice of the narrator and change the voice to a challenging, sarcastic tone for the Hangman. The tone is ominous and the narrator's voice changes from informative (section 1) to explanatory (section 2) to accusatory (section 3) to defensive (section 4).

BACKGROUND LANGUAGE

The poet uses descriptive language, so listeners will be able to visualize the Hangman, the gallows, and the community in spite of some unknown words. Students will need to know the words *scaffold* and *gallows*, as the meanings of these words may not be a part of their background knowledge.

1.

Into our town the Hangman came,
Smelling of gold and blood and flame,
And he paced our bricks with a
    diffident air
And built his frame on the
    courthouse square.

The scaffold stood by the
    courthouse side,
Only as wide as the door was wide;
A frame as tall, or little more,
Than the capping sill of the
    courthouse door.

And we wondered, whenever we had
    the time,
Who the criminal, what the crime,
That Hangman judged with the
    yellow twist
Of knotted hemp in his busy fist.

And innocent though we were,
    with dread
We passed those eyes of buckshot lead;
Till one cried: "Hangman, who is he
For whom you raise the gallows-tree?"

Then a twinkle grew in the buckshot eye,
And he gave us a riddle instead of reply:
"He who serves me the best," said he,
"Shall earn the rope on the gallows-tree."

And he stepped down, and laid his hand
On a man who came from another land.
And we breathed again, for
    another's grief
At the Hangman's hand was our relief.

And the gallows-frame on the
    courthouse lawn
By tomorrow's sun would be struck
    and gone.
So we gave him way, and no one spoke,
Out of respect for his Hangman's cloak.

2.

The next day's sun looked mildly down
On roof and street in our quiet town
And, stark and black in the
  morning air,
The gallows-tree on the
  courthouse square.

And the Hangman stood at his
  usual stand
With the yellow hemp in his busy hand;
With his buckshot eye and jaw like a pike,
And his air so knowing and businesslike.

And we cried: "Hangman, have you
  not done,
Yesterday, with the alien one?"
Then we fell silent, and stood amazed:
"Oh, not for him was the gallows raised."

He laughed a laugh as he looked at us:
"Did you think I'd gone to all this fuss
To hang one man? That's a thing I do
To stretch the rope when the rope
  is new."

Then one cried, "Murderer!"
  One cried, "Shame!"
And into our midst the Hangman came
To that man's place. "Do you hold,"
  said he,
"With him that was meant for the
  gallows-tree?"

And he laid his hand on that one's arm,
And we shrank back in quick alarm,
And we gave him way, and no one spoke
Out of fear of his Hangman's cloak.

That night we saw with dread surprise
The Hangman's scaffold had grown
  in size.
Fed by the blood beneath the chute,
The gallows-tree had taken root;

Now as wide, or a little more,
Than the steps that led to the
  courthouse door,
As tall as the writing, or nearly as tall,
Halfway up on the courthouse wall.

3.

The third he took—we had all
  heard tell—
Was a usurer and infidel,
And "What," said the Hangman, "have
  you to do
With the gallows-bound, and he a Jew?"

And we cried out: "Is this one he
Who has served you well and faithfully?"
The Hangman smiled: "It's a
  clever scheme
To try the strength of the gallows-beam."

The fourth man's dark, accusing song
Had scratched out comfort hard and long;
And "What concern," he gave us back,
"Have you for the doomed—the doomed
  and Black?"

The fifth. The sixth. And we cried again:
"Hangman, Hangman, is this the man?"
"It's a trick," he said, "that we
  Hangmen know
For easing the trap when the trap
  springs slow."

And so we ceased, and asked no more,
As the Hangman tallied his bloody score;
And sun by sun and night by night,
The gallows grew to monstrous height.

The wings of the scaffold opened wide
Till they covered the square from side
  to side;
And the monster cross-beam,
  looking down,
Cast its shadow across the town.

4.

Then through the town the
    Hangman came
And called in the empty streets
    my name—
And I looked at the gallows soaring tall
And thought: "There is no one left at all

For hanging, and so he calls to me
To help pull down the gallows-tree."
And I went out with right good hope
To the Hangman's tree and the
    Hangman's rope.

He smiled at me as I came down
To the courthouse square through the
    silent town,
And supple and stretched in his busy hand
Was the yellow twist of the hempen strand.

And he whistled his tune as he tried
    the trap
And it sprang down with a ready snap—
And then with a smile of awful command,
He laid his hand upon my hand.

"You tricked me, Hangman!"
    I shouted then,
"That your scaffold was built for
    other men.
And I no henchman of yours," I cried.
"You lied to me, Hangman, foully lied!"

Then a twinkle grew in his buckshot eye:
"Lied to you? Tricked you?" he said.
    "Not I.
For I answered straight and I told
    you true:
The scaffold was raised for none but you.

"For who has served more faithfully
Than you with your coward's hope?"
    said he.
"And where are the others that might
    have stood
Side by side in the common good?"

"Dead," I whispered; and amiably
"Murdered," the Hangman corrected me;
"First the alien, then the Jew . . .
I did no more than you let me do."

Beneath the beam that blocked
    the sky,
None had stood so alone as I—
And the Hangman strapped me, and no
    voice there
Cried "Stay" for me in the empty square.

33 The Sunday School Bombing/ Ballad of Birmingham

by Dudley Randall

SOURCE: *Dudley Randall was both a skilled poet and a successful publisher. He founded Broadside Press in 1965 and published the work of many famous African American poets.*

READING SESSIONS: 2
(one session for each passage)

SUMMARY

A magazine article reports on a Black church in Birmingham, Alabama, that has been destroyed by a bomb. Inside the church, at the time of the bombing. Sunday School classes were just ending. Four young girls who were in the bathroom were killed.

In "The Ballad of Birmingham," this horrific incident is told through the eyes of a mother of one of the little girls killed.

LANGUAGE AND VOCABULARY

Share the chart below. You may do it as a group activity or ask students to make their own charts. Before hearing the article, ask students to share what they know about Birmingham and the Civil Rights movement. Then list what they have learned from hearing the article. Encourage them to share questions or opinions. After listening to the "Ballad of Birmingham," ask them to share what new thoughts they have.

What I know . . .	What I learned . . .	Thoughts I now have . . .

THINK, TALK, AND WRITE ABOUT TEXT

What were some of the feelings expressed in this article? How did the article make you feel?

There were more than four little girls killed that day. **Who** else lost their lives that day? How?

When listening to the "Ballad of Birmingham," **ask yourself**, who is narrating the ballad?

What was the ironic tragedy of this ballad?

The Sunday School Bombing

Sunday morning, September 15, 1963, was cool and overcast in Birmingham. Sunday School classes were just ending at the 16th Street Baptist Church. Three 14-year-old girls, Carole Robertson, Cynthia Wesley, Addie Mae Collins, and 11-year-old Denise McNair were in the bathroom in the basement when the bomb exploded at 10:22 A.M.

READ-ALOUD TIP

This is a powerful pair of texts. It shows this country's long struggle with racial unrest. Emphasize the emotions from the quotes in the article—the panic, rage, despair, and disbelief.

BACKGROUND LANGUAGE

Point out to students that the article was written in 1963 and that the language in the article reflects the language of the times. African Americans, for example, are referred to as "Negroes," a commonly used term at that time.

Inside the church, a teacher screamed, "Lie on the floor! Lie on the floor!" Rafters collapsed, a skylight fell on the pulpit. Part of a stained glass window shattered. A man cried: "Everybody out! Everybody out!" A stream of sobbing Negroes stumbled past twisted metal folding chairs, past splintered wooden benches, past shredded songbooks and Bibles. A Negro woman staggered out of the Social Dry Cleaning store shrieking, "Let me at 'em! I'll kill 'em!" Then she fainted.

Police cars poured into the block. Rescue workers found a seven-foot pyramid of bricks where once the girls' bathroom stood. On top was a child's choir robe. One worker lifted the robe. "Oh, my God," he cried. "Don't look!" Beneath lay the mangled body of a Negro girl.

Bare-handed, the workers dug deeper into the rubble—until four bodies had been uncovered. The head and shoulder of one child had been completely blown off. "Oh, my God!" screamed a girl. "That's my sister! My God—she's dead!" All four girls were dead. The law may have ended segregation. But hatred still lives on.

The church's pastor, the Rev. John Cross, hurried up and down the sidewalk, urging the crowd to go home. Another Negro minister added his pleas. "Go home and pray for the men who did this evil deed," he said. "We must have love in our hearts for these men. Tomorrow we will have a rally for peace." But a Negro boy screamed, "We give love—and we get this!"

A man wept: "My grandbaby was one of those killed! Eleven years old! I helped pull the rocks off her! You know how I feel? I feel like blowing the whole town up!"

The Birmingham police department's six-wheeled riot tank thumped onto the scene and cops began firing shotguns over the heads of the crowd while Negroes pelted them with rocks. Later, Negro youths began stoning passing white cars. The police ordered them to stop. One boy, Johnny Robinson, 16, ran, and a cop shot him dead. That made five dead and 17 injured in the bomb blast.

Several miles away, two young Negro brothers, James and Virgil Ware, were riding a bicycle. Virgil, 13, was sitting on the handlebars. A motor scooter with two 16-year-old white boys aboard approached from the opposite direction. James Ware, 16, told what happened then: "This boy on the front of the motor scooter turns and says something to the boy behind him, and the other reaches in his pocket and he says, *Pow! Pow!* with a gun twice. Virgil fell and I said, get up Virgil, and he said, I can't, I'm shot."

And so six died on a Sunday in Birmingham.

Ballad of Birmingham

by Dudley Randall

"Mother dear, may I go downtown
Instead of out to play,
And march the streets of Birmingham
In a Freedom March today?"

"No, baby, no, you may not go,
For the dogs are fierce and wild,
And clubs and hoses, guns and jails
Aren't good for a little child."

"But, mother, I won't be alone.
Other children will go with me,
And march the streets of Birmingham
To make our country free."

"No, baby, no, you may not go,
For I fear those guns will fire.
But you may go to church instead
And sing in the children's choir."

She has combed and brushed her night-
dark hair,
And bathed rose petal sweet,
And drawn white gloves on her small
brown hands,
And white shoes on her feet.

The mother smiled to know her child
Was in the sacred place,
But that smile was the last smile
To come upon her face.

For when she heard the explosion,
Her eyes grew wet and wild.
She raced through the streets
of Birmingham
Calling for her child.

She clawed through bits of glass
and brick,
Then lifted out a shoe.
"O, here's the shoe my baby wore,
But, baby, where are you?"

34 Bird in a Cage

by John Malcolm

SUMMARY

Maria Reyes has grown up in gang life. By age 5, she has lost family members to violence and prison. At 11, she is jumped into a gang. When her high school English teacher Erin Gruwell assigns *The Diary of Anne Frank*, Maria reluctantly reads the book and is surprised that she identifies with Anne. Maria starts to question her place in the world and is forced to make some difficult decisions.

SOURCE: *From the book* Life and Death, *which is part of On the Record, a supplemental ELA program featuring paired profiles of fascinating contemporary figures. www.scholastic.com/ontherecord*

READING SESSIONS: 3

LANGUAGE AND VOCABULARY

Engage students in a discussion about the words *respect* and *pledge.* What does it mean to gain or earn respect? What are examples of showing respect? What are examples of showing disrespect? What does it mean to make a pledge? *(Make a promise)* What are some examples of people who make pledges? *(Schools pledge allegiance to the flags, politicians make pledges to help them get elected)*

Have students finish this sentence and discuss: "I wish the governor would make a pledge to _____."

THINK, TALK, AND WRITE ABOUT TEXT

Why would a gang put a new member through such a violent "jumping in" ritual? Why did Maria endure it?

As Maria sat in that courtroom, what were some of the options before her? What might be some of the consequences of those options?

What did Ms. G mean when she said that Maria might find herself in the book about Anne Frank? Did Maria see herself? How?

Ms. G suggested that education might be a "way out" for Maria. What did she mean by that?

How do you think education changed Maria's life? How did education change her Dad's life?

You may wish to have students **write** a personal response to this question: In order to do what she felt was right, Maria had to break the trust her fellow gang members had in her. Have you ever felt torn between your loyalty to friends or family members and the desire to do the right thing?

Bird in a Cage

by John Malcolm

Maria Reyes had a choice to make. Sitting in a courtroom with all eyes on her, and the weight of life and death on her mind, she was about to choose whether to protect her family at any cost. Having grown up in the tough neighborhoods of East Los Angeles, Maria had experienced violence and heartache at an early age. She felt ready for anything. But when a new teacher appeared in Maria's 9th grade English classroom, everything she thought she knew was turned upside down. What would Maria do, and where would she turn?

READ-ALOUD TIP

In this narrative nonfiction text, Maria goes through many stages of introspection as she examines her life and questions whether there is another way to live. Use a hard tone when Maria talks about her life and gang membership, then change to a softer, questioning voice to help listeners separate the details of Maria's life from her thinking.

BACKGROUND LANGUAGE

Many students will have heard of the Holocaust, Nazis, World War II, and Anne Frank and her writing. It is critical that students know something about Anne Frank's life and death to understand the powerful impact of her words on Maria's life.

The court officer stepped into the lobby and called her name. *Here we go,* Maria thought. She followed the officer inside and walked the lonely center aisle to the witness stand.

The previous spring, Maria had been jumped by several members of a rival gang. She and her best homeboy, Paco, had tracked them down, and Paco had shot one of them. It was payback, the oldest rule of gang life.

A member of the rival gang had been arrested for the murder, and now he was on trial. Maria and Paco had been subpoenaed as witnesses, and they both planned to testify that the innocent defendant had been the shooter.

When Maria was seated in the witness stand, she looked around the courtroom. One side was filled with her homies, the members of her gang. They had pledged their lives to protect each other. The members of the rival gang, who sat on the other side of the courtroom, had made the same pledge to their fellow members.

As Maria scanned the courtroom, she made eye contact with an African American woman. The woman had tears on her face and a young daughter on her lap. Could she be —?

Maria was in court to testify that an innocent guy was guilty of murder, and here was his mother. Maria tried to push the image from her head. She had a job to do. She was there to fulfill the code of her family and the gang—protect your own. But she couldn't help seeing her own mother in the woman's sad face, and herself as the little girl.

Protect your own. It was that simple.

Maria looked over at Paco. She noticed he didn't look nervous at all.

He was completely positive that she would lie to protect him—even if it meant sending an innocent man to prison. Her whole gang expected her to identify the rival gang member as the shooter.

She could hear her father's advice ringing in her head. He had grown up in the gang and remained loyal, even in prison. He had already told her she needed to lie for Paco.

But recently Maria had felt her loyalty shaken. New ideas were taking root, planted by new friendships at school and the books her English teacher kept assigning. Maria had begun asking herself questions: *Does it have to be this way— hating and fighting and shooting and dying? Could there be something better? Could I choose something better?*

But if she told the truth, she knew she might pay a terrible price. If she named Paco as the murderer, her own gang would probably turn on her. They might even kill her.

Maria tried to act cool as the lawyers began laying down questions. "Why did those guys attack you? Where were you on the night of the shooting? Who were you with?" Maria answered each one. Her gaze shifted between the two sides of the courtroom.

The questions pushed Maria toward the point of no return. Should she uphold the code of the gang? Or should she speak the truth and deal with the consequences?

Lives—including her own—hung in the balance.

For Maria, joining the gang was never really a choice. Gang life was part of her world, from her earliest memories on. She had been born in East Los Angeles, a tough neighborhood with a deep history of poverty and crime. East L.A. was a gritty, ragged place. Swirls of gang graffiti layered bridges and walls. Steel bars and metal gates sealed off houses and shops from break-ins. Broken beer bottles sparkled in the gutters, and weeds overran empty lots.

But Maria didn't know anything different. East L.A. was home.

Her dad and grandfather were *veteranos*—veterans in their Latino gang. Her dad had once dreamed of being a boxer, but most dreams died in East L.A. Her mother was a great cook and a hard worker, but she never got past second grade.

For her fifth birthday, Maria had hoped for a mountain bike. Instead she opened a box to find a pair of shiny red boxing gloves and a note from her dad: "Life is tough. When it knocks you down, I want you to get up swinging." Maria took his words to heart.

Shortly after that birthday, her family visited her grandparents' house. Her mother tried to catch Maria to braid her hair; maybe even put a dress on the little tomboy. Maria escaped by climbing the tree in the front yard, out of her mom's reach.

She was still hiding in the tree when she heard sirens closing in. Her older cousin was coming up the street. She liked him a lot. He was tall and strong and told her bedtime stories. As he approached the house, Maria heard five shots. Her cousin fell to the concrete, shot by police for reasons that never became clear. He died shortly after, another victim of gang life in East L.A.

Maria was still in grade school when the violence hit even closer to home.

Her father was arrested for a gang-related crime he didn't commit. The judge sentenced him to ten years in a maximum-security prison.

Overnight, Maria's mother was left alone to raise three young kids. She worked three jobs, day and night. She cleaned the homes of rich people, scrubbed toilets at big hotels, and sewed fancy clothes in sweatshop factories. Even so, she struggled to pay the bills and keep food on the table. "We don't have the luxury of crying," Maria remembered her grandfather saying. "Because for people like us, if we started, we'd be crying for a lifetime."

Maria wasn't much for crying, anyway. Whatever sadness or despair she felt quickly turned to anger. She would fight with anyone, no matter the punishment. In the fourth grade, she was expelled from a school for punching a teacher.

Maria was short, but by age 11 she had proven she was plenty tough. She was sitting on the porch one summer evening when a member of her father's gang walked up. "Do it now?" he asked her.

Maria nodded. She wasn't scared. She didn't even feel excited. Joining the gang was just the next step in growing up, and it was time to get it done. She was about to get "jumped in"—endure a major beating to earn her place in the gang.

Gang members gathered in an alley across the street from Maria's house. For the first round, a group of older girls circled around her. Maria knew she wasn't supposed to fight back. That was the custom. But when someone slugged her in the nose, her instincts kicked in. She threw a punch.

For round two, gang members formed two facing lines—ten *cholos* on the right, ten *chicas* on the left. Maria's mission was to pass between them. This time she could return the punches and kicks. But she had to be standing at the end.

She strode into the human tunnel. She ducked and battled while taking blow after blow. She fell near the end and someone stomped on her leg. She fought her way to her feet and stumbled to the finish.

To Maria, the ten-minute ordeal felt like it had taken two hours. Her nose was broken. One of her eyes was swelling shut. At the hospital, doctors found she had a broken arm and leg. But the pain was worth it—she was now a warrior like her dad. She belonged to the gang, and the gang belonged to her.

* * * * *

In 1992 Maria and her family moved from East L.A. to Long Beach, a city 20 miles south of downtown Los Angeles. Its neighborhoods are a patchwork of white, Latino, black, and Asian communities.

Maria brought her gang connections with her. She was only 12, but she was already a "working soldier"—an active member in the gang. She wore the belt buckle and the colors, with the bandanna dangling from the back pocket of her jeans.

Maria refused to hang back like many of the older girls in the gang. She belonged to a new generation of *chicas* who were determined to act as tough as the guys. She fell right into step dealing drugs, selling guns, and fending off challenges from rival gangs.

Before her one-year anniversary in the gang, Maria had already been

 Riveting Read-Alouds for Middle School © Janet Allen and Patrick Daley, Scholastic Inc.

arrested and locked up. The police caught her in a stolen car. They found drugs in the trunk and in her pockets. The driver of the car had slipped away, and Maria refused to name him. The result was her first stint in a juvenile detention center, or "juvie," as everyone called it. To Maria, getting locked up in the detention center seemed like just another step in growing up.

Maria was one of the youngest girls in the center, but she knew how to protect herself. When older girls tested her, she fought back. It was the only way to make them respect her, she figured.

During what should have been her middle school years, Maria spent more time in juvie than she did in school. She was busted seven times before the age of 14. Cops would see her on the street in gang colors and stop her for questioning. Once she was locked up for carrying a gun. Usually she was busted for violating the terms of her probation.

After one arrest she chose to go to a boot camp program instead of juvie. The boot camp guards enforced military-style discipline—5 A.M. wake-ups, cold showers, push-ups, and laps around the track. The guards barked orders like drill sergeants. "You may be something on the street, but you're nothing in here!" they shouted in her face. Maria couldn't stand it. She left the program and was bused back to juvie.

The early 1990s were an especially harsh time to be a kid in the poor neighborhoods of L.A. and Long Beach. To a lot of people living there, it seemed like a war zone. Latino gangs, black gangs, and Asian gangs battled for control of the streets. They trapped entire neighborhoods in an ongoing cycle of attacks and revenge. Drive-by shootings were daily events.

Gang life was dragging Maria down, but she felt she couldn't leave. It seemed that the only thing she could do was embrace the violence. No one made it out of her neighborhood anyway. She figured she'd be pregnant by 15, like her mom. Or locked up like her dad. Or dead like her cousin and other gang members she'd run with. She had already attended more funerals in her life than birthday parties.

At 14, Maria was arrested for fighting, skipping school, and missing appointments with her parole officer. All three offenses violated her probation. She served another couple of months in juvie and then joined a line of teen gang members in front of a judge. She was dressed in a blue jumpsuit with "Property of Juvenile Hall" stenciled on the back. Her wrists and ankles were cuffed.

The judge stared down at her. "It's clear you haven't learned anything, and I don't know what else to do with you," he said. "You have violated parole time after time. It seems clear you're on your way to becoming a career criminal. If you're ever in my courtroom again, you'll be behind bars until you're 18."

Maria glared back. *Who is this guy kidding?* she thought. *The game is rigged. I'll mess up or the cops will cook up some bogus charge and I'll be right back here. It's just a matter of time.* She thought about giving the judge the finger, but the cuffs made it impossible to lift her hands.

Maria was beyond caring, but her parole officer stood up for her. He got her sentenced to house arrest. Maria would be able to leave home only to go to school. The officer also got her enrolled at Woodrow Wilson High, a school across town. He hoped it would be far enough from her neighborhood to help her stay out of trouble.

Maria was already on edge when she entered Room 203 of Wilson High. Her face was marred by a black eye from a recent fight. Still, the staff had insisted on taking her ID picture—the photo that would appear in the yearbook. She was wearing an ankle monitor so her parole officer could keep track of her movements. And she didn't know a single person at the school.

I might as well wear a prison jumpsuit with "Jump Me" taped on the back, she thought.

She dropped her backpack and took a seat in the back of the room.

She scanned the rest of the ninth-grade remedial English class. It was a mix of blacks, Asians, Latinos, and one white boy who looked terrified. Most of them took buses from the poorer neighborhoods of Long Beach. Several classmates gave Maria suspicious looks, and she glared right back.

But Maria also noticed the defeat in everyone's eyes. They were all no-hopers, kids everybody knew were on the fast track to dropping out. Through the years they had all gotten the message from teachers and classmates— you're lazy, you're dumb, you're doomed. The teachers seemed to *want* them to quit school so they could focus on the "good" students.

The teacher had scribbled "Erin Gruwell" on the chalkboard. She was really young, really white, and faced the class with a goofy smile on her face.

She wore a polka dot dress and a pearl necklace and had chalk dust on her butt. *This lady ain't going to last a week,* Maria thought. That was one truth she knew all classmates could agree on.

Maria had a lot of reasons for hating school. Teachers seemed to get a kick out of making her feel stupid. She remembered her shame when grade-school teachers had made fun of her "Spanglish"—the mix of broken English and Spanish she had grown up speaking. And she had only fallen further and further behind while stuck in the revolving doors of juvenile hall. She was sick of people saying they wanted to help and then turning on her when she disappointed them. *As soon as you catch me messing up, or see what a lousy student I am, you'll bail, too, Erin Gruwell,* Maria thought.

Maria skipped school sometimes, but most days she made the long bus ride to and from Wilson High. When she wasn't in school, her probation required her to be at home.

None of her homies pressured her to run with the gang during this time. When Maria said she didn't want to do something, it was begging for trouble to ask twice.

One day in school, Ms. Gruwell laid down a line of tape on the floor. "We're going to play a game, the Line Game," she announced in her cheery voice. "I'm going to ask a question, and if it applies to you, I want you to stand on the line." She asked a couple easy questions, like "How many of you have the new Snoop Dogg album?" Almost everybody put their toes on the line.

Then the questions became more serious.

Riveting Read-Alouds for Middle School © Janet Allen and Patrick Daley, Scholastic Inc.

"How many of you have been shot at?" Most people touched the line. Then they stepped back for the next question.

"How many of you have a friend or a relative who was or is in juvenile hall or jail?" Maria stepped forward. Many of the other kids put their feet on the line, too.

"How many of you have lost a friend to gang violence?" Almost all of the class stepped on the line. "Two friends?" A few students stepped back. "Three?"

Maria kept her face still as the class played Ms. G's "game." But it struck her as she glanced at the other students: *We're all different colors and come from different gangs and neighborhoods. But we're all dealing with the same stuff. We feel the same pain.* They were like soldiers who had all survived combat. She felt a strange bond with the rest of them.

When it came time to write in her journal, Maria didn't hold back. It was another assignment Ms. G had given the class—to write every day about their experiences, thoughts, and feelings. "Write the truth," she had said.

Want the truth? Maria thought. *Okay, here it is.* "I hate Erin Gruwell. I hate Erin Gruwell," Maria wrote. "If I wasn't on probation, I'd probably shank her."

Maria handed in her journal. She was sure Ms. G would finally call her probation officer. Then it would be a quick trip to juvie and Maria's lousy life would be back on its lousy track.

But nothing happened. When Maria got her journal back she flipped to what she had written. The only comment Ms. G had made was a big smiley face in red pen. Maria looked at it in disbelief. *What is with this woman?* she wondered.

It was that April that Maria got jumped by the rival gang. A few weeks later, she was in the car with her friend Paco when he spotted the gang's leader. Paco got out of the car and, as Maria watched, gunned the guy down. Then Paco turned to Maria and said, "This is for you."

Another man was arrested and charged with the murder. Maria was an eyewitness. She would be subpoenaed to testify at the trial about what she had seen that day.

* * * * *

Maria returned to Room 203 for her sophomore year. She was annoyed that Ms. Gruwell was back again. But she noticed that other kids in class were warming up to their peppy English teacher. Unlike most teachers, Ms. G seemed willing to listen just as much as she talked. Maria still thought she was a fake, but she had to admit that Ms. G was no quitter.

Ms. Gruwell told the class that the theme for the school year was tolerance. She handed out the first book. It was *The Diary of a Young Girl,* by Anne Frank—a true story about a Jewish girl and her family who were forced to hide from the Nazis during World War II.

Maria frowned at the girl's picture on the cover. *Another book about some white kid,* she thought. "Why have I got to read this?" she asked Ms. Gruwell.

"I think you're going to find yourself in the pages of this book," Ms. G replied. Maria laughed in her face.

Maria was still under house arrest. Her mom hadn't been able to pay the electric bill, so there was no TV. Maria had nothing better to do, so she went ahead and started reading. She wanted to prove to Ms. G just how wrong she was. *Find myself in a book? Get real,* Maria thought. *They don't write books about bad girls like me.* But Maria got caught up in the story. Anne Frank had guts and a sense of humor. Maria wondered how Anne's romance with a boy in the hiding place would turn out. And when the Nazis started closing in on Anne, Maria was rooting for her. Maria even found herself talking about the book with Ms. Gruwell.

Then Maria read a passage that hit her like a ton of bricks. While Anne wanders through the family's secret hideout, she feels trapped within its walls like a bird in a cage. She longs to be able to fly away.

The words stunned Maria. That was how *she* felt, trapped in her violent, luckless life. But she'd never had the words to express it.

When she finished the book, Maria held it in her arms and cried. She felt knocked off balance, like someone had tilted her world.

The next day Maria threw the book at Ms. Gruwell. "Why didn't you tell me?"

"Tell you what?" asked the startled teacher.

"Why didn't you tell me Anne Frank didn't make it? She died." Maria was in despair. If a nice girl like Anne couldn't make it, she asked Ms. Gruwell, what hope was there for someone like *her*?

Ms. G stammered, trying to come up with a response. Then a classmate, Darius, spoke up. "She did make it, Maria," he said. "She's going to go on living even after she died because she wrote. How many of our friends have died and they didn't even get an obituary?"

The idea landed hard on Maria. Her dead friends from the gang were gone with hardly anyone to remember them. But one brave girl who shared her story of fear and hope would never be forgotten.

In the weeks that followed, Maria's class studied more about the Holocaust—the systematic murder of millions of Jews by the Nazis. They took a field trip to the Museum of Tolerance in L.A. They sat down to dinner with Holocaust survivors to hear their stories firsthand.

Maria felt something changing in her heart and mind. Here she was, reading about and meeting people who had suffered from the most terrible hatred and violence. Yet even as they faced terror and death, they refused to give up hope for a better world. If they still felt that way after all they been through, why couldn't Maria?

Back in the *barrio,* Maria's gang-mates noticed the changes in her. "I feel you slipping away, a little each day," Paco said. "And at times I have a hard time recognizing you."

Maria tried to explain. New thoughts and feelings were pulling her in a different direction. She felt alone and confused, caught between worlds. But her longtime homies didn't get it. It was like she was speaking a language they didn't understand.

Meanwhile, the trial for the murder of the rival gang member was approaching. Maria knew everyone expected her to protect Paco in court by identifying the innocent defendant as the shooter.

Maria visited her dad in prison a few days before the trial. She loved and trusted him deeply. He told her it was her duty to the gang to lie for Paco's sake. Telling the truth would dishonor the family and put her in danger.

But Maria's soft-spoken mother surprised her. Before Maria left for court, her mother asked her what she was going to say on the witness stand. "I'm going to protect my own . . . you know how it is," Maria answered.

"I know how it is, but why does it always have to be that way?" her mom replied.

In her whole life, Maria couldn't remember her mom ever questioning the gang code. The family had always obeyed it, even though it landed Maria in juvie and her dad in prison. It was the law of the hood, of life.

Why does it always have to be that way? The question echoed in Maria's mind.

In the courtroom, all eyes were on the witness stand. The lawyer finally asked the question Maria had been waiting for: "Who shot the guy?"

Maria felt a kind of peace settle on her. Her thoughts were clear. Doing things the same old way never changed anything. Paco had pulled the trigger this time. Next time, they'd hunt down Paco and shoot him. It would never stop.

Meanwhile, brave people like Anne Frank had looked into the ugly face of hatred and had still been able to feel hope. It was suddenly obvious what Maria had to do.

"Paco did it," she answered. "Paco shot the guy."

The courtroom froze for what seemed like hours. Then the world began to move again. As he was led out of the courtroom, Paco glared at Maria. "Of all people, you're the last person I thought would betray me," he said.

Maria returned home and went back to school. She felt bad about sending Paco to prison and trashing the loyalty she had promised the gang. She knew she had destroyed her ties with them. That

usually meant a trip to the hospital—or the cemetery.

Her father was furious when he found out what Maria had done. "You're no daughter of mine," he told her on the phone. "You have brought shame to the family." But deep down, Maria knew she had made the right choice.

Paco was sentenced to 25 years in prison, and Maria received multiple threats afterward. But nothing happened. No one drove by and blasted her as she got off the bus after school. No one knifed her on the way to the store. It seemed like the word had been passed—*keep your hands off Maria.* Her family's reputation must be protecting her, she figured.

Maria felt like she'd started a race toward a distant finish line, a race she was not sure she would finish. But she was running *her* race. She wasn't just sprinting wherever gang life told her to run. Ms. G was always telling the class that education was the best way out—the way out of being poor, powerless, and in prison. Maria was starting to believe her. She felt a new kind of strength growing inside her.

Two years later, Maria stood in line, listening for her name to be called. For some reason, it reminded her of waiting in line at juvie to see the judge. She wished the judge could see her now, graduating from Wilson High. She was the first in her family to complete high school. In a couple of months, she would be the first to go to college.

Maria heard her name called and walked across the stage in the bright sunlight. Beyond the fence, she heard her family members whooping. She glanced into the audience and spotted her mom and dad. Her dad had gotten out of prison and quit the gang. He and Maria had made their peace. The graduation gown Maria wore felt like wings.

Maria's father went on to earn his General Educational Development certificate. Today he works in a gang prevention program.

Maria and other students in Ms. Gruwell's English class published their writings in a book called *The Freedom Writers Diary*. Money from sales of the book was used to create the Freedom Writers Foundation and help pay for college for the students from Room 203. Their story was later told in the movie *Freedom Writers*.

Maria Reyes graduated from California State University–Long Beach. She travels to schools across the U.S. to share her story with students and teachers.

35 In the Line of Fire: A Story About D-Day

by Tod Olson

SOURCE: *Tod Olson is author of the narrative nonfiction series LOST, and the historical fiction series How to Get Rich. He lives in Vermont with his family, his mountain bike, and his electric reclining chair.*

READING SESSIONS: 4

SUMMARY

It's the summer of 1944. Keith, Tim, and Jake are young American soldiers who have been waiting to invade France and fight the Nazis. Leading up to the invasion, they can't imagine what it will be like. But when D-Day arrives, it is terrifying: death is all around them. Those who survive are celebrated with a parade, but Keith can't imagine what to say to people back home, and he can't forget the horrors he's seen.

LANGUAGE AND VOCABULARY

Use the chart below as you read this extended read-aloud. Ask students to list war words, feeling words, and other thoughts or words they might have.

Before the Battle	During the Battle	After the Battle

THINK, TALK, AND WRITE ABOUT TEXT

The questions below can be used to prompt **discussion**. Some may be asked at any time during the reading. They can be revisited, too.

- Why was the Battle of D-Day so significant to World War II?

- How was preparing for the battle very different from the actual battle?

- What were the soldiers learning—about war, survival, courage?

- How might the phrase "fighting for your country" take on new meaning for these soldiers?

- What did you notice about the actual battle? What feelings did you have?

The soldiers suggested that they might not say much about the war when they go home. **Why** do you think they came to that decision?

Think about the implications of the Battle of D-Day. How might lives have been changed because of it?

In the Line of Fire: A Story About D-Day

by Tod Olson

D-Day was one of the most important events in World War II. On June 6, 1944, American troops sailed to the beaches of Normandy to fight the Germans, who were occupying France. The operation was extremely difficult and made worse when many of the ships ran aground against sandbars, causing the soldiers to have to wade through the cold ocean water before they reached land. In this story, you will hear about this experience from the perspective of "Keith," an American soldier fighting for the Allies during World War II. Keith is fictional—he is not a real person—but his experience in D-Day is based on real events.

READ-ALOUD TIP

There are several voices in this narrative account of real events in World War II. Reading this text will require changing voices so students understand that there are several young soldiers talking, in voices sometimes filled with false bravado. Keith is introspective, so a softer voice will demonstrate that he is being pensive. When an officer steps in, change your voice to represent authority.

BACKGROUND LANGUAGE

Students probably have heard of Hitler but may be unaware of other terms or geographic locations: *D-Day, English Channel, medic, bunker,* and so on.

Introduction

In 1944, the world was at war, and all of America had a hated enemy—Adolf Hitler.

Hitler's Nazi Party had come to power in Germany in 1933, and it ruled with an iron fist. The Nazis believed that they belonged to a race that was better than all other races. They took everyone else's rights away.

Jews were the Nazis' main targets. They weren't allowed to vote. Their businesses were shut down or burned. And, eventually, they were sent to prison camps where they were used as slave labor—or murdered.

In 1939, the Nazi war machine began to move. Nazi tanks rolled through Poland, and World War II began. The next spring, the Nazis took control of Denmark and Norway. Then they overran Belgium, France, and Holland. By the middle of 1940, Germany controlled most of Europe.

The United States finally entered the war in December 1941. Americans joined the British and the Russians to form the Allied Forces. Together, they fought against Germany, Italy, and Japan. But the Germans still held firm in Europe.

The Allies hatched a secret plan called Operation Overlord. Allied soldiers would surprise Germany with a major attack. They would invade Europe and push the Germans out of the countries they'd occupied.

Early in 1944, American troops began arriving in England. Most of them were young, and few had ever fought in battle. They were just kids from places like California and New York and Kansas.

Even the officers—the men who led the troops—lacked experience. Many had been rushed through three-month training courses. They were called 90-day wonders.

By late May, there were two million Americans in England. They knew they were there to invade Europe, but they had no idea when they were leaving or where they were going. They had been told that German soldiers were fierce, and they expected the enemy to fight to the death.

D-Day, the first day of Operation Overlord, was June 6, 1944. On that day, Allied soldiers landed in German-occupied France. They were part of the largest invasion force in history—an invasion that would determine the fate of the world.

This is the story of an American soldier who took part in the D-Day invasion. His name is Keith Taber. Keith is not a real person. But his story is based on what real soldiers went through.

Follow Keith as he finds out what war is really like.

D Minus 32 Days

"Hoooo, yesss! Listen to those things fly! We're coming to get you, Hitler! Better watch your Nazi behind!"

I lifted my face off the beach and spit out some sand.

Tim was on his knees with arms open wide and his head thrown back. His face was turned up to the sky, and tracer bullets burned the air inches above his head.

I grabbed his pack and pulled him down. He landed in a heap next to me. "Are you nuts?" I hissed. "Those are real! Do you want to live to see France, or what?"

"Relax, buddy," he said. "Those are our guys firing. Nobody gets hurt in these things."

Then I heard Lieutenant Mabry: "Let's go! Elbows and knees! Move it up the beach!"

I rested my forehead in the sand. The lieutenant saw me and yelled, "Taber, I know it's early, but we don't take naps during an invasion! Now crawl!"

I looked at Tim. It was 0640, or 6:40 in the morning. It was midnight when we got the order—2400. That's the way it always happened. Seven times we had done this.

Each time was practice, but it sure seemed real. We were hustled out of bed and into the landing ships. I'd have 50 pounds of gear on my back. Then there'd be waves, and I'd usually lose whatever food I'd eaten.

We'd get close to the beach. Then we'd wade out, and the firing would start. They were our guys, but they were shooting real bullets. They wanted us to know what the real thing would be like.

I pulled myself up on my elbows, and little by little I started crawling.

"I'm telling you, man, this is the worst part," Tim grunted, "all the training and waiting and stuff. It's got to be worse than the real thing."

I inched forward like a worm in the sand. A mortar shell blew a hole in the beach to my left, and the sand landed like rain on Tim and me. "Holy—you sure those aren't Germans up there?" I yelled.

"The Germans can't shoot that straight," he said. "Remember, bud, this is as tough as it gets."

Up ahead, a soldier stood up for a second. Then I heard him scream, and he disappeared from sight.

"Medic!" I heard from up ahead, and then, "Keep moving!" It was a sergeant's voice.

We kept crawling. In a minute or two, we saw the soldier. He was lying on his back in the sand, his left arm bleeding onto the beach. Someone had tied a bandana around his shoulder, but the blood still poured out into the sand. People just kept crawling past.

"That's a million-dollar wound," Tim said to me. "He's going home. Doesn't even know the fun he's going to miss."

I turned and lay for a second in the sand, looking back at the guy who was bleeding. His arm was almost half off, and his head was thrown back on the sand, but on his face was the faint hint of a smile.

"Move it out, Taber," barked the lieutenant. "There's no time for rubbernecking!" He shoved my pack, and I rolled sideways. Then I picked myself up and slithered, inch by inch, up the beach.

• • • • •

D Minus 12 Days

"Hey, Country, pound of dark chocolate says we're here another month." Jake leaned over his bunk and looked down on Tim.

"No way," Tim said. "We'll be gone in a week." Tim was from a farm in the South, and Jake grew up in New York City. They were always betting on something or challenging each other to contests. Who could eat a roast beef sandwich faster? Who could shoot a can with an M-1 from 50 yards?

Neither of them could shoot straight, though. Me, I was shooting jackrabbits from 80 yards when I was ten. Shooting Germans couldn't be that much different.

We'd all been drafted a few months back. None of us knew a thing about war, but we'd been through plenty of training together. Jake always called the exercises games. And the guns were toys. No matter how hard it got, it was always games and toys. "They buy expensive toys," he'd say, "and we have to use them."

Jake didn't think much of the Army. But then, he had more to miss than the rest of us. He'd gotten married just before he was drafted—Mary was her name. When he left, she was pregnant. Jake was always joking about stuff, but there was no joking about Mary. You couldn't say a thing about her.

"What do you think, Cowboy?" Jake asked me.

"I don't know," I said, "but I know I'm sick of waiting."

"You've got to admit, though, the food's great," said Tim. "Steak last night—all you can eat—and then ice cream. I ate like a pig."

"That's exactly what the Army thinks you are," said Jake. "They're fattening you up for the kill."

We all laughed. Then Tim replied, "The only pigs dying this month will be German ones. It'll be sausages for dinner in Paris, baby!"

We'd been in England for three months now, and we all knew why— the Germans had taken over the rest of Europe.

There were all these little villages. People there were just minding their own business—then the Nazis came in with tanks and heavy guns. They just ran right over everyone, and now they were making them live under German laws.

What if they didn't stop there? Next thing you know, we'd have German tanks running through Idaho. At least, that's what the Army said. I didn't know if it was true, but it had a lot of us scared. We had to go to France and get the Germans out.

But before we went, the Army had to teach us how to do it, so we attacked empty beaches. They were nice places, too. They probably used to be full of nice British guys getting sunburns with their girlfriends.

But now the beaches were full of holes. We'd blown up one empty beach after another. I couldn't believe all the bullets we'd buried in the sand.

Now that all the training was over, we just waited. We slept in tents near the water. Someone said there were two million guys—English, Americans, Canadians. We all knew we were going to France, but nobody knew exactly when or where.

Parking lots full of tanks just sat there, all of them covered by nets. The nets were painted to look like the ground, so when German planes buzzed over, they wouldn't see a thing.

We had to stay in our camp at all times. A few guys snuck out to a bar once. When they got caught, they were stuck on kitchen duty for a week.

Everyone was going crazy waiting. There were fights every night, and yesterday some nut threw a clip of M-1 shells into a burning barrel. It sounded like the Fourth of July.

Sometimes I went down to the English Channel and just looked out over the water. We had a few miles of water to cross to get to France and all those Germans. Sometimes it seemed like you could spit on their heads from here, and sometimes it seemed like they were a world away.

"Have you ever met a German?" I asked.

Tim and a couple of other guys said no.

"See what I mean?" said Jake. "We're supposed to kill these guys, but who knows what they're even like?"

Two bunks over, a guy named Gabe spoke up. "Ever met anyone from 3 Troops?"

"Nope."

"Those guys are all Jews from Europe, and they hate the Nazis. They say Hitler's just wiping out all the Jews he can find. I spoke to one of them who said he'd never thought of himself as a Jew. He was even in the Hitler Youth, training to become a good Nazi.

"But the Nazis found out that his great-grandfather was a Jew, so they kicked him out of the Hitler Youth. Then his mom and dad disappeared, and some uncle or something helped him sneak out of the country."

"What happened to his folks?"

"He doesn't know, but he figures that they're dead."

"Just because one of them had a Jewish grandfather?"

"I guess."

The tent got quiet. I dreamt that night that the Germans just gave up—that it really was just a game. We bombed the right number of empty beaches, and they had to surrender.

D Minus 3 Days

The model was perfect. They must have spent weeks making it. It was just sand and wood and clay, but it looked like a real beach. There were little tank barriers and little machine gun nests. There were even little bunkers up on the hill. It was supposed to look like the beach we were invading.

The whole thing sat on a table in the briefing tent, and we all stood around it like a bunch of shepherds looking at baby Jesus.

The colonel gave us the plan. It seemed so easy. At least that's the way he made it sound.

We'd be waiting off the coast by dawn, he'd said. At H-Hour minus 70 minutes, our planes would appear, dropping bombs like hail on the Germans.

The battleships would start firing, shells would rake the beach, and then we'd land.

By that time, the Nazis would either be dead or driven out. We'd blow up the barriers and move up the roads with tanks and heavy guns.

Then we'd find our way to Paris, and after that, Berlin—the capital of Germany itself. They had it all figured out.

"The world is watching you, men," the colonel had said. "Millions of lives depend on your work. French ladies want the Nazis out of their homes, Europe wants its freedom back, and three million American boys want to go home to their families."

I felt a nudge. Jake was standing next to me at the model. "That colonel can't read a map," he whispered. "The way home is over the Atlantic Ocean—not across the English Channel."

Tim leaned across me toward Jake. "I'm not leaving without Hitler's head," he said. "If we do, he'll be knocking on *our* doors in a year."

I looked at the miniature beach. The real one was supposed to be 300 yards deep at low tide, with steep hills and cliffs along the back.

On top of the cliffs were German bunkers. They were big square things, each one made of thick concrete. Inside were huge guns—155s, 88s, grenade launchers, you name it. They just sat there, pointing at the beach.

I started thinking the colonel was crazy. Anyone on the beach would be a sitting duck. The only place to take cover was a long, low wall of rocks halfway up the beach. If you made it there, you'd be safe—but only for a while.

"Suppose the Air Force guys don't take out those bunkers," I said.

"Then we're going to get chewed up," said Jake. "That's what I've been telling you. A guy in the 116th said we're cannon food. Nine out of ten won't make it."

"Geez, I'm sorry about that," Tim said. "I'm going to miss you guys."

I laughed, but it was a weak sound, and it died away fast. In a minute, we went outside and walked back to the tent. Nobody spoke.

Suddenly, a shot cracked the silence. A crowd was gathering up ahead. We pushed our way in.

Over a shoulder, I saw a guy on the ground, his rifle lying next to him. His hands gripped his left calf as blood poured from the boot beneath it. Pain squeezed his face into wrinkle. But his eyes looked bright. You just knew he had done it on purpose. He was going home.

"You bloody coward!" said a voice in the crowd.

"Bloody smart is what he is," Jake replied. "He knows the way home."

We pushed our way out of the crowd and walked back to our tent in silence. The lights went out at 2200.

"Hey, Taber," Tim whispered.

"Yeah?"

"You think we're going to make it, right?"

I didn't know what to say. I just grunted.

"Well, I'm getting out of my own stupid town when I get home," he said "I'm moving to New York City. I'll work construction, hang out with Jake, maybe even get married. Our kids could play together. You should come too, man."

"Yeah," I said, "maybe when it's all over."

I rolled over. Tim didn't say anything more. In a minute, I reached for my rifle. Its weight trapped my hand against the bed, and my palm felt sweaty on the grip. I tried to imagine pulling the trigger.

It would only take one shot, I thought. In a month I'd be walking again—and I'd be home. I'd be taking my little sister to the fair, and I'd be alive. What would it matter? There were two million more just like me. Let them be heroes.

I couldn't do it. It's not like I wanted to be a hero. But I didn't want to be a coward, either.

* * * * *

H-Hour Minus 70 Minutes

I gripped the side of the boat in the darkness, every new wave almost knocking me over. It was as if the sea itself was trying to throw me out of the boat.

For five hours, I'd been fighting the lump in my stomach. I'd feel it rise and then drop again—over and over. All I wanted was to get sick. I felt it rise again. I pressed my hand to my mouth, but it just kept rising. I leaned toward the side of the boat. A wave jolted me back in—and that's when it all came out.

I opened my eyes and saw my vomit floating in seawater at the bottom of the boat. It sloshed against Tim's legs. I looked up, expecting some wisecrack, but Tim

was holding the side of the boat like a wild horse's reins. His eyes were pinched shut.

I looked around at our unit. We were supposed to be cool, well-trained fighting machines, but Jake was bent over the side of the boat, trying to puke into the ocean, and Gabe had been knocked over by the weight of his pack. He wasn't even trying to get up.

Then there was Tim. His eyes were shut so tight it probably hurt. It made me think of my little sister. She used to close her eyes and say she was hiding. She was right there in plain sight, but she couldn't see the rest of the world, so she thought the world couldn't see her either.

When we boarded the boats, it hadn't been so terrifying. And there were so many of them. I didn't know that many could even fit in the ocean. They were lined up side by side along the coast, so close you could almost step from the deck of one boat to the next. I bet you could have walked from one end of England to the other on those boats.

Another wave rocked the boat, and I felt the lump rise again. I looked out into the darkness, knowing that somewhere out there was a beach. I didn't care how many machine guns were there. I just wanted to be off the boat. In my mind, I knew two things: Bullets could kill you, and seasickness could not. But it didn't matter. I'd take my chances with the bullets.

I was ready to puke again. Just then, the sky brightened in the east. The outline of a beach came into view, and you could hear the buzz of a thousand planes in the air. In seconds, the beach was lit by explosions, and towers of fire burst from the sand.

A cheer rose from the boat, and I could hear Tim yell above the noise. "Get 'em, boys," he screamed, pumping his fist in the air. I could see landing boats scattered across the water, each one full of men staring at the beach. Twenty yards away there was another landing boat, and for a second I caught the eye of a kid in it. He looked about 12, I swear. He must have lied about his age. He wasn't even watching the bombs. He just looked plain scared.

For maybe 15 minutes, our bombers did their work. Fire just rained from the sky. It was like every star fell and exploded on the ground. I imagined the German bunkers getting blown into big piles of dust.

Tim turned to me and yelled, "Didn't I tell you? It's going to be a piece of cake!" Just then, I heard a familiar whining sound as an explosion ripped through the water 100 yards away. Everyone in the boat ducked, and in a minute, the air was full of German shells. They were coming from the cliffs behind the beach.

They're shooting at me, I thought—at *me*—and this isn't practice. They want to *kill* me. I crouched down, leaning against the side of the boat. I knew it wouldn't protect me, but for some reason it made me feel safe. I let my head pop up, and there was that kid in the next boat again. Now he looked even younger than 12. He was crouching, too. Just his head stuck up over the side, and I could see that his eyes were shut tight. I think he thought he was hiding—like Tim, like my little sister.

Then he was gone. There was that terrible whine—and then the blast. A shell hit the kid's boat dead center, and a spout of water shot from the ocean.

H-Hour Plus 5 Minutes

"You're not dropping us here!" Lieutenant Mabry was right in the Navy captain's face. "My men will drown!"

Shells were still screaming all around us. "I can't get this ship blown up," the captain said. "I've got more guys to bring in."

To our right, a landing ship was unloading 500 yards from the beach. The ramp was down, and men were walking into the waves. Then they would disappear in maybe 10 feet of water. The lucky ones got rid of their packs. They dropped their guns and everything else so they could swim. The unlucky ones just didn't come up.

The lieutenant was bursting with anger. In a second he had a pistol in his hand. He pointed it at the captain's head. "I said take us in!" he shouted.

The captain stared at the gun. Then he started moving the boat in closer.

In a few minutes, we were 150 yards from shore. The captain looked at the lieutenant. "I'm dropping the ramp!" he said. Lieutenant Mabry didn't answer. He just stared at the captain.

Finally, he turned to us and said, "Let's go!" That was it—just, "Let's go!" There was no big speech like you see in the movies. We just turned and walked into the water. Tim and Jake were in front of me, and I watched them both go under. Seconds later, they popped up without their packs. I couldn't believe it. We were like those animals that follow each other off cliffs. They know they're going to die, but they do it anyway.

I think the lieutenant was the first to get hit. After that, I don't know—bullets just raked the water around us. I know it's weird, but the bullets looked like water from a garden hose, and I kept thinking about my mom. I could see her standing in her garden, watering the tomatoes.

I kept wading. I waded through potatoes and squash and peas. I waded through pole beans and carrots. And I didn't think about the bodies until I was on the beach. The water was littered with them, many face down like they were looking for fish.

But Gabe was face up.

His eyes were open, staring at the sky. The water was blackish red around him, and I counted three holes in his shirt. I brushed him away like a corn stalk, and two more bullets hit him. The force pushed him back toward me, and I pushed him away again.

I hit the beach and ran. At least I thought I was running, but I wasn't moving any faster than the guy next to me. He was limping up the beach, and blood was pouring from his leg. All around us, bullets hit the sand. They made little noises—*sip, sip*—like someone sucking air through their teeth.

I don't know how long it took. It seemed like hours, even though I think it was more like five minutes. But, finally, I made it to the wall of rocks. I lay against it and looked out at the Channel. Everywhere, guys were running in slow motion up the beach. Every few seconds, someone would go down. It looked like they'd just tripped, but they wouldn't get up.

I shut my eyes tight. I imagined my sister curled up in a chair with her hands over her eyes—hiding. I sat that way for a while. I couldn't see them; they couldn't see me. I almost shut it all out—the blast of the mortars, the *sip, sip* of the bullets.

And then the sound of weeping slipped through. Again, I pictured my sister. It wasn't a loud bawling, like the sound she makes when she wants everyone to hear her. It was more like the quiet, desperate sound she makes when some terrible nightmare wakes her up on a peaceful night.

I opened my eyes and looked to my left. It was Tim. He was sitting with his knees drawn up to his chest. His helmet was off, and he was sobbing like he'd never stop.

H-Hour Plus 4 Hours

We were still sitting behind the wall when this colonel walked by. I can't remember what he said. He was crazy though. He was walking along the wall. The machine gunners could see him clear as day, but he didn't care. He just strutted along, yelling at us.

"You can die here, or you can die killing Germans." It was something like that. It seemed like a funny way to get us moving. I mean, dying is dying. What do you care what you're doing when it happens?

But he was right about one thing: We were going to die if we sat there. The machine guns couldn't see us, but the mortar guys were zeroing in. Their shells were dropping closer all the time. They left big holes in the sand when they hit.

The mortars turned men into rag dolls. One second, a guy would be running. Then you'd hear that whine, and fear would hit his face for a moment. Then the sand would explode, and he'd be lifeless on the beach.

It was weird to think how quickly it happened. You work so hard to get to be 17. I mean, you worry yourself sick about homework and girlfriends and making the baseball team—and then it's all over in a second.

I turned to Tim. He'd barely moved in a couple of hours.

"Hey, man," I said. "You okay?"

He didn't say anything.

"Tim, come on! You've got to pull it together. We can't stay here."

He whimpered something through his hands. "What?" I said.

"He was carrying his arm," Tim was shaking his head slowly.

"Carrying what?" I asked.

"His arm. I saw him from behind. I thought it was a rifle at first, but there was blood everywhere."

"Oh, man, you can't think about it, Tim. We have to get out of here."

"I got up there and it was Jake. He just kept saying, 'I won't drop it. I won't drop it.'"

I didn't know what to say.

Tim was talking through sobs now. "I just ran by. I turned my head so he wouldn't see it was me, and I ran by . . . "

He sat up like he'd just realized he'd forgotten something important. "Oh, my God! I have to find him."

Tim stood straight up and started to look around. Machine gun fire tore at the top of the ridge next to him, but he barely noticed. I reached for his sleeve and pulled him back down.

He collapsed in a heap next to me, and we just lay there, leaning on each other.

I guess an hour passed. I don't know. Everything around me sounded like a bad radio station. You know, like the sound was coming in and out. I would hear things, and then the blast from a shell would break it all up.

I remember a sergeant saying our group was nearly gone. Only six of us were still alive—out of 30. Then there was a blast. I remember Tim saying something about Jake—then another blast—and then he was talking about his mother. I could hardly understand anything he was saying.

Just then, a shell blew up near us. It must have been an 88. It landed 20 yards to our right, and a boot with a foot still in it dropped near my hand.

Right then, a sergeant came running down the line. "Come on!" he was yelling. "I'm not dying on this beach. Let's get us some Germans!"

He went right over the wall. He was charging at the hills, and people started following. In a second, Tim was up and moving. Anger was in his face like a fever. I didn't really feel mad at anyone—not the Germans, not that colonel, not the sergeant—I was just plain scared.

* * * * *

H-Hour Plus 10 Hours

It was weird. You could see the machine gun. It was spitting bullets through a hole in a concrete wall. But you couldn't see a person. I felt like it was just a big piece of metal we were after—like there was no flesh involved, nothing breathing or beating.

The gun sat right over a road. It was the main exit from the beach. There were big tank barriers on the road. Our guys were trying to blow them up, but they were just getting mowed down by this gun.

We had gone around the road. We went up a grassy hill where the guns couldn't get us, but the German had buried mines everywhere. The worst were the Bouncing Betties. If you stepped on one, it shot up from the ground. Then it went off at waist height, sending metal into you like a hundred knives. I was walking on my toes. It was stupid, I know, but I thought that way if I hit one it wouldn't go off.

We made it off the beach. We were 100 feet up, and I suddenly noticed something really weird: I could hear mortars and machine guns, but none of them were shooting at us. They were all pointed at the beach—we were *behind* them!

For ten hours, I'd been ducking. Every blast had made me think how soft I was. I don't mean weak, really, just soft, temporary. It was my body against a whole lot of dumb metal, and I didn't stand a chance. But now I was safe—for a while.

I looked at Tim. He was crouched next to me in the bushes. He was staring at the machine gun bunker, but his eyes didn't seem to be focused on anything.

"How are you doing?" I asked.

"They shot his arm off!" he said, his eyes like steel.

"Maybe he made it anyway. You don't know." But Tim wasn't listening.

The sergeant crawled over. It was the guy who had led us up the ridge. He whispered to Tim: "Private, let's move out. You take the left. I've got the right." Then he turned to me: "Son, you shoot at any head that pops up."

The two of them started creeping toward the bunker, and the machine gun spit out another round of bullets. Tim and the sergeant moved closer. Then they split up, and I lost sight of the Sergeant. Tim moved carefully around the left side of the bunker and pulled a grenade from his belt. He pulled out the pin and stuffed the grenade through a tiny slit in the concrete wall.

The bunker muffled the blast, but I knew it was big. I saw a German soldier stumble out. He was hurt pretty badly. Tim pulled out his pistol, pointed it at the soldier's head, and shot. The guy's head jerked back, and he crumpled to the ground. Then Tim gave out a kind of yell, lifted his rifle, and brought the butt down hard on the guy's head.

He was still doing that when I saw another German come out of the bushes. It happened so fast I can barely remember. All I know is this: He was raising his arm as he walked toward Tim, so I leveled my M-1, sighted, and put five rounds in his chest.

Tim stopped when he heard the shots and crouched down like an animal. I waited a couple of minutes. Then I headed for the bunker. The sergeant and Tim were standing over the guy I shot.

"Good shot, kid," said the sergeant.

I didn't answer. The body was lying still, its arms and legs spread out in all directions. It was like death had pulled them off and a blind person had put them all back.

His face was white and scared and young. He looked like the kid on the landing boat, the one I had watched get blown up.

The sergeant and Tim walked to the edge of the cliff. I took one last look at the kid's body, and then I joined them. The machine gun was silent now. Down below, our guys were busy. They'd blown a big hole in the concrete, and a tank was crawling through.

Behind us, the sunset was rusting the sky. Tim stood next to me. His face was blank.

D Plus 11 Weeks: Paris

We rode in like movie stars or something. Paris was the capital of France. The Nazis had been there for four years, and the French hated them. Now the Nazis were gone, and we had chased them out, so the French *loved* us.

We rode in tanks and trucks and jeeps. I couldn't believe the crowds. Up and down the streets, people were cheering. Girls were coming up and kissing us—just like that. They wouldn't even tell you their names. They'd just hug you and kiss you. Then they'd say "thank you" in that cute French accent.

Tim rode next to me on the truck. He just sat and took it all in. He didn't say much anymore—not since the beach. I was pretty quiet, too. I just didn't have much to say. Next to bullets, words didn't seem all that important.

The days were okay. We were on the move, and there wasn't much to do. The Germans were on the run. We still had to watch out for mines, and there were snipers in the trees, but there wasn't that much danger.

The nights were the worst. Falling asleep was like trying to enter a heavily guarded room. I'd get halfway in the door, but then I'd hear a blast in my dreams— like mortars or grenades—and I'd be wide awake again. Then I'd start all over. We didn't talk about it, but I know it was the same for Tim.

We never doubted that we were fighting on the right side though. The French people would tell us stories about the Nazis. In one place, the Nazis found a radio. Some French guys had been calling in information to the British, so the Nazis took them to the town square and shot them, right there in the open.

One woman hadn't seen her husband or her two sons in months. They'd been taken away to work in a factory somewhere, and she hadn't heard a thing.

Another village lost about 40 Jews. They were sent to prison camps by the Nazis. No one knew if they were still alive.

"Taber?" Tim was looking out the side of the truck.

"Yeah?"

"What are you going to tell them all?"

"Who?" I asked.

"People back home—your parents, friends."

"I don't know," I said.

All the images came back to me: Gabe floating in the water, Tim sobbing into his hands, the kid I shot. Why couldn't he have just surrendered? A lot of the German guys were thrilled to surrender. Some of them would throw down their guns and hug you. They'd have these great big smiles on their faces. Why didn't this guy just do that?

I looked out into the crowd. Right in front, there was a tall guy with a little girl on his shoulders. She had blonde hair and pigtails, and her blue dress looked like the Montana sky. Her chin rested on the man's head, and she was playing peekaboo with the guys on the tanks.

I leaned out of the truck to watch her. In a minute, she disappeared into the crowd. I turned to Tim. "I don't think I'll tell them much," I said.

Tim looked at me and nodded. The truck banged on through Paris. That girl was probably still back there. I could just see her, perched up high. Her arms were out like she was welcoming the world, and she was beaming like she'd never heard of war.

Epilogue

It was August of 1944 when the Allies rolled into Paris. Eight months later, the war in Europe was over. Adolf Hitler killed himself in an underground bunker.

Many American soldiers stayed in Europe after the war. They helped the Europeans rebuild. It was no easy task. Thirty to forty million Europeans had died, and entire cities had been destroyed by bombs.

Most American soldiers simply went home. Some got married and had kids. Others got money from the government to go to college. Most of them were changed forever by the war. Many had seen men die. Some had killed with their own hands. But nearly everyone felt that one thing was true: Hitler had put the world in extreme danger, and they had found the courage to do the right thing.

TEXT CREDITS

Every effort has been made to contact copyright holders for permission to reproduce borrowed material. We regret any oversights that may have occurred and will be pleased to rectify them in subsequent reprints of the work.